Healing of the Soul
Shamanism and Psyche

D1617525

Healing of the Soul
Shamanism and Psyche

Ann Drake, Psy.D.

Busca, Inc.
Ithaca, New York

Busca, Inc.
P.O. Box 854
Ithaca, NY 14851
Ph: 607-546-4247
Fax: 607-546-4248
E-mail: info@buscainc.com
www.buscainc.com

First Edition

Printed in the United States of America

ISBN: 0-9666196-6-8

Cover design by Cayuga Digital Imaging and Helena Cooper, with additional thanks to Dan Yokum. Front cover art is based on Helena Cooper's original oil on canvas painting, "Finding Forms." For further information on the artist: www.helenaart.com/ or www.buscainc.com/helenaart/.

Back cover photography: Tanya Daniel

Composition: P.S. We Type for You

This book is meant to inspire its readers as well as clarify certain concepts. It is not intended as a prescriptive work. In no way does this publication serve as a substitution for medical, therapeutic, and other forms of professional assistance.

In Memory of Scott Richard Schoelch, 1974–1991
A beautiful soul who died too young but taught us much

And to my teachers,
Ismail Daim,
And those of you with whom I have worked
Who have opened your heart and soul to me and are my inspiration.

About the Author

Ann Drake has been a psychotherapist since 1972 and a shamanic practitioner since 1992. In the seventies and early eighties she worked in a feminist therapy collective with women who had experienced physical, sexual and emotional trauma. During this period she worked to define new models of treatment that went beyond the overmedication and long hospitalizations that were common at that time.

In 1984 Ann entered a doctoral program in clinical psychology school at the Antioch/New England School of Professional Psychology. Upon graduation, Ann joined the faculty in the doctoral program at Antioch. In addition to teaching, she maintained a private practice, wrote articles, and gave talks and workshops. Ann had begun a book on the role of cultural violence on emotional and psychological functioning when she went to Borneo in 1992 and met a shamanic healer who transformed her life.

Ann was initiated into the Unani tradition of shamanic healing by the Bomoh, a wise and gifted healer. Upon her return, she devoted herself to the study and practice of shamanism and worked toward a clinical and theoretical synthesis of psychology and shamanism. The results of her healing work have been so powerful and dramatic that she has written a book and offers workshops and training for those who wish to seek an integration of the shamanic and Western psychological thought.

For more information about Ann and her work visit the web at www.anndrakesoulwork.com and www.fullcirclecenter.org.

Contents

Acknowledgments

In addition to the Bomoh, Ismail Daim, to whom I am profoundly grateful, I have studied with many wonderful teachers and learned much from many people. My first teachers are my parents, John and Eloise Schoelch, and my brother, Dick, who taught me about family, relationships, how to be in the world, and how to love. My son, Josh, taught me the joy of unconditional love and the magic of watching an incredible soul grow from infancy into manhood. Along my shamanic path, I have studied with gifted teachers who have greatly influenced my work—Tenzin Wangyal Rinpoche, Larry Peters, Sandy Ingerman, Michael Harner, Nan Moss and David Corbin, and the late Linda Crane. I have been blessed with two incredible mentors who have shepherded me along my path and from whom I have learned so much, Robert Bosnak and Mary Jonatis.

There is a wonderful group of people who are my peers, colleagues, students, teachers, editors, and, most importantly, friends without whose love and support this book might not have been brought to life. My peer study group: David and Sylvia Hammerman, Claudia Harris, Starr Potts, Carin Roberge and Miriam Greenspan several of whom are also in the shamanic study group that also include Carol Caton, Joanna Duda, Fenton Hendrickson, Paul McCormick, Barbara Miller, Kay O'Laughlin, Patti Pearce, and Sharon Polk-Sadonik. Much gratitude goes to all of you as well as to my shamanic sister and peer Julie Soquet.

I did not start this project as a writer and have many to thank who have edited and re-edited and taught me how to write. Kathyrn Watterson took on the task of being my book doctor and saved it from being a dry academic tomb. The mantra she gifted me with was "show, don't tell" which rings in my head each time I become pedantic. There are many others who offered their time, energy, and thoughtful comments in editing the book—

Marie Cantlon, Amy Elizabeth Fox, Emily Weidman, Sandra Nunnes, Paula Fuchs, Sandra Farrel, Pete Wilson, and many of the folks listed above.

I have enormous gratitude to my editor and publisher, Michael Cooper, who has been more than I could ever have dreamed for one in this role. His comments and feedback have been helpful and wise, and he has given me enormous latitude in making this book my own. Michael's enthusiasm for *Healing of the Soul* and his willingness to bring it to print is truly a gift from spirit.

My two dear friends, Cassie Reese and Georgette Kelley, accompanied me to Borneo on the early trips and grounded and supported me through the early initiations. Cassie, a fellow Peace Corps volunteer, shares my love of Malaysian people and helps me to remember through her presence their beautiful open hearts. Georgette, my dear friend who has walked by my side since freshman year in college, has supported and loved me every step of the way. Since we were young women, she has challenged me to go with her into the deepest places of the heart and soul—a truer gift one could not receive. I also want to thank Georgette for the generous use of her cabin in Vermont where the bulk of this book was written. And to Hawk, my writing guide, who circled the cabin daily as I wrote and who majestically flew off over the mountain when the last page was complete.

And last but not least, I want to thank the Boston Red Sox, the New England Patriots and the Boston Celtics who lured me in from the outdoors to sit silently by the computer as I wrote this book.

PART I

Introduction
A JOURNEY INTO THE MAGICAL

This book is an account of my process as I was confronted with phenomena that I could not explain. Many of the experiences and observations that I make may appear fanciful and difficult to take seriously. I wrestle with those reactions myself. But there are thousands of people around the world who work in very sacred and profound ways, ones that are outside of the western way of understanding. I hope that my own struggle with coming to new explanations, flawed as they may be, will encourage others to do the same. Thus I write this book as an invitation to you, the reader, to ponder existence from new and varied perspectives, taking what makes sense, validating it with your own internal wisdom, and creating your own meaning from it.

Chapter 1
To Borneo and Back

It was the summer of 1953. I was eight years old. My good friend, Jane, and I had just finished playing on the teeter-totter at the park. We were lying on the grass looking up at the clouds. As the clouds entranced me, I was overcome with a sense of the immensity of the universe. I asked Jane if she ever wondered why she was born a girl at this time and place rather than a boy in China or Africa. Jane said that she had never thought about it. I remember that day as clearly as if it were yesterday. Although I spent most of my fifth year of life fervently attempting to dig my way though the center of the earth to China, this was my first conscious memory of a lifelong curiosity about the universe and how everything in it functions.

Growing up in the Heartland

I was born and raised in Shelbyville, Indiana, a small town 32 miles southeast of Indianapolis. The population has stayed between 14,000 to 16,000 people for the last 50 years. For most of my youth Shelbyville had the honor of having the best corn crop in the nation. My father and his father owned the local shoe store and my mom's parents lived with us. Our family was one of those stereotypical all-American families. My parents were pillars of their church, The Christian Church, which has a fundamentalist philosophy similar to that of the Baptist Church. They were on boards and committees and served as elders and deacons. They were also very involved in civic and community affairs. In their mid-eighties they moved to a retirement community outside of Shelbyville. Both their church and the city government presented them with plaques and other signs of appreciation for all that they had given to the community. My older brother, Dick, and

I were very active in the church and in all of the activities at school, serving as class officers and presidents of clubs. Dick was captain of the football and baseball teams. My boyfriend was captain of the football and track teams. Since there were no organized sports for girls at this time, I had to be satisfied with a vicarious experience.

I was constantly fascinated with the meaning of life during my childhood. From the time that I was quite young I attended church services and soon perfected leaving my body to merge with the stained glass image of Jesus in the Garden of Gethsemene in the church window. It was quite a rush to merge with the divine, and I assumed that this must be what people meant by a religious experience. Of course, since no one ever spoke of such things, I did not know if what I was experiencing was normal or something special. On youth Sunday my senior year I gave a sermon on "What is Man." I remember listing the minerals that we are composed of and stating that the monetary value of man is $1.29; of course with inflation we are worth considerably more now. The theme of my sermon was that our value is not in our physical being but in our soul. Today I am still trying to understand and define exactly what the soul is.

I also loved politics; John F. Kennedy was my idol. When I was 13, I decided that I wanted to go to DePauw University and major in political science. There were several hurdles to overcome with this plan. I had a fairly serious learning disability, and needed tutors from the first grade until the first year of college. At that time no one understood dyslexia so everyone thought that I had significant difficulty with learning. When I was in the fourth grade, my teacher told my parents that I was not smart enough to attend college.

Despite my learning problems, I worked hard academically and was a leader in my class. On the strength of my "extra-curricular" activities, I was accepted at DePauw University. My freshmen advisor informed me that I did not have the intellectual abilities to major in political science and should major in elementary education instead. "Besides," he told me, "this is a man's field." His pronouncements made me even more determined. After much debate, he "allowed" me to take the freshman prerequisites for a political science major, predicting that I would fail. As he listed the courses that I would need to take, he named one that I had never heard—anthropology. I ran back to the dorm and looked up the word in the dictionary, mortified to discover that there was an entire area of study in my chosen field that I did not know even existed. There was a sinking feeling in my stomach when I realized that the sheltered world from which I had come had barely prepared me for what I wanted to accomplish. The courses were indeed challenging; I functioned on only four hours of sleep a night in order to finish my work, but I loved all of the things that I was learning, and at the end of the semester I proved my advisor wrong. I did not fail.

Four major events transformed me from an all-American girl from the heartland to a political activist. The first was a job the summer between my freshman and sophomore year, as a College Board model, at the largest department store in Indianapolis. Girls from the different colleges in the area worked as sales clerks in a special section of the store for college bound customers. Part of the job required modeling clothes in the tearoom each noon. I was told to make sure that I spent enough time at the executives' table so that each had a thorough chance to "feel" the full textures of the fabrics while I was wearing them. The table was large with eight men sitting around it. I was expected to walk up to each of them, turning around as they touched various parts of my body while examining the clothes. When I complained to my supervisor about this groping, she told me to get used to it, adding that I should feel flattered that such powerful men found me attractive. Her words did not quell my outrage and sense of violation, but I stayed on the job, not quite having the courage or know-how to take on this battle.

The second transformative event came during my sophomore year with several other young women in the Alpha Phi sorority house who were on a similar quest to understand the meaning of life. Although we were all active in campus activities and involved in dating, we quietly formed a religious study group that continued through our senior year to ponder all the questions that were floating around in our minds. When I was home at Christmas, I met with my childhood minister to discuss some of the things with which I had been struggling. I posed this question to him: "I had always been taught that if people did not believe in Jesus Christ and God that they would go to hell. What happens to all the people in Africa and Asia that have never heard about Jesus and God?" He replied, "If they have not accepted God as their personal savior, they will go to hell. That is why," he pronounced, "We need more missionaries." I was taken aback. The God I believed in would not condemn a person to hell just because that person had never heard of God. In fact, I was beginning to question if my God would send anyone to hell.

After a few courses in the religion and philosophy department, I had studied several new concepts such as the doctrine of free will, which asserts that God so loves us that He has given us the ability to choose our own way.

In these teachings God is seen as a benevolent, compassionate, non-judgmental being. These various philosophies delved into the complexities of the soul and the psyche in ways that excited and challenged me and resonated with my intuitive sense of how the world operates. These realizations paved the way for a growing disconnection from my family, my church, and my past.

The third transformative experience occurred the summer of 1965 following my sophomore year. I worked as a congressional intern in Washington, DC. It was the year that LBJ launched the Great Society and the debates on Vietnam were beginning to gather steam. It was an exciting time to be in D.C. and I soon found that if I smiled and chatted with the doorman I could get into any committee meeting or session of Congress that I wanted. But there was a downside to being allowed entrance to the seat of power. I discovered that many of our elected officials were neither that bright nor that honorable. I also encountered the pesky problem from the summer before. As the low person on the totem pole in the Congressman's office, I was given the task of accompanying lobbyists to lunch whom the Congressman did not want to deal with but did not want to insult. Instead of figuring out that they had been given the shaft, all too many of them considered me an offering of some sort. The seeds for a feminist consciousness were taking root by this time. I came away from this third eye-opening experience with a naïve and optimistic idea of how things should be and a growing sense of cynicism as to how adults ran the world.

The next summer cities were burning as blacks let centuries of repressed rage erupt. At the core of my being I identified with their struggle and felt estranged from all that opposed their expression of rage. It was through this identification that I realized that the transformation was complete. There was a growing rift within my family as they felt confused and angered by my beliefs. When I returned to school in the fall, I joined the Students for a Democratic Society and two months later was engaged to marry Bob, the young man who founded the SDS chapter on the campus. It was an intense time with much internal struggle and conflict. I was president of my sorority, yet opposed everything a sorority stood for. I spent far more time in meetings and intense conversations than I did studying. Bob and I decided to marry and go into the Peace Corps after graduation. At the time it seemed like the noble and correct thing to do. In retrospect I see that it was the safe thing to do. Had we acted on the power of our beliefs, Bob would either have gone to jail or we would have moved to Canada to register our resistance to the Vietnam War.

The gap between my family and myself widened; they felt abandoned, judged, and betrayed by my political views, which appeared to them to be a total rejection of their way of life. My brother, Dick, had just finished business school at the University of Michigan and had enrolled in officer training for the Navy. Dick was on the right path. My family could not comprehend why the man I was marrying was a draft dodger and had no interest in having a career in which he made a lot of money. As much as I tried to convey that my religious upbringing had been the foundation for my political beliefs, they became more entrenched in their views as I did in mine.

After a formal wedding, Bob and I left for training in Hawaii. It was the fall of 1967. We were to serve for two years in Malaysia, a newly formed country that was just four years old. Bob's draft board initially refused to let him go for training because they said he was leaving the country before all of his appeals had been exhausted. Bob had to point out to them that Hawaii was our 50th state and part of the USA. While we were in training, we learned that his appeals had been exhausted and that he was to be drafted. The Peace Corps decided to make this a test case and sent us overseas despite the draft order. General Hersey, the officer in charge of the draft board for the United States government at that time, did not want to take on this political hot potato and granted Bob a two-year deferment.

Borneo

We were assigned to teach elementary school in Sarawak, a state of Malaysia within Borneo. A British family named Brookes had ruled Sarawak for over a hundred years until 1946 when Sarawak became a colony of Britain. In 1963 Britain relinquished control of several colonies in Southeast Asia to form the Federation of Malaysia. The educational system was still British and required students in the 6th grade to take exams to go on to the next level. Only one third of all students went to secondary school, and 99% of those came from missionary schools in the larger towns. It was our job to see that students from our remote village had a chance to make it to the seventh grade.

We traveled to a small village near the South China Sea called Matu where we would live for the next two years. It took two days to reach Matu by boat. First we took a prop plane from Kuching to Sibu, the nearest large town to Matu. Then we took a "launch," which was a wooden boat with space for cargo underneath and hard wooden benches ringing the top level. It went about as fast as one could swim. In the middle everyone put all of his or her belongings or "barong" as it is called there. Our vast collection of supplies and what we deemed as essentials filled much of this open space. The boat trip took 26 hours and included a rough ride in the shark-infested waters of the South China Sea. As we floated down the Matu River toward the village, we saw monkeys swinging in the trees of the lush and dense rainforest. Approaching the shop area, there were a few houses built on stilts lining the riverbank. This was the Chinese area of the village. The commercial area consisted of three sections of wooden shops built high off the ground with a wooden gangplank connecting the sections.

As we disembarked, everyone turned to stare at us, not knowing what to make of these two large white people with more things than most ever dreamed of having. The villagers were unaware of the existence of the United States; they thought we were from New Zealand since, according to them, that was where the white man lived. For most people, I was the first white woman they had seen. All aspects of western culture were totally foreign to them. Our dress and manner of being was undoubtedly quite bizarre. They stared at us while giggling and whispering. After what seemed like an interminable amount of time, the head of the district council came running to greet us and introduced us to the villagers.

It was December, the height of the rainy season, and the whole area, including our quarters, was flooded. The only way to get around was by boat. For awhile we stayed with the Tua Kampong, who was the head of the village. Then they moved us to temporary housing in the district office guesthouse, which was next to the district office. It sat squarely between the Chinese and Melanau sections of the village, not a part of either kampong. The day they moved us they forgot to leave a boat, and we were stranded in a strange little house. Both of us cried that day wondering how we could spend the next two years in this place, yet, we knew that the other alternatives would be worse. Fortunately it did not take long to fall in love with Matu and the people who lived there.

In 1967 Matu was a sleepy little village of less than a thousand people with their own language called Bahasa Melanau which is unwritten and spoken only by those who live in nearby villages. Three-fourths of the people are Melanau and are Muslim, while another quarter are Chinese and Buddhist. The Chinese are the shopkeepers who live in a separate compound across the riverbank. In the sixties the Melanaus tapped rubber from rubber trees that they sold to the Chinese for processing in smokehouses. This was the Melanaus only cash crop. They were very poor, frequently only having rice and dried fish to eat. Growing vegetables was difficult, as the land was flooded several months of the year. When the earth was dry enough to plant, the monkeys swooped down and took anything that was growing. My students and I tried to build tall fences of tree branches that extended across the top of the garden like a cage, but the monkeys seemed to have an easier time getting into the garden than we did.

Houses with thatched roofs perched on stilts lined the river surrounded by dense rain forest as the backdrop. Out-houses were built over the river. The river was the only source of water except during the rainy season. Everyone drank from and bathed in the river. When I first saw these conditions, I swore that I would never get in the water. However, as soon as the rainy season was over, I had no choice other than to bathe in the river. With the infant mortality rate in Matu at 50% either a newborn quickly developed immunities to the contaminated water or died of diarrhea. Most people, including myself, had worms. There was no electricity. Yet despite all of these physical hardships, I experienced a peace and tranquillity I had never known before.

Neither Bob nor I had been trained to teach beyond the seven weeks of training we received from the Peace Corps. There were few books or supplies in the school. As established by the British, school was taught in English because there were 57 different languages spoken in Sarawak at the time. Only one of the teachers spoke English. The other teachers read from the English text but had no idea what they were teaching. We began teaching by identifying all of the objects in the classroom in English and having the students teach us the objects in Melanau. After a couple of months we had enough of a working vocabulary to actually begin to teach. At the end of two years, we had succeeded in getting half of the students into secondary school. But long before we achieved these results, we realized that the students who left Matu to be educated in the city would forever experience life in a much different way than they now knew. Western culture was beginning to creep into the larger towns. There were cars and buses, and open markets where one could buy fresh vegetables, fish, and meat. With a ninth grade education one could become a nurse, teacher, administrator, or government official. The government determined the job a student trained for and where he or she was stationed based on one's aptitude and the need for the acquired skill. By chance a student from Matu might be assigned to Matu, but most would never permanently live there again. There was a bitter irony to the fact that by doing our job, we were in essence, destroying the fabric of the culture. This was especially painful for me as I had grown to feel at home in Matu in a way that I had never felt in my native land. There was a peaceful sense of community and ease that soothed my soul.

In addition to teaching, a myriad of health problems needed to be addressed in the village as well. Bob and I carried with us the bias that our system of health care was superior to that of Matu and that we needed to get them to change a few things. It seemed to us that the logical first task was to get everyone boiling their water to bring down the infant mortality rate and other contaminated water related health problems. Convincing villagers to always boil their water for at least five minutes was difficult. Drinking boiled water only part of the time lowered people's resistance to the water, creating more health problems. It did not take long for us to encounter illness ourselves and to seek out healing in the traditional methods that had sustained the Melanaus for centuries. Once I had a fever of 104 totally broken by the skilled hands of an incredible masseuse and healer. Soon Bob and I discovered that all our well-intentioned schemes for bettering the lives of the people in Matu were really beside the point. The real benefit of our being there was to learn from them.

The people in Matu were incredibly cooperative. Initially it took several months to discern who was related to whom as they flowed in and out of each other's lives, nursed each other's children, and cared for one another in illness and hard times. Natural leadership was accepted; there seemed to be little competition. As was the British custom, there was a class prefect at the school. I thought it would be a good idea to rotate this position, giving several students a chance at leadership. This attempt was met with vigorous opposition. Daud was their leader; he had always been and everyone felt uncomfortable with my trying to change this.

The student's favorite game was trying to see how long a group could keep a ball in the air without the ball touching the ground; it was a game of cooperation. When they played rounders, a game similar to kick ball, the players did not keep score. Initially I did. When I called out the score, they looked at me quizzically, questioning the purpose of scorekeeping.

The people in Matu were extremely aware of everything around them. Once a poisonous snake was about to attack me, but before I was aware it was there, the person next to me whipped out his knife—"parang," as it is called—and cut the snake in two. At times I felt like the ugly American, trying to impose my way of doing things upon them while often being ignorant of what is truly important. Fortunately the people in Matu are very understanding and would just laugh at our ignorance and arrogance and then explain why they do things as they do.

There was nothing in my early life to prepare me for living in such a different culture. My hometown of Shelbyville was a small, conservative,

Midwestern town steeped in its own culture and traditions. The town was racially segregated and staunchly in support of the Vietnam War. There were strict customs such as never wearing white shoes before Memorial Day or after Labor Day. Most of the homes were very neat and clean. There were no rats, poisonous snakes or lizards running around. Despite these differences, I felt very much at home in Matu within a matter of a few months. Regardless of our different ways of doing things, the people there were warm, loving, and accepting of us. The notion that reality is a created construct dependent upon one's culture soon became clear to me. For instance in the village of Matu, men touch each other freely as do women, but it is taboo to touch a member of the opposite sex in public, even if you are married. It is an insult to point one's foot at a person just as it is an insult to point one's third finger at a person in the American culture. I began to see that the rules, rituals, and customs of a culture are at once both the fabric that binds the community together and totally arbitrary. From this experience the rules and customs that had so dominated my life in growing up became less powerful; as I saw that these rules were not hard truths but cultural artifacts. Realizing this it became easier for me to step into the culture of Matu without judgment, and to be more accepting of the customs of my own culture.

The Spirit in All Things

Living in Matu was one of the most profound experiences of my life. I learned about community and acceptance on a level I had not experienced in America. I felt what it was like to live within a place of peace by being intimately connected with nature. We awoke at dawn and would go down to the river to wash and relieve ourselves. The roosters were crowing and there was a hum of activity as everyone prepared for the first meal of the day and got ready to work. There was always time to stop to chat and there was a steady stream of people who stopped in on the way to their morning activities to say hi, ask a question or favor. Since we lived in a one room hut, I became very good at dressing and undressing under a sarong all the while holding it in my mouth and talking at the same time. The sarong is an all-purpose piece of beautiful batik material that is sown together like a large tube. It can be wrapped around and worn as a skirt, or tied above the breast to wear when bathing. It is also used to carry babies by slinging it around the neck and placing the baby inside. It allows for the baby to be constantly carried while the mother has both hands free to do her work.

There was a structure and formality to the day at school that stood in stark contrast to the natural flow of village life. The first year I had 45 ten-year-old students all of whom sat obediently with their hands folded waiting to learn from me. Even though in the beginning they scarcely understood a word I was saying or I them, there was never a problem with discipline—just respect and cooperation. We had few text books and most of the lessons and materials we created ourselves. For the most part the children were anxious to learn, but at times it was so hot that it was hard to focus. We had a two-hour break from 12 till 2 to rest and have the mid-day meal. This seemed to be the only time that the pace slowed and the flow of people stopped. Bob and I used this time to prepare lessons and catch up with each other. School went until four, giving little time for errands and chores. Being a woman, I was expected to do all of the cleaning, cooking, and washing while Bob and the other men gathered at each others' houses or at the little shops sprinkled throughout the village that sold coconuts, bananas, rice, spices and occasionally sweets.

At dusk, the sky and air would turn a vibrant rose as everyone gathered at the river's edge to bathe and prepare for the evening meal. Before we came, the people of Matu had never seen or used soap or shampoo. We went through an entire bottle of shampoo each time we washed our hair as all were fascinated with having their heads covered in white suds. In the evening our house was filled with visitors. Unmarried men and women were not allowed to be alone together or even seen talking together as they walked through the village. Thus our house became a safe meeting place for young people to mingle with the opposite sex. Our parents had sent comic books from America. The young men and women would hide behind the comic books, giggling and taking notice of one another. On most nights our small house was filled with people of all ages wanting to exchange stories of life and customs in each of our respective "villages."

From the people in Matu I learned how beliefs can create reality. The villagers believe in ghosts and indeed ghosts do exist there. There were many reported sightings of ghosts near the graveyard. The school was next to the graveyard, which made it impossible to have classes in the evening for the adults as most were afraid of the ghosts. Each month there was a young woman, named Fatimah, who became possessed at the time of the full moon. She ranted and howled at the moon. Most of the villagers came and sat with her as she howled hoping to catch messages from the spirits. In a day or two she would be her normal self until the next full moon. There was one ghost, named Pontianak, who was a vampire. She was a young woman with fair skin and long dark hair, similar to me. Reportedly Pontianak would come out at night, seduce men and then suck the blood out of them. As a result,

I was warned never to leave the house alone, even for a trip to the out-house, or I might be mistaken for Pontianak and killed.

The people of Matu believe in magic and the existence of spirits in all things. The spirits are powerful and can bring great benefit or harm. The people pay attention to the signs from the spirits and to the rhythms of nature. There were ceremonies and rituals for all major events in the village in order to ensure the spirits' blessings. The local shamans blessed new houses before the occupants moved in; ceremonies of protection were held before major transitions. Bob and I were given a wonderful ceremony of protection and blessing before we left to return to the States. We sat up against a wooden post with our legs straight out dressed in traditional clothing. The local shaman put a substance like white paste on our foreheads, arms, and feet while saying incantations. He asked the spirits to grant us safe passage to our home and bless us with many children. He also asked the spirits to assure our return. The entire village came, and there was a feast afterwards.

I had several deja vu experiences while in Borneo, which caused me to wonder if deep within my being, on a cellular level, I had knowledge of this place. In addition to becoming open to the possibility of reincarnation, I began to understand that I was awakening to the powerful interconnection among the natural forces of the earth, an awareness that is lost in American culture, but one that lives dormant ready to awaken within each of us.

The month before we were to leave Matu, Bob received his draft no-tice. During the course of our time there, Bob had decided to apply to divinity school, one of the few remaining draft deferrals. This was not an entirely utilitarian decision, but stemmed from hours of spiritual discussion between us. In my heart I was jealous of Bob because I would have loved the opportunity to study religion, but I needed to get a job to support us. So instead of the leisurely six months trip through Asia and Russia on our way home, which we had planned, we had one month to get to Boston and Harvard Divinity School.

Turmoil and Growth

We arrived back in the states in January of 1970 to strikes, political demon-strations, and protests. After two years of daily live radio reports from Saigon and Hanoi on the events of the Vietnam War, we immediately became in-volved in the anti-war movement, anxious to release two years of listening to horror with no direct avenue to vent our displeasure. I was hired to work as a tutor and counselor in the Cambridge schools with "acting out" black boys, under the assumption that I had experience in dealing with dark skinned kids. I quickly realized that I did not have the skill or knowledge to address the pain and suffering these boys were experiencing. Even though I had never had a psychology course, I decided to go to graduate school to become a school psychologist.

For the next 20 years I struggled to integrate political, psychological, and spiritual ideas. As soon as I became comfortable and settled in one idea, I found myself challenged in new and unexpected ways. The intensity of this period was not always easy. I spent several years in psychotherapy and took a five-year hiatus from owning a television as I searched to find my own voice and true heart. My husband and I continued to be involved in left-wing politics while trying to enact change through conventional channels. Bob was a student minister in a suburb of Boston, and I had a job as a school adjustment counselor responsible for covering nine elementary schools. This meant that I was the therapist for 3,000 children and a consultant to their parents, teachers, principals and learning specialists. In the evenings we ran an alternative high school program in the parsonage where we lived.

I was increasingly uncomfortable with trying to work within the system, and convinced Bob to buy a run-down farm on an incredibly beautiful piece of land in New Hampshire to use as a weekend and summer retreat. This place became my haven, my soul's home where I began to learn to listen to my heart much as I had in Borneo. I can remember clearly a day when I was working on the farm. I looked up at the mountains around me, struck with the realization that there were two distinct voices in my head. One carried all of the messages and beliefs I had been taught throughout my life. The other contained what I really thought and believed. I realized that for a number of years these two voices had been at war. Later in my life I came to know that the true voice arose from the wisdom and knowledge that is in my soul.

Soon after our son, Josh, was born, Bob and I separated. Bob was edging toward a more conventional life style while I was becoming ever more deeply committed to the feminist movement and to political action that called for the eradication of racism, classism, and sexism. Acting on these beliefs, I lived in a political commune in which we were all committed to putting our beliefs into action. During the day I worked in a feminist therapy collective, seeing women of all economic backgrounds, regardless of their ability to pay, and spent almost every night in some form of meeting, political action, or consciousness-raising group. It was an exciting and growth-producing time. Bob and I remained good friends and jointly raised Josh.

During this period I largely ignored my spiritual life, yet at times I felt a hunger for further exploration in this area. Occasionally I read spiritual books and attended workshops and teachings from a variety of Asian masters, but the political line from the left regarding spirituality and religion was that it was an opiate that ignored the suffering of the masses. In the early eighties, I began to experience inner tension with my all consuming political lifestyle. Often I felt as if I were not doing enough to promote radical change within society at the same time feeling that I was drifting further and further away from myself. The challenges of my professional life also demanded that I pay more attention to my work life. Frequently I felt as if I were choosing between devoting my energies to my clients or my political commitments. Women who feared labeling and victimization by the traditional mental health system were attracted to the feminist therapy movement. Many of these women had suffered sexual, physical, and emotional abuse as children and were deeply wounded. I started questioning whether I had the knowledge and skills to adequately help these women. My empathy and compassion for what they had gone through helped form a trusting alliance, but I had not been adequately trained to deal with the extensive psychological damage that this type of trauma causes.

During one weekend political retreat the clarity for which I had been searching materialized. Lately there had been a great deal of political infighting amongst the various committees of the political organization to which I belonged, City Life, regarding the direction of the organization. We were nestled in a bucolic setting in the countryside, yet stuck inside a meeting room. I cannot remember the specifics of the debate, but it was difficult for us to listen to each other as each was trying to make his or her own point. There was constant jockeying for power and supremacy; personal issues seemed to color and, at times, overtake the political discussion. The next morning I awoke with a sense of clarity. I realized that healing the psyche is necessary before there is any possibility of real political change or we will just keep repeating the same patterns that cause those in power to become arrogant and hungry for more power. I decided to go back to graduate school and get my doctorate in psychology.

Despite my learning disability, I thrived in graduate school. I attended Antioch/New England Graduate School, an institution known for its progressive educational style and commitment to political change. The faculty viewed my radical past as an asset to the program. I pushed to better understand the role of culture and society in the formation of the psyche and the faculty appreciated me for this. Upon graduation, the school offered me a part-time teaching position in the doctoral program teaching ethics and clinical skills. During the six-year trek through graduate school, internship, and licensing, I had become remarkably mainstream. My parents heaved a sigh of relief that I had finally come to my senses. I had a thriving private practice, specializing in working with those who had endured some form of trauma. I had also reconnected with my spiritual life through Vipassana meditation, a form of Buddhist practice. I loved teaching and finally believed that I had found my niche. But once again, circumstances challenged me to open to radically different ways of perceiving reality.

Chapter 2
UNEXPLAINED MYSTERIES

I peered out the window looking for a client who was late. In the six years I had worked with her, Jenny always had been exactly on time. Suddenly someone was coming up the walkway, a woman I had never seen before. As she came closer I realized she strongly resembled my client yet, eerily, did not seem to be her. Searching for the right door, the woman looked around as if she had never been to my office. She rang the bell, apparently having forgotten the combination to the lock. As I opened the door to the office, my client stared at me blankly, sat down and looked around the office. Finally she said in a voice I had never heard, "Hi, I'm Julie."

I had read about multiple personalities but had always remained somewhat skeptical, believing it to be a rare condition if, in fact, it existed at all. So, nothing had prepared me for how I felt in encountering this whole new being that inhabited Jenny's body. After the first session with "Julie," I had a splitting headache. I felt confused and off center. In addition to my concern that I might not have the skill and knowledge to adequately treat someone with multiple personalities, I was unsettled, and struggled to make sense of something that was outside my frame of reference. How could a whole energy force take over a body? Where did the part I knew as Jenny go when Julie was present?

There had been hints over the last few months that Jenny might have other personalities; she reported that at times she was unclear how she had ended up in places with people she did not know, who seemed to know her. In the past she had explained away these occurrences as "black outs" since she was addicted to several drugs. As she began to control her addictions, she struggled to explain these bizarre encounters.

One Body, Many Lives

Julie was the first of five distinct personalities to emerge from within this client—three females, two males. They ranged in age from a three-year old to a grown woman of 35. Each had a different voice and unique mannerisms. A distinctive manner of dress and style of hair signaled to me from the onset who was present that day. One had a tic; one was farsighted, while another was nearsighted. Some had perfect vision. All but one carried a story of a horrible trauma that had occurred at the age in which the speaker was frozen. The personality that spanned the ages from early childhood to the present functioned as the "mother" for the different alters as they are called in psychological terminology. She had always been older than the rest and carried the energy of the perpetrators of the abuse that Jenny had endured as a child. She was extremely loyal to those who had abused and tortured the others and had internalized the abusers' voices and judgments. If the "mother" personality could not control the other parts of Jenny, she would torture them in ways that they had been tortured as a child. At times, the voices of her abusers would rage at me through the "mother" personality. It was clear there was another energy force present within her in those moments, separate from the six parts of Jenny. Initially the most challenging personality with whom to work was the "mother" alter, who saw me as the enemy. She too had stories of horrific abuse and, on occasion, had been present to absorb some aspect of all the others' trauma.

Each personality had specific stories and traumas to work through. As the stories unfolded, there was a total re-experiencing of the traumas down to feeling the physical pain of the torture as if it were happening in the moment. At times the body would manifest the scars of the abuse. The work was long and hard. Jenny showed remarkable courage to face the pain and horror of what had occurred to her. After each alter worked through his or her stories, he or she was then free to join or "integrate" into Jenny's conscious being.

At the same time I was working with another client, named Sara, who was a survivor of childhood ritual abuse. One day she began to recall a horrific memory. As Sara began to give voice to the image she was seeing in her mind, suddenly, she fell onto the floor writhing in pain. Her body was rigid and shaking violently. When I was in training in the early seventies, I witnessed a client receive electric shock treatment. Sara's body reminded me of this. When Sara stopped shaking and finally was able to speak, she reported that she felt as if she had just been electrocuted. Each time she got close to remembering the trauma, she again experienced the pain of electrocution. This phenomenon is commonly called "programming" where through torture and hypnosis the programmer inserts behaviors, beliefs, and responses, which are activated upon an external trigger. Sara struggled for weeks with the urge to electrocute herself. On several occasions she called me crying hysterically, telling me that she felt compelled to draw a bath, get in the water and then throw a turned-on hair dryer into the water. I referred Sara for hypnotherapy where she learned how to seal away the internal messages that told her to kill herself by electrocution. Yet this self-destructive energy hauntingly remained, and she continued to be plagued with thoughts of killing herself.

The Limits of Psychological Theory

The arrival of the new personality named Julie and the witnessing of Sara's "electrocution" occurred within weeks of one another. All of a sudden I was forced to grapple with phenomena for which words and theory were inadequate. Until recently, psychological literature had defined the process of different personalities residing in one body as multiple personality disorder. Now this phenomenon is referred to as Dissociative Identity Disorder by the diagnostic manual for the American Psychiatric Association. Although psychological literature used descriptors to confirm what I had witnessed, the theory seemed inadequate to explain the complexity of different voices, consciousnesses, physiologies, and even appearances residing in one body. Mysterious happenings had occurred; the language and ideas used to explain these happenings were flat, inadequate to match the depth and richness of what I witnessed.

My first encounter with programming had been in the movie, *The Manchurian Candidate*, a sixties hit dealing with the psychological manipulation of an American soldier in the Korean War in order to have him become a political assassin. Programming has long been a plot line for political thrillers and seemed confined to the intrigues of the CIA and foreign espionage. What did it mean that young girls were being "programmed" to kill themselves if they began to remember what had happened to them? How does one reach into the mind to gain control over another? I knew that programming can occur via some forms of hypnosis or when one is being tortured, but again these theories did not adequately explain how this really worked. I was simultaneously upset and intrigued both psychologically and politically as to how and why young girls were being tortured in ritualistic ways, resulting in the alteration of their physiology and psyches.

Over the years I had also struggled with more commonplace concerns. Many clients reported feeling there was a big hole inside of them—as if nothing were there. Some felt anxious, and feared that if the anxiety was taken away, they would have to face the nothingness that they intuitively knew was at the core of their being. Many of my depressed clients were already living in the dark hole feared by those filled with anxiety.

At times I wondered if it was possible to heal the pain that many had endured. I wanted to believe clients' wounds could be healed and the clients made to feel whole again by the safe and consistent "holding environment" of the psychotherapeutic relationship, which ideally allows for the processing and release of painful emotions. And for some, this did happen. Little by little I could observe them filling up with their natural energy and returning to wholeness. But others clung to the darkness, or the fear of this darkness, making outward or structural changes but never really feeling whole and content. For years I sat with a sense of disquiet, not quite having language or theory to explain my unease.

In the early 1990's my theoretical belief system was challenged, and reality as I had known it was altered, as a result of my work with Jenny and Sara and other clients like them. My professional life was just where I had dreamt it might be, when I discovered that I had many more questions than answers. Frustrating for me, many of my fellow therapists did not seem to be struggling with these same concerns. Some focused on new techniques and medications to treat the phenomena with which their clients presented, with little curiosity as to the root of what causes the psyche to rupture into separate or distinct parts or allow the voice and will of another to enter.

Other colleagues simply chose to deny or ignore occurrences that did not fit their existing constructs. In 1990 while teaching a seminar in the Boston area for medical students on the impact of psychological problems on the body, we discussed the possibility of multiple personalities. I told the students about a staff psychiatrist at the training hospital who had a patient with this diagnosis. One of his client's personalities had Crohn's disease, a severe intestinal disorder of such debilitating pain that often part of the intestine needs to be removed. The psychiatrist reported that the other personalities had no symptoms of Crohn's disease. All the medical students agreed this was impossible to explain scientifically. From the implausibility of this account, they went on to conclude that the phenomenon of different personalities residing in one body, not explainable by western medical theory, did not, therefore exist.

There are many within the medical and mental health professions who have reached similar conclusions. If observable phenomena did not fit within the existing framework, then the observation must be flawed and the observer and/or patient are describing a reality that does not exist. There are others who struggle to explain and understand occurrences that do not fit existing paradigms. The tension between these positions is on-going and part of a dialectic process. Whenever there is a theory, there are exceptions to the theory that eventually force the creation of a new theory. Usually most people will resist the new theory, but then it becomes the norm only to be challenged once again by exceptions to it. The dialectical process then begins anew.

A Return to Borneo

In the midst of my professional and intellectual crisis, I went on a long awaited trip to Asia that included a visit to Matu, my home for two years while I was in the Peace Corps. Like a magnet I felt pulled to return to the place that had been so important in my life. On my return visit to Matu in 1992, I was shocked by the changes. Most of the men are now loggers and that has led to significant changes in the environment and in the community. Open spaces and roads connect Matu to neighboring villages and to thriving garden plots away from the riverbanks. There is electricity, and even women ride motorcycles. With the land cleared there are few monkeys, bugs, or poisonous snakes. Another significant change is that the men who are off logging only return home two or three times a year. The few men left in the village are government workers, most of whom are my former students who had learned enough English to go on to secondary school. Finally, the standard of living has changed dramatically in Matu as it has in all of Malaysia. The homes have furniture, televisions, and telephones. Unfortunately the plumbing or lack thereof remains the same, but there is now a village water supply free of contamination. With a post office, library, small hospital, and two brand new well supplied schools, Matu has jumped from the 16th century to the 20th in twenty-five years.

The Bomoh

I traveled with my good friend, Georgette, a member of the religious study group back in college, who is a Jungian analyst. We were sitting in a "kadei" or shop having tea talking with one of my former students, Latip. He has the best command of English of all in the village and has one of the higher governmental jobs as director of parks and open spaces for the sixth division, which is a huge expanse of land including many villages. Georgette and I had just visited India and Nepal. In order to better understand the different cultures we were visiting, we decided to ask those we met about their spiritual and healing practices, especially as it pertains to the mind and emotions.

Georgette and I had visited the new hospital earlier in the day. We asked Latip how the villagers were mixing western medicine with the traditional healing methods of the past. He explained that most use a blend of the two, going to the hospital for vaccinations, pre-natal care, and broken bones, but that most still feel more comfortable calling on the Bomoh, the name given to a male traditional healer or shaman. The Bomoh mediates between the spirit world and this reality. He divines the origin of a problem or illness and the cure needed. He is also a master of removing spells and hexes, and has the ability to foretell important events or occurrences, such as weather changes or the sex of an unborn baby. Georgette asked Latip if he could arrange for us to meet the Bomoh. As it turned out, the Bomoh is the father of a student, named Yakuup, who I had taught 25 years earlier while in the Peace Corps. I had known Ismail Daim—the Bomoh's given name—before when he was just beginning on his shamanic path.

The Bomoh is a small, shy, unassuming man with an intensity and presence that becomes more apparent the longer you are with him. He rarely looks you in the eye and is often seen gazing out the window, distracted or entranced. Yet when he brings his full focus to a question or a task, I feel the power of his energy and the clarity of his intention. He is incredibly agile and, even though he is in his sixties, he can scurry up and down trees like a child of ten. The Bomoh's frame is quite small, yet his hands and feet are wide and strong and appear to belong to a man twice his size. Prior to his calling to be a shaman, the Bomoh had tapped rubber, fished, and did carpentry like the others in the village. When he was in his thirties, a water spirit appeared to him on the riverbank as he was grieving the recent death of his younger sister. Instead of being afraid when he encountered the spirit, he listened to her message, which directed him to become a healer, so that others would not have to suffer the pain he was feeling from losing a loved one at such a young age. His grandmother had been a shaman and he comes from a lineage that is tied to the Islamic Unani tradition as well as centuries old indigenous practices. The Unani practices date back to the time of the ancient Greeks and work with the power of intentionality, meaning that energy is transformed through focusing the mind.

Soon the Bomoh's house became a gathering place with many of my former students present as we talked about the different healing practices of our two cultures. I knew nothing of shamanism except for what I had seen and experienced while there 25 years ago. Georgette had done considerable reading on the subject and knew the right questions to ask. They were impressed that we were doctors of the "mind" and were intrigued to learn how the West deals with "gila" or madness. We were fascinated to hear the stories of a native healer and to learn how he deals with psychic distresses.

The Bomoh told us that various spirit guides, or genies as he calls them, have taught him most of what he knows. He has different guides for different illnesses and problems and works extensively with herbs and plants of the land. New spirit guides have appeared over the years to teach him new techniques and lessons. Ancient Unani texts written in traditional Arabic script are also used. For three years he studied with his grandmother until he mastered these teachings. The texts contain powerful prayers for various aliments and conditions. These prayers work at the deepest level of our being, altering the basic imprinting of the personality by shifting the vibrational field, thereby allowing healing for the soul. The Unani tradition works with the power of intention in conjunction with spirit guides.

The Bomoh travels throughout Sarawak to heal. The government sent him a document certifying that he is a bona fide healer and a white doctor's coat to wear when he does healings. He laughed at this and refuses to wear the white coat, because he says, he feels silly in it. He has been invited into hospitals to heal people western medicine has failed. He proudly told me the hospital pays him $75 an hour for his time. Traditionally the Bomoh does not charge for his services. People make whatever offerings they can to express gratitude for what he does; frequently he receives food or a prized object. The Bomoh was flattered that we were so interested in his way of healing and invited Georgette and me to go with him on healings. Even though I was curious about his method of healing, it did not occur to me initially that he would provide me with answers for many of the questions I had been pondering.

Uncharted Territory

The next day we went by boat to a distant village, built entirely over water, where a man was near death. I had never seen anyone look quite like he did. His body was simultaneously bloated and emaciated. His swollen feet looked like clubs; his skin had a greenish tinge; and he appeared to be about ninety. He was lying in a barren room being cared for by a young woman who I assumed was a daughter or granddaughter. I later learned that she was his wife; the man was in his late thirties. The Bomoh went into a trance state; he cleared his own energy by stilling his mind so that his spirit guides would take over and do the healing. He did this by lighting incense, "smoking" a white bowl with the incense, then pouring water into the bowl and blowing into it. The blowing released the spirits or genies into the room. He worked on an energetic level, only touching the man's body to apply a green paste and oil used in pulling out the illness on the man's belly and feet. He covered the man with newspaper while he said incantations and waved a knife to ward off evil spirits.

After the healing, the Bomoh told us the man was a fisherman. His boat had capsized two months before in the shark-infested waters of the South China Sea. It is rare for anyone to survive in these waters. In this case he was lucky to have been rescued before he was devoured. He returned home in sound physical health but dispirited. Over two months his health deteriorated until he was near death, but no one knew what was wrong. The Bomoh's spirit guides said the man's soul had left him from the shock of facing certain death at the jaws of a shark. In a trance state the Bomoh was able to find the man's soul and bring it back. He then asked the family to make an offering to the spirits to ensure his soul would stay with him. That evening the man's family called the Bomoh to say that he was sitting up; his normal color had returned; and he was able to eat. Soon he regained his full strength. He had been dying because a major part of his spirit or soul had left. Without this part, his physical body could not survive.

The idea that part of one's soul or essence could leave the physical body when faced with a terrifying or traumatic situation was my missing piece to the puzzle. Like tumblers on a lock falling into place, I connected with a deep understanding that had been just beyond my conscious awareness. The sense of emptiness many clients reported feeling was explained by the fact that part of their soul indeed is missing. It dawned on me that this might be a major cause of depression. How energy moves in and out of the body resulting in different states of consciousness, some subtle like the taking in of a parent's critical voice, or some dramatic as in the case of those with several personalities, became clear. The Bomoh described how other spirits or entities might enter the body when there is soul loss; they can hang around, haunt you, and make you feel "mad." The Matu woman, Fatimah, who had howled at the moon each month while we were in the Peace Corps, was believed to be possessed by a spirit. Many, at the time, listened carefully to her ranting in hopes of receiving information from the spirit world. If Fatimah chose to rid herself of the spirit, the Bomoh could remove it with relative ease.

Much of the Bomoh's work involves the removal of spirits or spells. Less reputable shamans are easily bought to perform black magic and cast a spell on someone with whom one is angry or perceives as an enemy. There was a widespread story of a fellow Peace Corps volunteer in Sabah who suddenly developed debilitating headaches. A few days after the headaches began, a woman was spotted squatting below the volunteer's window chanting. Identified as a local shopkeeper well versed in the practice of magic, the woman was angry at the volunteer because she had stopped shopping at her store. The shopkeeper decided to hex the volunteer.

The Bomoh and one of my students, Abdul Rahman, relayed a similar story. Many in Matu still practice the custom of arranged marriages. Abdul Rahman's mother had promised him to be married to one of his cousins. While studying in secondary school, he met a young woman with whom he fell in love and married. Abdul Rahman's mother was furious and banned them from living in the village. Because Abdul Rahman ran the library and his wife was a teacher, they lived in government quarters outside of the village. Soon his wife began having debilitating headaches so severe that she was unable to work. The Bomoh came to see her and found a stone in the back of the cabinet where she kept her clothes. This stone had been used to hex her. The Bomoh removed the stone and in doing so the hex was gone. He then went straight to the home of Abdul Rahman's mother who is also the Bomoh's first cousin. She had hired a man who works with black magic to place the hex. The Bomoh returned the stone and told her to stop this foolishness or the stone would be used to hex her. Knowing that the Bomoh is the most powerful healer in the area, she complied and her daughter-in-law's headaches were gone. Finally ten years later and after the couple had had six children, Abdul Rahman's mother begrudgingly accepted his marriage.

Soul loss can also cause physical illness, which can enter the body in the vacuum created by the loss of part of one's essence or soul. When the Bomoh treats someone with a physical illness, he is always mindful to look for the underlying cause of the problem, as in the case of the fisherman, as well as treating the person's body with healing herbs.

The Bomoh is held in high esteem by both the Chinese and Melanaus in Matu. Historically a shaman has been much more than a healer. The shaman would frequently be one of the community's leaders as a result of the shaman's ability to see beyond the concrete into the subtle interconnection of the spiritual, material, political, and psychological aspects of existence. Cultures that practice shamanism believe in an interconnection among all things. In shamanism the entire ecological system is utilized and understood in healing. Humans are just one part of this system. Healing ceremonies involve the entire community and extend beyond the healing of an individual. There are ceremonies done for harvests, new dwellings, and seasonal changes to name but a few. In order to truly heal the individual's soul, society as a whole must be healed. The Bomoh carries the knowledge and connection to the spirit world for all.

The evening before we were to leave Matu, the Bomoh invited Georgette and me to stay and train with him and be initiated into the path of the shaman. His spirit guides had come to him to tell him that we were called to follow this path. He asked if we were willing to accept the gift of spirit. Although we could not stay to train at this time, we assented and were initiated that evening even though we had no idea what to do with this gift or how it could change our lives. Since this ceremony is sacred, I am not at liberty to describe it here. The Bomoh's genies told him we were to learn this way of knowledge and healing and take it back to our country. By initiating us into this path, he extended his energy and wisdom to us through a process called transmission. Just as one can cast spells or sends negative energy, it is possible to extend part of one's wisdom and positive energy to another. A powerful energetic shift occurs when this happens.

We took the initiation seriously and were perplexed as to what to do with this calling. That night after the ceremony we lay awake waiting for the spirits to appear, terrified of what we might experience. As we waited, Georgette and I got the giggles; I am sure we kept everyone in the house awake with our nervous laughter, but nothing happened. No spirits appeared. We left early the next morning for a trip into the interior of the rain forests. As we sped by boat down the Rejang River, I wrote in my journal trying to assimilate what had happened. Suddenly I was aware that I was writing on the nature of good and evil from new perspectives and a more compassionate and comprehensive viewpoint. I could see that those who do evil acts are in soul wrenching pain and need to receive compassion in order to heal. In the following week as we wandered through Java, my mind was full of new insights, but no spirits appeared.

A week later while staying at the Gandhi Ashram in Bali, I began to feel and experience the spirits. Madam Oka, a venerable woman who had been a close friend of Eleanor Roosevelt, ran the ashram. Although we had written in advance requesting to stay there, we had to undergo a personal interview given to all guests. The ashram is a place for spiritual retreat, and Madam Oka wanted to ensure that each guest was sincere in his or her quest. Apparently we passed the test. She put us in the end cottage where the ocean waves virtually lapped the porch at high tide. An inlet on one side flowed into a lagoon behind us. Behind the lagoon was a beautiful terraced mountain. Madam Oka smiled and said, "the energy in this cottage can be a bit intense, but I think you girls are up for it. Few people can tolerate staying in this cottage so let me know if it is too much for you." The cottage was a duplex so we each had our own room. Neither of us slept much that first night. Energy swirled around our rooms moving objects as we drifted in and out of a heightened dream state. The next morning we awoke to find that the herbs and medicines the Bomoh had given us were removed from their bags and rearranged. The lid of the bottle containing cancer medicine had been removed and was carefully placed next to the bottle. Although neither of us saw any spirits, it was clear that energy forces were present. I could feel the presence of other beings in the room and felt the energy reverberate within my body; the power of these beings was overwhelming. In no uncertain terms, I experienced the power of the energy available to me and was both humbled and terrified by it. We had an urge to ask Madam Oka for a more energetically tame cottage, but decided to stay put and ride out several nights of intense energy with vivid dreams. When it was time to go, Georgette left her herbs behind, foreshadowing her decision not to continue on this path.

I tried to integrate the experience at the ashram and the teachings of the Bomoh with my western way of thinking. Part of me wanted to walk away, pretending that nothing had happened or to catalogue it as an interesting experience I had on my summer vacation. A stronger voice within told me I had no choice but to pursue this path. Georgette also struggled with her experience. Eventually she decided to continue her work of combining Buddhism with Jungian practice, allowing the shamanic to flow in where it would.

Chapter 3
SHIFTS IN AWARENESS

When the plane landed in San Franscico, I felt as if I had hit concrete. The magical and spiritual energy of Bali and Borneo had made me feel whole and at peace. Now I was confronted with the energy of a land focused on material gain and physical signs of success seemingly unaware of spirit. Would I be able to hold onto that magic, or would I fall back to sleep, lulled by a culture based on rationality and materialism?

Following my initiation by the Bomoh, I was full of excitement and anticipation but did not have any idea how to integrate all that I had learned, nor how to make sense of what had happened. I got in touch with a wise old mentor named Mary, who works as an intuitive and astrologer. Mary told me that my path was to integrate shamanism with psychotherapy. She suggested books for me to read and people with whom I should study. Before I could fully embrace these two disciplines, she said, I needed a better understanding of shamanism.

Prior to my trip to Asia I had been writing a book about the impact of violence in our culture on an individual's psychological well being. Mary told me to put the book on hold as I only had one sixth of the information that I needed. She said that the topic was much more complex than I was currently capable of conceptualizing.

I continued to work as a traditional western psychotherapist and to teach, all the while reading and taking courses in shamanism. My academic and intellectual training was strong and could not easily be dismissed. I needed to find a way to combine the two models. Having been a psychotherapist all of my adult life, that way of viewing reality was ingrained in my being. At first glance it seemed impossible to translate the teachings of the

Bomoh into a practice that would be acceptable in western culture. I doubted that there were many who would feel comfortable with my covering them in green paste while banishing evil spirits with knives in order to heal a psychotic episode.

Contemporary Shamanism

As I set out to better understand just what shamanism was, I decided to study with Sandra Ingerman and Michael Harner, two noted shamans in the United States. Shamanism, I learned, is an ancient healing method that has been practiced in virtually every culture at one time or another for at least 60,000 years. Anthropologists[1] have discovered a commonality in the shamanistic practice of culturally unrelated and religiously diverse peoples. The rituals associated with healing vary by culture, but there is a core process common throughout. At the apex of shamanic healing is "journeying," a practice of entering a trance state to seek information in realms of non-ordinary reality for the purpose of healing another. Shamans also can journey to gather information for themselves, for friends and family, or for the community at large.

The Bomoh shifts into a trance state by lighting incense, "smoking" the bowl with incense, adding water to the bowl, then blowing into the bowl; it is his way of calling in the spirits. His shift in consciousness is almost imperceptible to an observer, yet I could "feel" another energy working through him. Other cultures use drums or rattles to shift into a trance state, while some rely on psychotropic plants. In some cultures, the shift into trance is an elaborate performance with loud drums and bells, exotic costumes and spirits moving through the shaman in dramatic fashion. Given my quiet nature, I was appreciative that my teacher taught me to go into trance in a very gentle way.

While journeying, or being in a trance, one meets with spirit guides, power animals, and plant spirits. Power animals live in the lower world, a vast multi-layered realm inhabited by the healing wisdom of the animal kingdom. Power animals ground us in our instinctual energy—an energy that is needed to be fully in the body. Plant spirits connect us to the earth and the middle world; we live in the middle world. Each plant and tree has energy and wisdom. When we take time to be still and listen to a plant with our heart, we can sense what gifts the plant has to offer us and how we can work with each plant for health and healing. Spirit guides are teachers that live in the upper world. The upper world is also a multi-layered realm, which houses the vibrations of the great teachers and masters, as well as other beings and spirits. Spirit guides introduce the journeyer to universal knowledge. They also inform the person in trance what steps to take for healing another. In a trance state one is able to *see* traumatic incidents that resulted in soul loss or energy intrusions that have caused mental or physical illness. For some this *seeing* may be an auditory, visual, or sensory experience or a combination of all. Trusting one's guides, inner wisdom, and intuition is the basis of shamanic healing. Wisdom exists on different levels of reality, which we can tap by being still and going into trance. Some believe Carl Jung was talking about these other levels of reality when he described the collective unconscious and the well of wisdom that is available to all.

In the fall of 1992 I traveled to New York to attend a two-day workshop given by Michael Harner on shamanic journeying. More than one hundred people gathered in a junior high school gym in downtown Manhattan. Michael said that if we could journey here in this noisy crowded room we could journey anywhere. Michael taught us to journey via a drumbeat. The drum induces a trance state by entraining the right and left hemispheres of the brain, creating a theta or trance state.

During the workshop we often worked in pairs, journeying for each other. This helped to dispel the fear that we were just making up what we saw. The highlight of our work was retrieving a power animal for one another. Each of us has spirit guides and power animals. It is extremely important to know and work with these beings as they are our teachers and guide us through the labyrinth of non-ordinary reality. My partner and I had very powerful and confirming experiences. I first journeyed for Stefan. He had told me that he was sure his power animal was a lion, thus this is what I expected to find. Michael Harner told us that when we encountered an animal we would need to see it three times and/or have it enter our body before we would know for sure that it was the true power animal. He also told us that we could just ask the animal if he were the power animal. Almost immediately upon going into trance I saw a tiger that kept pacing back and forth. Finally I asked if he were Stefan's power animal. He looked me in the eye and jumped into me. Fortunately I was lying down or the force of the energy entering my body would have knocked me over. Michael had told us that once we had the power animal that we were to blow it into the heart and crown chakra of the person for whom we were journeying and then rattle around to seal in the energy. Without saying a word, I blew the tiger into Stefan's chest. He bolted up and said with excitement, "Wow, it is a tiger instead of a lion."

When Stefan journeyed for me, he was gone a very long time. I had been doing some journeying on my own prior to the workshop and had encountered various animals, but did not trust my own skills enough to be sure who my main power animal was. I had seen a fierce mythical bird a few times, but I had not known what to make of him. Finally, Stefan returned and told me that he was very confused by what he had found and he was not sure what it was. He had seen a large creature with wings and a beak like face, but this being also had powerful legs and arms like a very strong man. He had told Stefan that he was my guide so Stefan brought him back for me. As soon as Stefan described him to me, I knew immediately that it was the Garuda.

The Garuda, a shape shifting bird-man in appearance, is an important figure in both Hindu and Buddhist mythology. The Garuda is the protector of Shiva, the God of destruction and transformation in Hindu theology and is one of the four protective deities in the Shambala teachings of Buddhism. While I was in the Peace Corps, Bob and I had gone to Ankar Watt in Cambodia and had purchased a five-foot temple rubbing of the Garuda holding up Shiva. This hanging had been in my living room for the past 22 years. It seemed that the Garuda had been with me all these years, yet I was unaware of its significance to me. From this experience, I became convinced of the existence of the realms of non-ordinary reality and of the incredible wisdom that resides there.

After this powerful experience, I knew I needed to learn more about shamanism, as my rational mind needed feeding. I discovered that obtaining knowledge from other realms of reality was ignored and nearly lost to the West through the movement toward materialism during the Scientific Revolution, the Reformation, the Age of Reason, and finally the Industrial Revolution. During the Spanish Inquisition, nine million healers were labeled as witches and killed. In the New World Native Americans, who continued to value the spiritual above the material, were viewed as ignorant, superstitious, and primitive, which further diminished the value of spiritual information and knowledge in western cultures.

For a long period of time westerners thought that shamans were psychotic or mentally ill, not worthy of study or consideration. Not until anthropologists began to look seriously at shamanism as an important aspect of indigenous cultures did western social scientists begin to study shamanic practices.[2]

In recent years, there has been a resurgence of interest in ancient methods of healing. Initially this interest was confined to the "new age movement." But as people have begun to experience health and wholeness as a result of these ancient methods, modern science has begun to rediscover the importance of the mind/body connection in illness and healing. The acknowledgment of and pull to understand other realms of reality were popularized in the media through TV shows like the *X-Files* and *Buffy the Vampire Slayer*, and novels made into movies such as, *The Sixth Sense*, the *Harry Potter* and *Lord of the Rings* series. All of these explore the supernatural and other dimensions of existence.

Concepts from shamanism can be found in many aspects of western culture. In Judeo-Christian religions, followers pray to God, guardian angels, or other saints for help, guidance, and protection. Asking for help, guidance, and protection from one's spirit guides and power animals is a similar practice. Music and poetry throughout the ages are replete with images of soul loss, and of giving part of one's heart to another. Janis Joplin's famous line "take another piece of my heart" exemplifies this imagery. Further, this awareness is shown on an unconscious level when we speak of people "not being themselves" after the death of a loved one, surgery, or some other form of trauma. Whether we consciously acknowledge it, we are aware of an energetic difference when there has been soul loss.

From the workshop with Michael Harner, I learned that he has a foundation, which loosely oversees shamanic drumming circles throughout the country and runs a host of advanced workshops and trainings. I discovered that there was a gifted shamanic practitioner named Linda Crane, who ran a shamanic drumming circle out of her home in the magical coastal community of Gloucester, north of Boston. I went to see her to experience a shamanic healing from her. Linda performed a soul retrieval for me bringing back parts of my being that had been lost when I was a child, as well as the energy of a bone from my shamanic ancestors to help me on my path. I had not told Linda about the Garuda, but she reported seeing a magical bird-man figure assisting her in the retrieval. After the soul retrieval, there was a subtle shift in how I felt. I felt calmer, more peaceful, centered, and sure of myself. Everything looked and felt vibrant and alive; there was a quiet joy within me.

I began to attend the drumming circle and deepened my confidence in traveling in the realms of non-ordinary reality. I began to ask my guides about some of my clients and found their guidance extremely valuable. They seemed to cut right to the heart of the problem with a clarity I had not experienced in professional consultation or supervision. When I tried my guides' suggestions in sessions with my clients, it facilitated an opening to a deeper level of the therapeutic process. Despite these successes, I continued to hold back from introducing shamanic journeying to my clients or to talk about shamanism with my professional colleagues. I still feared judgment and ridicule.

In the spring of 1993 Bonnie, a friend and colleague, asked me to journey for a client of hers named Leah who had expressed a desire to do shamanic journeywork. I told Bonnie that if I contacted spirit guides for Leah, there was no way of knowing beforehand what I would find or what the problem might be. This lack of a map initially made me quite nervous, for, as a therapist, we are supposed to have a plan and be aware of where we are going. Thus with great apprehension, I met with my first shamanic client. During the journey a snake appeared. I was afraid that Leah would be displeased with the imagery of a snake for her power animal, and I was anxious about bringing the snake back. This fear was my mind's own projection, based on my perception of how people negatively view snakes in American culture, even though in many cultures the snake is a powerful healing and regenerative feminine symbol. Realizing my projection, I left it aside and told Leah about the snake and the snake's message. She then rolled up her sleeve. On her arm, there was a magnificent tattoo of the snake I had seen on the journey. The snake was the power animal for Leah and had given me the answer to the question she was asking, fanciful and metaphorical as that answer seemed to me. The metaphorical message made perfect sense to Leah, freeing her to make changes in her life. I heaved a sigh of relief and began to believe that maybe I could actually do this work.

Still, my fear held me back. I decided to attend a workshop designed to unblock the creative energy in the second chakra, which is the energy center below the navel that regulates emotions, creativity, and sexuality. As part of the workshop, we journeyed to a past life in which traumatic events had occurred that resulted in blocking our creativity in this lifetime. During the journey I found myself in France or Germany in the 16th century. As the vision came more into focus, I saw myself in a dark stone house with only the light of the fire to see by. I was a midwife and healer, attending a middle-aged woman who was giving birth. It was a long and difficult birth with many complications; the woman died. Death during childbirth was common at this time in history. However, the grief-stricken husband who was left with several children and no wife to care for them, vented his rage on me by declaring me a witch and a heretic. While I was preparing supper for my husband and three small children the next night, a group of men came and carried me away. I was placed on a stake in a field with two other women who were similarly accused. We were left there to freeze and starve to death. Our families were told that they would be killed if they tried to rescue us. It was a slow torturous death. One of the other women died first and I watched as vultures ate her body, knowing that this would soon be my fate. Then I saw myself die, felt the pain of the death, and watched as my body was dismembered.

I came back from the journey with the knowledge that I had been one of the nine million healers who had been killed by the church. Rather than fear that I would meet a similar fate in this lifetime, I felt a strong conviction to carry on the work I started in a previous life and to avenge that wrongful death. When I thought about it, the worst thing that could happen in the 21st century was that I would lose my psychology license and thus my ability to take insurance payments. Given that dealing with insurance companies is the bane of my existence, this did not feel like much of a deterrent. I left the workshop once again impressed with the power of journeywork to free up blocked areas in the psyche and with a renewed resolve to integrate shamanic and psychological techniques.

Soul Retrieval

That summer I took a five-day workshop with Sandra Ingerman in order to learn how to do soul retrievals. The workshop was held in a beautiful setting in upstate New York. While I was registering, I saw the name of the clinical supervisor that I had worked with for four years while I was in graduate school. I turned around and there was Loretta. We hugged and laughed and both said at the same time, "Why didn't you tell me that you were interested in shamanism?" I was thrilled and relieved to find someone I loved and valued as a psychotherapist on a similar path.

That workshop was a powerful and transformative experience for me. Sandra is an excellent teacher with the ability to be clear and concise while also transmitting the power and magic of the spirit world. She conveyed a plethora of information, much of which is detailed in her book, *Soul Retrieval*.[3]

Sandra had learned how to do soul retrievals from her spirit teachers, then she began studying anthropological literature and found that this same method had been practiced throughout the world for centuries. My first introduction to soul retrieval had been when I watched the Bomoh return the fisherman to health by retrieving the part of his soul that was lost when his boat capsized and he feared being devoured by sharks.

The key in doing a soul retrieval is to work with one's own spirit guides and power animals. Often the guides and power animals of the person for whom the soul retrieval is done are central in directing the healing. The guides and power animals do the work with the journeyer acting as the assistant. Essentially the journeyer has two jobs. The first is to be a clear channel so that she can report what is seen and done during the soul re-trieval while always holding a clear intention that the healing be for the person's highest good. The second job is to be the physical conduit through which the soul parts are returned. A healing is done for the soul parts before they are returned. Often this involves some form of energy work, done by the guides. Although each healing is unique, usually they remove any en-ergy belonging to another person or entity, heal it and send it on its way. Then they channel in healing energy from the divine source of light.

Frequently soul parts are found frozen energetically at the scene of the trauma. For example, it is not unusual to find someone's soul in the arms of a loved one who is deceased. Neither of them is free or whole in this state; the deceased's soul needs to be able to go to the other side and the incarnate person's essence needs to go back to ordinary reality. What is seldom known is that communication can continue through personal journeying with those on the other side. Spirit guides do any healings or rituals that might be necessary and assist the deceased in crossing over to the other side. Some-times part of one's essence has been taken by another and must be retrieved from this person. It is not uncommon for a parent to unwittingly take some of a child's soul energy. In many intimate partnerships one person might take part of another's essence. A healing is done for the person who has stolen the essence part as well as for the person whose soul part has been stolen. One would have no need to take part of another if there was not a hole in his or her essence body. We need to treat those that harm or take from others with love, compassion, and an understanding that harm is done as a result of pain and suffering.

During the five-day workshop with Sandra, we were deeply immersed in spirit and non-ordinary reality. I came away from this experience know-ing that this was my path. My way of viewing life had expanded and in that expansion was joy and peace and an inner knowledge that there was so much more to learn.

I came home resolved to share this experience with my clients. When my clients asked me about my vacation, I decided to tell them about the workshop. Some responded with great excitement, wanting to know more, hoping to shift our work to incorporate some of what I had learned. Others barely seemed to take in what I had said and went on to focus on their own issues, while a few others were anxious and worried about what I was telling them, afraid that I had changed. The truth was I had.

One of my clients was particularly excited by the idea of soul retrieval. I had seen "Sue" for several years in psychotherapy, long before I became involved in shamanic work. Sue had worked very hard in therapy and had clear insights into the dynamics and issues that held her back. Over the years she spoke frequently of feeling that a part of her was missing, that there was a black hole of emptiness that had the potential to engulf her. Sue, who was on medication to counter her depression, had done quite a bit of reading regarding alternative ways of healing. When I told her about the workshop, she wanted to know more. I talked to her about soul or essence lost, and the concept deeply resonated with her. Sue asked me for something to read, and I referred her to Sandra Ingerman's book.

The next week Sue came in reporting that she had been unable to put the book down, that it made perfect sense to her, and asked to have a soul retrieval. We discussed the pros and cons of my doing the work for her given her long psychotherapeutic relationship with me. I told her about Linda Crane's wonderful work. After a thorough discussion, Sue decided that she wanted me to do the soul retrieval. We scheduled a special time to do this since more than the usual one-hour allotted for psychotherapy was needed. Because soul retrieval is really a ceremony, Sue invited some people close to her to attend.

I began by asking those present to journey with me if they liked, or to meditate and concentrate on bringing healing energy to Sue. Then I checked Sue's energy field by running my hands above her body to see if there were any blocks or leaks in it. When there is soul loss, a vacuum is created in the energy body. In shamanism it is believed that the vacuum from the lost soul energy is the opening for emotional and/or physical illness to enter the energy field. Energy from other people or beings, as well as germs from the environment, can enter the field and cause all sorts of problems. Thus it is important to remove this energy through an extraction before beginning the soul retrieval. If the foreign energy is not removed, there will not be room for the returning soul parts and spirit guides. Sometimes during the soul retrieval, I *see* energy that needs removal. I also can direct the spirit guides and power animals to do the extraction work while the soul retrieval is in progress.

I brought back several soul parts for Sue but one was particularly important. During the journey, I was drawn to a desolate desert where I found an exhausted frail young woman lying alone on the sand. One of my spirit guides began to blow energy into her, but the energy would not penetrate her being; it kept bouncing back. A power animal that does the extraction work emerged and began removing rusty nails and iron, which was like a suit of armor. The power animal took the armor and formed it into a beautiful statue. Negative energy must always be transformed into positive energy before the healing is complete. Now it was possible for the spirit guide to blow the remaining energy into the body of the young woman. Soon a beautiful strong young woman stood tall and radiant.

When essence parts, spirit guides, and power animals are brought back, I blow them into a crystal that I have been carrying while I journey. Usually I blow through the crystal into the heart and crown chakra of the person, but some feel uncomfortable having me blow directly into them so I blow into the crystal and immediately give it to the person to hold. With Sue's permission I blew the soul parts and guides directly into Sue, then I gave Sue the crystal to hold and to keep. I took a rattle and shook it around her to seal in the energy that was brought back. Before I relayed my own experiences on this journey, I asked Sue and her friends what they had seen and experienced. One of the young women had seen Sue lying, void of energy on the sand in the desert and had become alarmed that I might have brought back this part to Sue. I explained what I had seen and the healing that had taken place before the soul parts were brought back. One never brings back an unhealed soul part.

After I blew the soul parts and guides into her, Sue said, she immediately felt a difference. I brought back three soul parts, but the young woman was the one that most resonated with Sue. After the shamanic healing, I asked Sue to take some time to meditate on what the returned soul parts and spirit helpers needed in order to stay and to listen for any messages they might have for her. Frequently a soul part wants to make sure that the conditions that caused the part to leave in the first place have changed; other times the parts or guides may have information about an event to share. I played a Tibetan Prayer Bowl during the meditation. The Tibetan Prayer Bowl, when played, releases a beautiful high-pitched sound that assists in altering the vibrational frequency. The overall purpose of extraction and soul retrieval work is the alteration of the vibrational frequency, returning it to a state of wholeness. At the end of the meditation I struck the gong for each soul part and spirit guide, asking Sue to invite them into her being on the deepest level if she wanted them to stay. Then I ask her to find a ritual to welcome the parts back and to do this ritual for the next ten days. Shamanic healings move energy, which alter the body's frequency level. Through ritual and loving attention to the returning parts, Sue was able to honor this shift in energy to ensure that the frequency on which she had been operating shifted. It is much easier to change old thought forms and patterns if the frequency is altered.

Rituals are a wonderful way in which to alter frequency and vibrational levels and free oneself of old habits and beliefs. Rituals are not a focus of life in western cultures; thus it takes creativity and dedication to bring them into one's life. If one does not work on integrating the energy that has been brought back, the soul retrieval is less effective. Sometimes the soul parts wander off again if the client does not properly integrate them. A ritual can be as simple as welcoming the soul parts and spirits helpers into one's being each day by a simple prayer or remembering, or a ritual can be more elaborate involving offerings, songs, or some form of artistic expression. The intention behind the ritual is the key in altering the person's frequency level; the form the ritual takes is immaterial.

After the soul retrieval, Sue felt strong and whole in a way that she had never experienced before. She took seriously her role in the integration process and created beautiful rituals for each of her soul parts, spirit guides, and power animals. Her confidence grew as did her ability to connect to friends in deeper ways. She was no longer depressed. Soon Sue went off her medication and felt fine. Both of us had difficulty trusting the power of the work as it was such a dramatic change, and thus we did not terminate our sessions altogether, but reduced them to once a month.

Ten months later, Sue encountered a situation that was similar to what had caused the soul part of the young woman in the desert to leave. The soul part that was found in the desert had left after having her heart broken. Her current partner had informed her that she had a crush on another woman, and thus Sue had great fear that she would be left again to face the unbearable pain of a broken heart. Returned soul parts tend not to stay if they encounter a situation that is similar to the reason they left in the first place. By the time we met again, her partner had recommitted to her, and the potential loss was diverted, but Sue was depressed again. When she came to see me for her next appointment, she felt so bad that she was considering going back on medication. I took a moment to journey and saw the soul part of the young woman floating near by. Since the situation that had caused her to leave had been positively resolved, the soul part wanted to come back. I reached out to bring her back. I opened my eyes and told Sue I had something to hand her. I handed her the essence part and told her to take the part into her heart. Sue felt the energy soar into her and immediately felt the depression leave. Several months later, Sue still felt whole and happy and we terminated our therapy sessions.

I strongly feel that one of the reasons Sue's soul retrieval brought such dramatic changes in her life was because she had worked very hard in therapy and had altered the negative patterns and thought forms which had caused her suffering. The soul retrieval would not have been as effective if she had not done this work. But conversely despite all of her hard work in psychotherapy, Sue remained depressed. It appeared that the depression was the result of soul or essence loss that needed to be addressed on an energetic level. Once her full energy body had been restored, the feeling of the void inside was gone. This example also shows how sensitive our essence energy is and how easily it can be shattered. The soul part that embodied the young woman was so afraid of re-experiencing the intense pain that caused her to leave in the first place that she left again. More than likely this part would have reintegrated on its own as it seemed to be waiting for an opportunity to return when I found her, but the shamanic work sped up the integration and healing.

Opening to a New Way of Being

The first two years after my return trip to Borneo in 1992, my outer life appeared the same as before, but inside the way that I felt, understood, and experienced life was changing. One day I became aware that I had crossed a line from which I could not return. I had not set out to do this, yet all of a sudden I saw and experienced the world differently. I could sense spirit and energy in everything. I began to remember on a cellular level the contentment that flows from knowing that you are connected to everything and everyone. I had awakened to a deep knowing that there is life and energy in all things, even rocks, trees and plants. The way life is structured in America began to feel alien, like a blip in the history of humanity when we lost touch with our connection to each other and the natural forces around us. At this point I was living among wonderful friends in Cambridge, an exciting, culturally diverse city. After almost 25 years, it was home to me. One night I dreamt that I was to move to Gloucester, the coastal town an hour northeast of the city where Linda Crane, the shamanic healer, lived. Gloucester is a beautiful fishing village edged with craggy cliffs holding back the surging ocean, and a wondrous wooded interior. Soon after this dream, I began to make plans to move with an inner certainty I had not known before.

My professional life was also affected by the inner changes that I experienced. I stopped teaching in the doctoral program in which I had been both student and faculty member, because I found it difficult to teach just one aspect of human behavior. I realized that psychological thought seems to stop at an edge just short of understanding the integration of energy and spirit into psyche. Carl Jung came very close to this integration years ago. Some believe that Jung was a shaman but that he knew the western world was not quite ready for such a deep level of synthesis of psyche and spirit.

Over time my psychotherapy practice also began to change. My new depth of understanding about how energy, spirit, and psyche interfaced altered how I came to understand my clients. I began to combine shamanic work and psychotherapy with many of my ongoing therapy clients. Others who came to see me solely for shamanic work may not have known that I was also a psychologist. In my clinical work I talked more about energy. I asked clients where they felt energy was stuck in their bodies. Most seemed to intuitively know, and were relieved that I would consider such things. Many clients knew or sensed that there was helpful energy around them. At the same time I continued to see clients who had no idea that I did shamanic work. Yet my work with these clients was greatly influenced by this shift in perspective as I was gathering information from my guides as I worked.

From a shamanic perspective it is not important what one calls oneself or the language used to describe what one does. What is important is meeting each client where she or he is and the intention that one brings to the work. Many theories, ancient practices, and techniques abound about how we heal because there are so many different levels on which to work and so many different ways to enter into the healing circle of an individual. The key is to find the right entry level for that particular person.

Chapter 4
PARALLELS BETWEEN
SHAMANISM AND PSYCHOLOGICAL THOUGHT

I have had the benefit of living in an indigenous culture in which receiving information from journeys or spirit guides is as natural as receiving information from the nightly news. When I am in Borneo, the way people do things seems natural and flows; just as when I am in America the way we do things feels familiar. It is relatively easy for me to step back and forth between these radically different cultures, but at the same time it is difficult to find a common language to explain one way of life to another. As I pondered these cultural differences and how to bridge them, I became aware of how powerful the media and the intellectual community are in shaping what we think. They clearly influence the formation of our thought forms and the boundaries and range of what we allow ourselves to consider as reality. We frequently dismiss thoughts as fanciful that have not been formally sanctioned by the culture either through media coverage or academic scrutiny.

Commonalties in Theory and Practice
As I strove to find my own integration of shamanism and psychotherapy, I realized that there are key elements of shamanism within each of the main theoretical traditions of psychology. When my former supervisor, friend, and colleague, Loretta, asked me to do a day-long workshop for psychotherapists, I was forced to find the language and theory to bridge the worlds of psychotherapy and shamanism. Those in the field of psychology have long struggled with the tension between regarding psychology as a science or an art. Psychologists strive for legitimacy through scientific research; yet they sense that the art of healing the psyche is largely a magical and mysterious process. In my work I discovered that each of the major psychological

theories is better understood by including an understanding of energy. Each of us is an essence or soul that carries an awareness of our higher purpose and place in the universe. Within the soul are the emotional, mental, energy, and physical bodies. I now believe that the major task of psychotherapy is to heal the personality so that one's true essence can emerge.

There are many levels to healing the soul, which range from the micro, or inner world of a person, to the macro or societal context. Psychodynamic and object relations schools of thought deal with the intrapsychic life of the individual. These theories focus on the inner workings of the psyche. Most of us spend a great deal of time focused on our inner world, a world to which we seldom give voice. Many of us find ourselves stuck in images and feelings from childhood. These images and feelings create an energetic imprinting. The hurtful, rageful words of a parent stick to a child's energy field like velcro, haunting the child with feelings of shame and inadequacy. Frequently, blocks to the removal of this energy can be found in our thoughts or cognitive processes. Through shamanic work these hurtful words can be energetically removed.

Cognitive therapy focuses on the rational aspects of the mind. This theory investigates how irrational thoughts and feelings cause emotional suffering and devises therapeutic treatments to alleviate these destructive thoughts and feelings. In shamanism, thoughts are believed to be energy. Many thoughts are quite fluid and come and go such as noticing changes in the weather or contemplating what we are going to eat or wear. Thoughts, such as "I am an inadequate person or a disgusting person," may become rigid belief systems or thought forms creating an energy form that is a non-material entity. Often I *see* and *feel* these rigid thought forms as burrs or spikes intruding into a person's energy body.

By using shamanic extraction techniques, I have found that it is possible to remove these thought forms through the help of my spirit guides by pulling them out of a client's energy field and transforming them into some form of healing energy. But first the client must understand the issues embedded in the thought forms and be willing to relinquish the old thoughts and patterns or the mind will re-create the energy forms causing the non-material entity to re-materialize. In some traditional cultures this is not the case. There is not the attachment to the workings of the mind that we have in industrialized countries. Traditionally a shaman can remove a strange object such as a thorny branch from a person's field, without any understanding of what it represents and the person will be healed. In my western practice, I have found that if I remove something that has not been con-

sciously dealt with, within a few weeks it re-materializes. Once when I journeyed for a client, I saw her covered in the dark cloud of her mother's pain.
The client had been led to think she caused her mother's suffering and thus
believed she was deserving of this pain. This belief operates like spikes holding the tent of her mother's energy in place. The spikes or beliefs first must
be understood and processed emotionally and then removed energetically
before healing and transforming the pain in which she is enshrouded.

On the macro level there are interpersonal and societal beliefs that
shape and influence the inner workings of the mind. Cultural, religious,
and governmental beliefs frequently become rigid thought forms, appearing as truths when they are merely a set of beliefs or thoughts. In America,
for instance, we are told that it is our responsibility to be the policeman for
the rest of the world. This belief justifies spending billions of dollars on the
military while millions of our citizens-including one out of every five chil-
dren-go to bed hungry at night. Our environment is at risk as the result of
governmental and business practices tied to military preparedness. The notion of defending against attack seems to outweigh a sense of caring for our
most vulnerable citizens

The societal belief that one must be prepared to fight for what is right
is transferred to the interpersonal level. People get into violent fights for
cutting each other off in traffic and women are battered for minor perceived slights such as not having dinner ready on time for their companions. Domestic abuse, incest, and rape are all too common within the United
States.

Societal and interpersonal violence have destroyed the psyche and soul
of millions of Americans. Many seek treatment for trauma and abuse, for
psychological problems caused by another's violent action. Trauma survivors are prone to addictive behaviors as they attempt to fill the emptiness of
soul loss and protect the mind from painful images. Frequently, trauma
survivors experience periods of dissociation, a process where part of the
psyche separates from the whole. A key aspect of healing traumatic experiences is to help a client bring dissociated experiences or memories back into
consciousness. For more than 60,000 years, shamans have facilitated the
healing of dissociation by bringing back a person's lost soul parts.

I conceptualize and *see* the psyche as being comprised of different layers. Interestingly the various psychological theories reflect each of these layers. There is a spiral of interconnection among the differing layers of the
psyche from the inner workings of intrapsychic processes, to the cognitive
or rational aspects of the mind, to the contextual. Systemic thought asserts

that the contextual—meaning the family, community, spiritual, and cultural heritage of an individual—has an enormous impact on the inner psychological make-up of a person and on the beliefs a person holds. Cultures that practice shamanism believe in an interconnection among all things. Everything is viewed as part of the whole, mutually dependent and valued. The shaman is charged with holding the vision of the whole, in all the layers and meanings from the physical elements of this realm to the magical of the spirit realms. As my shamanic practice deepens, I can *see, sense,* and *experience* the layers of complexity that make us who we are.

Case Study

In my work with Patti, a trauma survivor and a scientist, I did psychotherapy without utilizing shamanic techniques directly; yet, I brought my awareness of the energetic to guide the course of healing. I was just starting to integrate traditional shamanic techniques into my practice and felt cautious about explaining these practices to a scientist trained in the West. Patti had many of the classic symptoms of posttraumatic stress disorder such as nightmares, numbing, difficulty concentrating, startle reactions, and sleep problems. Frequently she dissociated in session—her mind far away from me and the room we were in. I began to ask her where she goes when she dissociates and what it is like there. As she paid more attention to this space, she was able to describe it as safe, a place where she likes to go. Patti was even able to identify that she does not like it when I ask her where she is because she prefers being over there to being in the room with me and dealing with painful feelings. Over the weeks as we explored this more, she began to tell me about a little girl she saw hiding in a corner. The little girl was in abject terror, matching the feelings Patti had been having for months. We worked with this realization for several weeks. Then she began to see what the little girl was afraid of; she was watching another little girl being hurt by a big man. Gradually the story unfolded that the big man was the little girl's father and he was raping her. More time passed and Patti realized that she was the little girl who was watching. She experienced all of the feelings of the little girl watching. This freed her to go on to experience herself as the little girl being abused. Finally after intense processing, Patti experienced the little girl as separate from her, living in this room far away. She created a ritual to invite the little girl to come to live within her and the little girl left the separate space and joined with her.

Patti's story illustrates the process of a separated part of one's essence being brought back to the core essence over the course of several months of twice-a-week psychotherapy. As a result of my understanding of shamanism, I carried an awareness that part of the essence was split off and could be brought back. This directed how I worked with her. It was apparent Patti had varying degrees of connection to the lost essence part. There was a tug in the form of nightmares, depression, and affective states of terror that connected Patti to the little girl. Her experience also illustrates that, in addition to the little girl who was abused, there was the dissociated part that hid in the corner watching the abuse as it happened. The dissociated part that was watching needed to be healed before Patti could connect with the abused girl.

Now the question comes to mind, where was this little girl? Did she reside in Patti's unconscious or was she outside of Patti in another realm of reality that is easily accessed? Was this a process where energy re-materialized into conscious memory? This is where we run into the limitations of language and of existing constructs. To my understanding, psychological theory does not adequately explain where one is when one dissociates nor the process that occurs when one reintegrates from a dissociated state. This is one of the reasons that the topic of repressed memories is so hotly debated today. It is difficult to answer these questions with western scientific theory. Through exploring a shamanic approach to working with dissociative states, it is possible to find answers to these questions.

Grounding in Scientific Thought

In trying to answer some of the above questions and to understand the relevance of shamanism to psychotherapy, I discovered the importance of exploring the shifts in scientific thinking that embrace a fuller understanding of energy. The movement of energy, utilizing all aspects of the environment, is at the core of shamanic healing. Healing takes place by removing unwanted energy from the body or energy field and bringing back soul energy that is lost or stolen. Often spirits from plants, animals, rocks, minerals or crystals are called in to facilitate a return to well being. We are just beginning to understand and experiment with the power that can be marshaled by utilizing the human energy field and psychic energy. People are studying and working with energy from a variety of disciplines, including quantum physics, chaos theory, acupuncture, vibrational medicine, bioenergetics, Reiki, therapeutic touch, polarity therapy, the Feldenkrais method, and Alexander technique, to name a few.

Reflecting on these disciplines, which incorporate working with energy helped me understand shamanic practice within current scientific traditions. Ironically I had never been able to grasp western scientific thought. I now have a better understanding of western scientific theory as a result of my understanding of the energetic.

For the past three centuries, we have defined our experience in terms of three-dimensional space and linear time. The belief in linear time has profoundly affected our understanding of the after-life. Since the late 17th century, Newtonian thinking has dominated scientific and popular thought, asserting that reality is determined by what can be examined, measured, and quantified: in sum, that which exists has a material base. Within the Newtonian theoretical frame, people are viewed as solid objects and the universe comprised of fundamental building blocks called atoms. Religious teachings were based on interpretations of the stories in the Bible. The miracles performed by Jesus were seen as proof that He was the Son of God since there was no scientific way to explain what Jesus had done. Those healers who attempted to tap into the same divine energy, and who saw a more spiritual and mystical view of reality, were frequently labeled witches and heretics. Many were vilified and executed, sending the message that it was not possible to be simultaneously a follower of God and open to the incredible healing powers that God has made available to all of us.

The Christian belief that there is a heaven and a hell and that there are rules to be adhered to in order to reach the kingdom of God brings a concreteness to the interpretation of the teachings that does not fully address the power of spirit and the care of the soul. Nor does it add texture or dimension to the other realms. A growing number of Christians and Jews are beginning to explore the mystical traditions of their faith in hopes of connecting to spirit on deeper levels. It seems that there is a hunger to break out of the rigidity of thought from the past several hundred years.

In the twentieth century, Einstein's theory of relativity began to counter Newtonian materialism. According to the theory of relativity, space is not three-dimensional and time is not linear. Indeed there may be as many as ten dimensions or more. Space and time are intimately connected forming a fourth dimensional continuum, "space-time." Space-time is analogous to non-ordinary reality. Cultures unaffected by Newtonian thinking, such as Native American and Australian aborigine, have two kinds of time, the "now" and the "other time," which is also referred to as the "great time" or "dream time." When one is in the "other time," one is having experiences in non-ordinary reality and is in the fourth dimension that Einstein theorized.

Another important aspect of relativity theory is that energy and matter is interchangeable. Matter is simply slowed down energy; our bodies are energy, and so are our thoughts. Part of our energy can leave the physical body behind and exist in other places and in other forms; it can travel in our dreams and take shamanic journeys. We might do this when we drive a car along familiar routes. Suppose that you recently had a disagreement with someone. While driving you are back at that encounter, reworking and creating a new way of understanding it that makes sense to you. Your thoughts have created your version of what happened and more than likely a scenario for the next encounter. All of a sudden you are home with little awareness of having been in the car. You were on a different plane. Part of you was driving the car, carefully obeying the rules of traffic, while another part reworked the encounter and created a new one. This is also an example of the process of dissociation—existing in one reality while at the same time being in another.

From an understanding of relativity theory, some ancient beliefs have reemerged for consideration. One such ancient belief system is the human energy field. Barbara Brennan[4] describes the human energy field as a three to three and a half-foot "luminous body that surrounds and interpenetrates the physical body." Commonly referred to as the "aura" or the "auric body," it is the manifestation of universal energy and is holographic in nature, meaning that it can move in and out of matter and take on form or image as it needs to. Dr. Karl Pribram,[5] a noted brain researcher, has accumulated evidence over the years that the brain's deep structure is essentially holographic, as is the structure of the universe. For many people, the first introduction to holographs was in the movie, *Star Wars*, when Obi-wan Kenobi's ghostly image emerged. My understanding of the holographic is that at the core of existence everything is an energetic or vibrational frequency that has the capacity to materialize into matter as well as de-materialize and reconfigure much like Obi-wan Kenobi did. I had been told that some highly evolved spiritual practitioners were able to de-materialize or make themselves invisible. When I asked the Bomoh about this practice, he told me that it is a dangerous practice because it is extremely hard on the nervous system. He said that I should try it only if faced with a life-threatening situation. I have since realized that just as one builds up physical body strength, one must also develop and strengthen energetic capacities or great harm can result.

Karl Pribram and David Bohm[6] noted quantum physicists, who were driven to find answers to phenomena that were not explainable by existing paradigms, independently discovered the holographic model. According to Pribram, the brain uses a holographic process to abstract information from a holographic domain that transcends time and space. In the movie, *Contact*, based on noted scientist Carl Sagan's novel of the same name, Jody Foster's character, Ellie, took a voyage through the universe that lasted 18 hours by her account. Yet the voyage lasted only a few seconds in earth time. This aspect of the movie captured the transcendence of time and space on the physical plane when dealing with other realms of reality. When I return from a journey for clients, I am often amazed that so little time has passed on the clock as it feels that I have traveled so far and experienced so much.

The human energy field is an example of the fluidity of the holographic model. The aura is both inside and outside of linear time and three-dimensional space as it weaves in and out of the body, expanding and contracting energetically. According to Barbara Brennan[7] scientific study of the human energy field has been going on since 500 B.C. and many components have been measured in the laboratory including the electrostatic, magnetic, electromagnetic, sonic, thermal, and visual. Reportedly there are seven layers to the human energy field. The first three layers reflect the structures of our definable reality. These are the physical, emotional, and mental bodies.

The fourth layer is the astral layer, which connects us to other realms and other frequencies of knowing and understanding. We travel to the astral plane, another realm of reality, in the dream-state. Energetically we exit the auric body, which is the container for our soul, via the astral layer. We also interact with people on this level especially in the area of romantic attraction. Many people have had the experience of going to a party and sensed there is someone across the room that they would like to know. As they are talking to one person, a part of them is checking out a person across the room; a part of their energy is actually connecting with the other person's energy. In a little while they have a sense of whether they do or do not want to meet this person without even having spoken one word to him. This whole process is taking place on an energetic level that stems from the astral layer.

The next three layers are higher spiritual forms of the first three. In the fifth layer one's physical body is represented. Those who have the ability to read auras can actually see diseased organs in this part of the aura. Thus if you have a liver ailment, a diseased liver will be visible in the energy field about two and a half feet away from the physical body. Scientists have created instruments such as the x-ray and the CAT scan to capture what is within the potential of the human eye to grasp. The Bomoh is not only able to see within the body and auric field, but is also able to psychically remove tumors through the help of his spirit guides and the power of intentionality.

The sixth and seventh layers represent higher forms of spiritual connection. The sixth layer is where spiritual ecstasy and the feeling of unconditional love are experienced. On the seventh level it is possible for your energy essence or soul to become one with the creator or the creative energy of the universe. There is a protective field similar to an eggshell around the seventh layer. Pulling light energy in through the crown chakra and radiating this energy out the heart center strengthens this protective layer. This in turn strengthens and expands the outer edges of the energy body and sends loving energy to those around us.

The Dreambody

As I journeyed more for my clients, I began to *see* what psychologists call an ego structure appear as energy frequency bands. Those who were fairly solid in their sense of self had a wide frequency band with fainter bands surrounding it. Those who have experienced trauma and abuse had several thinner bands that would fragment or shatter into little pieces when upset or triggered by a memory of abuse. Other times there were several different and disconnected bands representing distinct but disconnected ego states.

A client I'll call Frieda came to me in an almost psychotic state. She had endured horrific abuse as a child. As I journeyed for her, I saw the core of her energetic band unraveling into separate, chaotic threads, almost like an energetic shattering. Frieda's and my guides set to work to contain and reconfigure the unraveled energetic bands much like one would do when making a ball out of string or rubber bands. Then we surrounded her in the divine light of the universe and called on all of her guides to encircle and contain her. After this Frieda felt calmer and more coherent, but still a bit dazed.

We are aware that energy exists on different frequencies. This is how our telecommunication system operates, with many frequencies sharing the same space and time. Psychically, people operate on different frequencies as well, making it easier for us to relate to some people more than others. The psyche is part of the soul. Within the soul are the energy and physical bodies as well as the psyche, which includes the emotional and mental aspects of the mind, all of which are vibrationally housed in the dreambody. The dreambody operates on various frequency bands. For instance the frequency wave of the physical body is denser than that of the energy body. Yet we need all of the various ranges of vibrations to be healthy and whole.

In journeys I have perceived the dreambody to be an energy form that fits like a hood around the top half of the body attaching at the solar plexus in the front and the kidneys in the back. It is holographic in nature and weaves in and out of the auric field and the physical body. Stored within the dreambody are the various frequencies that make us who we are including experiences in this lifetime as well as those from other lifetimes. Our consciousness or ego makes up the widest frequency band. Unconscious processes that are close to consciousness have a stronger vibrational frequency than those of past lives. When the unconscious processes become conscious, they merge with the dominant frequency band. Returning to the question of where Patti's various dissociated states resided, I believe that they were housed in the dreambody. Each image came more closely into focus until the unconscious or split off frequency band merged with the band holding consciousness, becoming integrated into the core ego structure or frequency band.

When I do an extraction and soul retrieval, I am removing energy or frequencies of others that do not belong in the main frequency band of my client and then bring in fainter vibrational frequencies, known as lost soul parts, into the consciousness of the main frequency band. The client must bring focus and care in the integration of the new soul parts or they can float out of this dominant band. Past life memories are also stored in the dreambody as faint vibrational frequencies. I had several déjà vu experiences when I first arrived in Borneo in 1968. These experiences alerted me to past life memories I had of Borneo when the frequency bands containing these lifetimes were brought into consciousness.

The dreambody detaches when we go into trance during a shamanic journey. In the movie *Contact*, we get a visual understanding of how this works. The structure sending Ellie into space created such a high frequency that Ellie's energy body sped through the universe while her physical body stayed behind. The movie brilliantly showed the energy body moving out from the physical body via the intense vibration that was created.

When the physical body dies, the dreambody carries our soul away. The more one journeys, the further one can extend the frequency range in which one can travel. Skilled shamans perform psychopomp, which is the accompanying of a deceased's soul to the other side and then the shaman returns.

To see auras and to psychically remove tumors, a healer shifts into higher frequency levels while staying grounded in the physical realm. As the shaman becomes skilled in shifting frequencies and going into trance while staying present in the physical realm, she brings focused intentionality to the trance state, making it possible to move energy around and do such things as remove tumors. A shaman usually practices for many years before getting to this skill level.

The Limitation of Language and Cultural Constructs

As I have deepened my shamanic practice, I have been struck with the difficulty of conveying the powerful images of my journeys to others, especially to my professional colleagues. Initially my understanding of what I was *seeing*, *sensing*, and *experiencing* was greater than my ability to find language and a common context in which to share this information. Words describing frequency bands and the dreambody are flat compared to the vivid images I experience in my journeys. My journeys are multi-dimensional, multi-contextual and metaphorical. Because they exist outside of traditional western intellectual frameworks, it is difficult to define such expansive experiences in a rational concrete way.

Language, which plays an enormous role in defining what we think and how we comprehend, can limit or expand our capacity for understanding. In Matu, one word, *tod*, embodies the concept of the "place" in the universe where one is—earth, town, city, state, country, and planet. This word is inclusive on one level, but excludes important political and geographic distinctions. In contrast the English language is very strong in describing distinction but weak in having words that embody inclusive concepts. The field of psychology also tends to specialize and break things down into small units. The diagnostic categories used to define mental health clients can limit how they are understood, as can the theories that have been created to define their behavior. Narrowing our understanding of a client to pre-existing labels and theories demeans the richness of the individual.

In contrast, shamanism does not work within the confines of a traditional diagnostic system. A person may have a cold, but the cold may be symptomatic of another problem. The shaman works with her guides to find the root cause of the problem, which may manifest itself as either a psychological or a physical ailment. When one contacts spirit guides on behalf of another, there is no pre-ordained idea of what one will find or what the problem might be.

Each healing in shamanism is unique; its meaning and symbols come from another source of knowledge, a wisdom to which each of us has access. In the West we have a theory, we diagnose, and we define what the problem is. When we work to place the dynamic energy of the person being treated into existing constructs, we narrow the possibilities. Yet many who practice psychotherapy also define magical moments with clients when the right words came at the right moment and there was a breakthrough. Chances are those words were spontaneous. Afterwards, when processing the session, the therapist finds theory to explain what she did. More than likely the therapist and client were so attuned to the same frequency level that the therapist could enter the client's energy field and find the correct place to enact change.

At times, conventional thought patterns prevent us from making the mental leaps necessary to understand the nonmaterial or energetic, thereby limiting our full understanding of a person. Traditional shamanic practice may need to expand to embrace the workings of the western mind, a mind in pain as a result of the complexity of our interpersonal and intrapsychic musings. Thus each tradition has much to learn from the other.

All of us have the capacity to be in touch with vast amounts of universal information if we allow ourselves to be open to another way of experiencing reality. The work I did with psychotherapy clients who had endured horrendous torture, at times resulting in the creation of other personalities, forced me to be open to other explanations. There was no other way for me to fully understand what I was witnessing when different people moved in and out of the same body. There simply were no adequate constructs in western thought to explain what was unfolding before my eyes. Thus as I embarked on my trip to Borneo in 1992, I was more ready than I realized for a new way of understanding the humans condition.

Chapter 5
Teachings from the Bomoh

In 1996, I returned to Borneo to study with the Bomoh. I approached my meeting with him with great anticipation and apprehension. On the one hand I feared he would take one look at me, see me as unworthy, and dismiss me. On the other hand I knew that if the Bomoh took me on as a serious student, there was the distinct possibility that my life, as I had known it, would be changed forever.

I traveled to Borneo with my friends, Georgette and Cassie. Both Georgette and Cassie had been to Matu with me before. Cassie and I were both in the Peace Corps in the late 60s and Georgette accompanied me on my previous trip in 1992. We arrived in Matu on a Sunday evening in August, tired and exhausted from a long day's journey that included a harrowing walk on a gangplank that connected the boat on which we were traveling to the shore. It was low tide so the thin piece of wood that was the gangplank extended vertically at a terrifying tilt. There was a twenty-foot drop into the narrow slit of water between the boat and retaining wall of the dock. The three of us looked at each other with alarm fearing that this was an impossible feat. We called on our spirit guides, kept our eyes focused on our feet and moved at a steady pace. We were all shaking as we hugged after we safely made it to the other side.

Although I had given the Bomoh's son Yakuup our arrival date, everyone thought we were arriving two days later and no one was prepared to receive us. Yakuup, his wife and four children were staying at the Bomoh's while Yakuup and his father built a new house for Yakuup's family; thus there was no room for us there. There was confusion as to where we were to stay and who was going to cook for us. There are no hotels or restaurants in

Matu. Things did not feel right. I was a nervous wreck, and according to my traveling companions, difficult to be around. Finally after much conferring and scurrying around, they decided to put us in a little cottage behind Latip's house, which was due to be torn down soon. It was a bit musty and two of us had to sleep in the one bed while the other one slept on the floor. With rats and other interesting creatures running around the cottage, I felt I should sleep on the floor since Georgette and Cassie had been kind enough to accompany me to Matu. Latip's wife, Eta, agreed to cook for us.

Early the next morning the Bomoh stopped by the cottage to tell us to come to his house after dinner. Although I spent the day visiting with many friends in the village, the day dragged on as I awaited my meeting with him. Finally it was time to go to his house. After pleasantries and an exchange of gifts, Yakuup, his son and our translator, asked, "What is it that you want from my father?" My heart fell to my feet. I replied, "I have come to study with your father if he is willing to take me on as a student." After what seemed like an interminable amount of time, Yakuup translated, "My father is willing to extend his guides to me through a ceremony of transmission. Did I want them to be outside of me or in me?" I felt taken aback. This was not the response I expected! I regained my composure, and replied, "Since I already have several guides around me, I would like them to be inside of me."

The Bomoh accepted my desire to study with him with a serious sense of responsibility. During the day I observed him sitting in a corner of his house, pouring over the ancient text from his grandmother, studying and preparing for my transmission and training. The ancient texts are written in Jawai, the Arabic language. It is unclear if they are solely from the Unani tradition or also contain the wisdom passed on orally from the native people in Borneo. Frequently the Bomoh called to his wife for help in translating the text. In the lineage tradition of the Unani, the teachings are passed directly from one person to the next. Although others from his country had wanted to study with him, I was the first student he had accepted. Yakuup had expressed some interest in the practice but was not yet at a point in his life that he could make a commitment to follow his father's path. Our agreement was that the Bomoh would teach me and then one day I would teach his son.

During the days following our first meeting, I accompanied the Bomoh on healings. My memory of the language had faded and there was no translator during the day; thus our communication primarily consisted of gestures and facial expressions. Frequently I was confused about where and when we were going, and how we were getting there. Transportation was an issue. The Bomoh traveled by motorcycle, but I did not know how to drive one so they had to find someone with a car that could drive us. I often felt anxious and disoriented and was also concerned about how Georgette and Cassie were doing. During the healings, the Bomoh beckoned with his hands for me to come and sit beside him as he did his work. Occasionally the Bomoh motioned for me to do the healings myself or to offer my sense of what the problem was. Because of language difficulties, it was hard to ask questions or receive information about patient's symptoms or problems. I had to totally trust the spirits and my intuition. Because I had no diagnostic map to follow, the only information I had about a person's problem came from what I could sense from looking at the person before me. Sometimes I had no idea what was happening and struggled not to feel like a failure or a fraud.

One day the Bomoh asked me to tell him what was wrong with Kassim, a young man I recognized from the previous visit, who had come for help. He did not look ill; he looked like his normal self. The Bomoh pointed to Kassim's face. I looked into it and his eyes seemed to flutter. The Bomoh asked, "Where is the problem?" I replied, "with the eyes." "Yes, it is the eyes, but what is the problem?" I did not know. The problem was that the Kassim could not find his money and had come to request the Bomoh's help in locating it. The Bomoh told him where to look and the man went home and found his misplaced money. Often I did not know how to approach the person or problem before me. I did not know if a person was suffering from emotional or physical pain or something as seemingly insignificant as a misplaced object. Yet that was just the lesson that I needed to learn; I had to stop thinking in categories so I could clear my mind and let the necessary information flow through.

In the evenings the Bomoh, Yakuup, and I met at the Bomoh's house. I asked questions about all that I had seen and observed during the day and took copious notes as he explained the magic of his work. The Bomoh works with herbs, ancient prayers, and the strong power of intention that flows through him from his spirits. One day I accompanied the Bomoh to see a Chinese woman who lived in the adjacent village and had become unable to walk. I watched him bring life back into her legs by pressing on various points on the body. I asked, "How did you know which points to press?" He said, "Not to worry—the spirits always guide you to the correct place." Many times he answered my questions by telling me not to worry, that the spirits would tell me what to do or that when I got stronger in the practice, I would know what to do. The amazing thing is, he was right.

After a few days, the Bomoh decided it was time for the ceremony in which he would transmit his guides to me. There were several things that needed to be gathered for the ceremony, including a white bowl and knife that I would then use in my work to call the spirits. Finding a ceramic white bowl was a formidable task and took several days. The Bomoh, Abdul Rahman (who was the librarian, a former student, and the owner of the only car in the village), Georgette, Cassie, and I traveled to several neighboring villages in search of a bowl. We traveled over barely passable roads in Abdul Rahman's tiny car, which managed to hit every bump in the road. We were quite a sight—three large white women crammed into the backseat of this little car. We created quite a stir going from village to village in search of the bowl. While Malaysia was racing toward westernization, many people wondered why I had come to learn the old ways. Finally a shaman in a coastal town of Kuala Matu had a white bowl, which he gave to the Bomoh. The Bomoh then presented it to me during the ceremony.

The Transmission

On the day of the ceremony, I retreated to my room to fast and mediate until that evening. I checked in with each of my guides who had come to me during the previous four years to ask their permission to proceed with the transmission. By this time I had a council of 12 spirit guides and a totem of seven power animals. Each of the guides and power animals appeared to me in journeys or during power animal dances at the shamanic drumming circle. Once when I started to dance and had invited my guides and power animals to move through me, I experienced another being close to me that I did not know. Hekate, goddess of the underworld and guardian of the dark moon, is a crone that assists in the deathing process. She appeared before me wrapped in black and white furs. Her eyes were fierce yet loving. We began to move to a gentle dance that contained elements of sadness and celebration. As she told me who she was, Hekate said that she would be one of the three main guides that would be present in healing work and that she would help me to understand about death and assist in my helping others with this process.

Each of the guides had certain teachings and functions. For example, a guide from Tibet and one from Mongolia were teaching me how to work with energy from their cultural perspectives; another from Chile taught me plant spirit medicine. The Iguana's role is to help me focus my mind and to assist in doing extraction work. I had been told by all but two of my guides that they had been my teachers in other lifetimes and had come to help me remember what I already knew. One of my guides whose function is to work with me during each shamanic healing had been a close friend who was killed in a car accident when she was 19. We have known each other in many lifetimes and often take turns being guides to each other when we are not incarnate at the same time. It is like having a best friend in the spirit world. I also have a spirit husband to whom I have been married in other lifetimes. The last two spirit guides had come to me the first week of the trip when I was visiting the village where Cassie had lived in the 60s. One was a Chinese acupuncturist named Chen Shi. He told me to learn the Chinese system of medicine. In particular he wanted me to learn about the spleen, liver, kidney and lung functions and how they relate to emotional states. My friend Cassie was experiencing back problems and he told me that the problem was with her kidneys and gave me instructions for how to help her.

The Garuda, my main guide, travels between the upper and lower worlds, and sits on the council with both the spirit guides and power animals. He accompanies me on my journeys. First I did a journey to the lower world and called all of my power animals to form a circle. I asked each of them if they gave permission for the transmission. They eagerly assented. Then I journeyed to the upper world where I sat encircled by my spirit guides. My spirit guides also assented.

When I arrived at the Bomoh's house for the ceremony, I discovered that the Bomoh had several questions for me. The Bomoh was giving me the water spirits that come from the sea and river. He asked, "How many water spirits do you want?" I replied, "I will take as many as you think I can energetically handle." I expected that he would say one or two. Instead he replied, "I will give you twelve." Then he asked, "Do you want them to be male or female?" Without hesitation, I said, "female." The Bomoh consulted with his spirits for a moment and then offered to extend six male guides to be on the outside for protection, increasing my outside guides to 18. Next he asked, "Do I want the spirits to be married or single?" He quickly added, "If they are married, their spouses will become jealous of me. It is better to have them be single." I chose them to be single, intrigued at the notion that spirit guides have feelings of jealousy.

The details of the ceremony are sacred and cannot be shared, but I can share my reactions. When the Bomoh blew the spirits into the crown of my head, I felt such a surge of energy rush through me that I began to vibrate. Georgette and Cassie witnessed the ceremony and sensed the power of the energy that came through. After the ceremony, the Bomoh performed several tests to confirm that the transmission had been successful. He asked me to taste different waters to determine which was from the sea and which from the river. Each time I got the answer right the Bomoh would break into a big smile and give me a thumbs up. The Bomoh said, "Most of the knowledge that I have you now have within you." He added, "The next time you come, I will give you the spirits of the forest and the crocodile spirit. After that transmission, you will have access to all the knowledge I have with the exception of the wisdom of one spirit that I cannot give you unless you convert to the Islamic faith."

Immediately after the ceremony, he had me copy ancient Arabic prayers to memorize and use in my work. One of the prayers remove the addiction spirit from a person's energy field. My hands were trembling so that I could barely write. Everyone was laughing at me and the atmosphere was relaxed and playful. I felt as if I were in such an altered state of consciousness that I wondered if I could walk back to our cottage.

The Integration of Energy

When I went back to my room that night, I fell fast asleep only to be awakened with a start a few hours later. For the next four hours each of the twelve genies or water spirits appeared before me; some were quite terrifying in appearance. They danced around me, moving through me and staring me in the eye to see if I had the courage to deal with the energy that was presented. Each carried the physical or emotional manifestation of the illness or problem they were expert in healing. One was to work with the problem of rage; thus she appeared as a rageful, frightening being. Others that carried the emotional aspects of existence were portrayed as greed, envy and jealousy, fear, low self–esteem, and madness. The six embodying physical ailments appeared as blood, bone, nervous system, organs, immune system, and muscle/tissue. The spirit that dealt with blood was transparent with all her arteries and veins showing.

After each spirit told me about her function and abilities, they all began to dance and swirl around with arms extended. Gracefully and rhythmically the spirits began to merge into one body with 12 heads and 24 arms thus demonstrating they could act as one and then they separated into 12 beings conveying their individual power. They told me that each would reside in one of my fingers and the palms of my hands. The emotional ailments were embodied on the left hand, the physical on the right. They told me to feel the sensations in my hands for a clue in diagnosing a problem.

Over the next few nights I met the protectors who were each accompanied by a power animal. Each represented one of the six directions—east, south, west, north, below, and above. Ailo and the white reindeer were from the east; Luis and a large black snake came from the south. The west was represented by Tall Oak Standing and the buffalo; Aunu and the polar bear were from the north. Thor, the horse and the tiger came from below or the lower world; Mohammed, the owl and the eagle were from above or the upper world.

Although my relationship with the Bomoh has a certain formality to it, our connection deepened after the transmission. I spoke freely to the Bomoh's wife, Hwa Jung, in their native tongue, yet the Bomoh and I always spoke to each other through an interpreter; we rarely looked each other directly in the eye. He would motion to me when he wanted me to accompany him. I always walked behind him and only sat beside him when we did healing work together. Yet on the spirit plane, we communicated freely with each other. The Bomoh offered to send me home with the essence of a powerful tree he uses in healings. The tree was deep within the rain forest where it was difficult to go. So I went into trance by smoking my white bowl with incense, thereby awakening the spirits, and journeyed to the tree, and asked permission to take the essence of it with me. This was granted. It was the first journey that I had done after the transmission. My energy body, which separates from my physical body when I journey, was big, awkward, and quite comical. I kept falling down as it felt like I was walking on stilts. I was aware that I had much work to do to integrate all of the energy. That evening the Bomoh commented that he was happy to see the tree had granted me permission to take some of its essence home. He was aware I had journeyed to the tree as he had *seen* me with the tree on a journey of his own.

The Bomoh and I had tuned into each other psychically before. Frequently, from my home in America, I had asked him questions and received answers. He would be equally aware of our exchange. One time on a journey, I saw that the Bomoh was ill and his lungs were weak. Later I called on the telephone and confirmed that he was ill and had a problem with his lungs.

After the transmission ceremony, the Bomoh began to teach me in earnest about herbs. Unfortunately what grows in Borneo does not grow in New England. He made clippings of several of his most valued plants, which, with the help of the protectors, miraculously made it through customs and home, but the plants were unable to grow in the cool temperate climate of the northeast.

The Bomoh also began to give me more responsibility. One day he took me to the home of Daud's mother. Daud had been one of my best students and was a high-ranking officer in the army. One of Daud's brothers had run over and killed a child with his motorcycle. The mother was so distraught that she would not eat or sleep. The Bomoh asked if I could heal her. I consulted with my guides who said that she had had considerable soul loss and that I should do a soul retrieval. The Bomoh told Daud's mother to come to his house after dinner for a healing performed by me. She arrived with about 40 other people, all curious to see what the white "dukun" (a female healer) would do.

I was used to doing soul retrievals the way Sandra Ingerman had taught me, working with crystals, rattles, and drums. I had none of these with me, but I had brought the Bomoh a crystal as a gift, so I asked him if I could use it. I told Daud's mother to lie down next to me while I went into trance. Everyone was talking and asking Cassie, who speaks the language well, what in the world I was doing just lying there. It was extremely difficult to stay in trance with all of the commotion and with the lack of a drum to guide me to the other realms. I did find that part of her had left with her husband when he died, thus making her more vulnerable to shock. When she learned of her son's accident, more of her essence left out of fear and grief. I brought these two parts back along with a bird with an orange beak as a guide and blew them into her. After the healing she still was unable to speak or eat, but I was told that she was doing a bit better the next day. As hard as Cassie, Yakuup, and I tried to explain, she did not seem to understand the importance of doing a ritual to keep the parts with her and seemed to prefer having part of her with her husband.

The people in Matu are used to the Bomoh actively healing them and did not understand the concept of taking an active part in one's own healing process, which is so important in the West. The idea that she had to do anything beyond giving an offering to the spirits was foreign. Again I was struck with the immense job I had in taking the spirit of the teachings and making them unique and applicable to each person I treated. Clearly the method I had been taught by Sandra was not appropriate to Matu. I needed to take the teachings a step further by asking my guides what to do rather than relying on a technique I had been taught.

At the end of my time with the Bomoh, I considered staying on and skipping the trip to Laos I had planned with Georgette and Cassie. I could not imagine leaving. There was still so much to learn, yet my mind and energy being were so full that I did not feel I could absorb another thing.

After checking in with my guides, I was told to go Laos. I needed the time to integrate my experience away from the intensity of life with the Bomoh before returning to the demands of my own life in America.

The trip to Laos was well worth it. For several weeks after the transmission, I slept very little, spending most of my nights in trance and meditation just trying to integrate the enormous amount of energy inside of me. I did not feel like myself and struggled to regain a sense of equilibrium. Neither Cassie nor Georgette wanted to share a room with me as I was up most of the night with all of this intense energy zooming around. I spent each day in Buddhist temples meditating, receiving teachings, and integrating the 18 guides in deeper ways. One day while we were shopping, Cassie came running to me saying that she had found a statue of the Buddha with 12 heads, 24 arms and six protectors surrounding it. It was a magnificent marble statue of Avolokiteshvara, the Buddhist representation of compassion. Since I am a Buddhist, I felt that this statue gave form and image to the power of the guides inside of me. After great effort both physically and politically, I was able to bring the statue home with me.

When I returned to America, I was aware that I had stepped through a veil to yet another level of reality. Things that I had been unable to comprehend were now clearer. I could see the layers and complexities of existence, from both this world and beyond in ways I had only glimpsed before. At the same time, I was struck with the magnitude of what I do not yet know or comprehend. Happily it all has allowed me to enjoy and participate in life with a deeper richness than before. Knowing that we are in physical form to experience and learn from being incarnate has given me a passion for life that I did not previously experience. It also challenges me never to be complacent or to attach to any one belief as the ultimate truth. Each time I confront a situation, problem or question, I journey or meditate to find an answer. Each answer pushes me to new understandings and new questions.

PART II

INTEGRATION OF SHAMANISM AND PSYCHOTHERAPY

After I started introducing shamanic techniques into my practice, I was continually amazed to discover how powerfully this ancient healing method complemented psychotherapy. The learning curve has been quite steep. In order to ground myself in what I was learning and experiencing, I needed to write. Each time before I began to write I called my guides to me. On several occasions new information flowed from them to the page, making writing another venue in which to receive teachings.

Through journeying and writing, my guides have taught me extraction—the removal of unwanted energy stuck in the body and the energy field, and have directed me to learn about the ancient metaphysical systems that work with chakras and energy cords to conceptualize how this occurs. They also guided me to envision the dreambody, which is the container for our soul and past life memories and the vehicle in which we leave our body. In the following chapters, using clinical examples to illustrate key concepts, I will weave the information I continue to learn from my guides and from clinical experience with psychological theory.

Chapter 6
EXCHANGE OF ENERGY

A man named Jeff came to see me for shamanic work. He is extremely gifted, but he struggles with a lack of organization and motivation and so he has difficulty actualizing his potential. During the healing I removed a great deal of gray cotton-like energy from the lower third of his body. My guides told me the energy belonged to his mother. When we were finished, Jeff said that he felt fear fall away from his hips as I worked on him. I asked if his mother had been fearful. He replied that she was extremely fearful, and he had always felt her fear was stuck to him.

In our day-to-day lives we speak of people who drain our energy. Others energize us, and we feel good around them. On one level we know that we have energy within us and energy fields around us. But in our culture, energy is not something with form and shape. The rational western mind does not readily accept its material reality. Traditional Oriental Medicine places energy, or Qi (also written as Chi), at the apex of the healing system. Working with energy has been the foundation of healing practices throughout the world for centuries. This awareness lives deep within our unconscious, but was lost to our public consciousness during the Renaissance when we turned away from the intuitive to Cartesian and Newtonian paradigms. Thus logical rational thinking replaced intuitive knowledge. As soon as I allowed myself to be open to an intuitive way of knowing, I could readily grasp the ancient healing practices that are being rediscovered in the West. On some level I felt that I had always known them. Many others have had similar experiences.

My client, Jeff, for instance, always knew he carried his mother's fear, but it never occurred to him that this was something tangible, something that could be removed. For years, working as a psychotherapist, I understood that a person could carry another's fear. The fear could dissipate through therapy if there was a significant breakthrough or a cathartic moment that resulted in a deep structural change within the psyche. It took an "ah ha" moment in which the client understood on a deep level that the fear they carried was not their own. The problem is that it is not possible to orchestrate these moments; they seem to happen on their own. Many therapists go months, even years, before a client experiences one of these cathartic moments. Yet when it does happen, there is a striking alteration in the client's demeanor and perspective; one might even say that there has been a radical energy shift.

There are several schools of psychological thought. As a graduate student in psychology I was particularly drawn to the object relationship school of thought, in large part I thought, because it deals with unconscious processes. I now wonder if I were drawn to object relation theory because it comes close to grasping how energy goes back and forth between people through understanding introjects and projections, two important constructs in object relation theory. Winnicot, a noted object relations theorist, described the nature of introjection and projection: "What is inside is part of the self though not inherently so, and it can be projected. What is outside is not part of the self, but again not inherently so, and it can be introjected."[8]

Simply put, introjection is the process of taking in key psychic energetic parts of another. This process occurs most frequently in infancy and early childhood when a part of the parents' or other important caregivers' feelings about the child are taken into the child's being. Because feelings have an energetic base the child can absorb this energy. For example, if a child is constantly shamed and told he or she is bad, this message can become a core part of the child's psychic structure. The message contains both a belief structure and energetic component that holds the belief in place. The process of introjection also involves taking in key mannerisms and attitudes of a parent. A child can easily internalize a parent's shame, confidence, or fear.

The corollary process, projection, is placing unwanted and unintegrated parts of the self onto or into others. In Jungian terms, it is the unintegrated shadow. Many parents project unintegrated parts of themselves on their children. A parent's unacknowledged desire to be taken care of can be projected onto the child by the parent viewing the child as selfish. The parent, denying his or her own feelings of need, feels anger at the child for expressing a need and labels this "selfish."

The process of taking in another's energy and sending it out is a complex one. When a child takes in a sense of herself as bad, this sense may come from a variety of sources. The child may be told she is bad frequently. She may believe that there is something wrong with her because she is often ignored and dismissed. If one or both of the parents feel worthless, the child may pick up that energy by taking in the parent's feeling of worthlessness as her own. Or since it is difficult to fully accept and integrate a view of oneself as bad, the child may project this feeling. She may identify others who share similar traits that she possesses and judge them as bad. She also may feel so badly about herself that she projects her own view and assumes that others see her as bad even when they do not.

When Winnicot spoke of aspects of the self that could be introjected and projected, he essentially was talking about psychic energy. Psychic energy is part of the soul. Part of one's essence or soul can be projected onto or into another. Part of another's essence can be introjected or taken in. This has many parallels to the Bomoh's description of how people send energy or cast spells on others. Yet psychic energy or essence energy cannot be exchanged unless there is an openness for this to occur. Winnicot went on to write, "The baby who adopts an object (part of another) as almost part of the self could not have adopted it unless it had been lying around for adoption."[9]

Winnicot's sentiments agree with a fundamental principle of shamanism: psychic energy or essence cannot be given to a person unless one is willing to receive it nor can it be taken away unless one is willing to give it up. As can be imagined, our unconscious processes are at times more willing to give up parts of the self or receive parts of another than the conscious mind would like to allow. When there is a case of soul loss, that loss leaves a vacuum that can allow unwanted energy to enter. Shamanic cultures notice when there has been soul loss and are quick to retrieve the lost soul parts to ward off other energy from entering the body.

Young children are particularly vulnerable to energy exchange. On the intuitive level a newborn is most connected to the life force as energy. She is also least able to protect energy from being seized or intruded upon. This is why key introjects are taken in at a very early age. Barbara Brennan,[10] the noted energy healer who is quite adept at seeing auras, reports having witnessed the difficulty of energy essence entering the body of the baby at birth. Brennan suggests that some of an infant's wailing results from the confinement of essence energy to such a small container. The energy of the infant may spill over and radiate out. One can easily be seduced by the purity of the newborn's energy. On an unconscious level a parent may take some of this energy, which results in soul loss for the child. For a child to surrender part of her essence energy is not uncommon.

I did a shamanic healing for a young woman with whom I had been working as a psychotherapist for almost a year. In the healing I undertook, I saw this young woman, lying with her mother on her mother's bed. Her mother looked comatose. The little girl was around six months old. I could see energy in the form of light rods flow from the little girl into the mother. On an intuitive or unconscious level, the infant knew she depended upon her mother for survival. In order for her mother to take care of her, the child needed to give some of her energy to the mother, leaving a hole in her essence. The little girl grew up and became severely drug and alcohol addicted by age 14. She continued to live in a comatose, drug induced state, as her mother had, until six months into her psychological treatment at age 23. For essence loss to be countered with addiction is extremely common. This soul loss also left the child vulnerable to taking in energy that did not belong to her. After the soul retrieval, her addiction cravings were gone and she was able to make some important changes in her life. I believe that the healing was successful because she was quite motivated and had worked hard in therapy prior to the soul retrieval.

Stockholm Syndrome
Adults are also vulnerable to soul loss or theft when exposed to trauma and loss. This is exemplified by an incident that occurred in the 1950's known as the Stockholm Syndrome, an incident that befuddled psychological experts for decades. When I first read this account, I too was puzzled and unable to come up with an explanation as to what had happened. After I began to work with energy, I was called to revisit this story to see if a shamanic perspective could shed light on what had happened. A bank robber took several employees hostage during a foiled robbery in Stockholm, Sweden. The hostage siege went on for several days while the robber and hostages stayed in the bank's vault. As the days went on, police saw that the hostages were leaving the vault to go to the bathroom on their own, making no attempt to escape or even communicate with the many police in the building. Observers assumed the hostages had been told that a fellow hostage would be killed if they did so. Finally, when surrender had been negotiated, the robber walked out arm in arm and surrounded by the hostages.

On debriefing, the hostages were found to be extremely loyal to and protective of their captor. None of the hostages had a history of psychiatric problems to explain why this happened. The experts were perplexed. Initially they supposed that it was a case of temporary identification with the aggressor. However, months went by without a shift in loyalty.

The difficulty psychological experts had in understanding this phenomenon speaks to the limits of current psychological constructs. Through considering an exchange of energy did what happen begin to make sense to me. In the initial moments of terror when the hostages were unsure if they would die or be horribly tortured, they dissociated, part of their essence left their bodies, creating a vacuum that the perpetrator's energy filled. The hostages then felt a bond with the perpetrator since part of his energy was within them. This occurred, I believe, because soul loss from the terror of being abducted created space for the robber's energy to enter. The robber's energy was scattered and diffuse because he was operating from a negative place; he himself was not whole. His charged energy readily spun off into others and created an energetic bond between them.

As a psychologist I have specialized in working with victims of trauma. Through years of listening to unthinkable abuse and torture, I have been struck by the power of abuse to kill the spirit, to freeze the victim psychically and physically in the trauma, and of the incredible pull to re-enact the trauma in some way. I struggled for years to understand why some of us feel compelled to harm others in horrific ways, forever leaving a mark. More often than not, these acts are perpetrated upon a loved one or on oneself, further defying explanation. As I began to *see* how energy is literally exchanged during traumatic encounters, I gained a new perspective on how and why abusive acts happen. This brought me to an increased sense of compassion for those who are victims and perpetrators of abusive acts. At the same time I saw new ways in which healing could occur through the removal of unwanted energy and the return to wholeness by soul retrieval. Looking at the impact of the societal and interpersonal problems of rape, war, and domestic abuse upon the psyche and the soul from an integrated perspective of the psychological and the shamanic provides us with new therapeutic understanding.

Rape

Rape victims often display aspects of having taken in the energy of their rapist. The rape victim frequently feels violated, shamed, and bad. Self-loathing is a common side effect. Of course many cultural messages re-enforce this self-loathing, making the person feel responsible for her victimization. Part of the disgust comes from having taken in the energy of the rapist who himself has likely experienced soul loss through abuse, neglect, or violation. As stated earlier, soul loss creates a vacuum that must be filled. Some fill it with addictions; some believe they can be made whole if they possess another. The most extreme way to possess another is physical and emotional violence. Victims of childhood rape quite often reenact the trauma by either becoming victims as adults, perpetrators, or both. A victim is driven to rid the psyche of the trauma by releasing it through re-experiencing the trauma or by projecting it into another. Those who commit violent acts attempt to do both. Some, particularly women but also men, re-experience the trauma by self-abuse such as cutting or burning a part of their body or by becoming prostitutes. Whenever I hear someone is abusive of herself or others, I first consider whether the person may be acting out behavior either experienced or witnessed at an earlier age. I ask the client if another person had done this destructive behavior to them. The answer, upon reflection, is usually "yes."

On numerous journeys I have taken for people who have been raped and violated, I can see energy flow out of the victim into the perpetrator, filling a hole caused by similar abuse done to the perpetrator. I also see the perpetrator's energy flow into the victim. Phoebe's father raped her at the age of five. When I saw this during a soul retrieval, I found part of little Phoebe on the ceiling, looking down in terror as she witnessed what transpired. Her father's face looked deranged and scary as he harmed her, he hit her head to quiet her before he raped her. Energetically he was weak, having lost much of his own soul essence through similar attacks on him as a child. I could see clearly his energy body sucking the life force out of little Phoebe. When he was finished with her, he left behind a gray sediment similar to that in a used vacuum cleaner bag that covered her energy field and made it hard for her to breathe. We brought Phoebe down from the ceiling and my guides did a healing for her. First they removed the gray sediment and healed it, knowing that they would use it later. Then they bathed her in clean water from a stream and surrounded her in divine energy as she lay on the grass to dry.

We then went to the land of the dead where people are stuck between worlds—usually as a result of too much soul loss and from taking other's soul energy—to retrieve the soul essence that her father had taken from her. A terrified energetic form of Phoebe was sitting on her father's lap as he grasped her tightly. We took Phoebe and her father to a peaceful island away from the land of the dead. The healed gray sediment that was the father's energy was returned to him in the form of a ball of light. As he reached out to grab it, he let go of Phoebe and we took her from him and did a healing for her as well. Phoebe's father was then able to acknowledge the harm he had done to her. He stated how much he had loved her and had wanted to possess her sweet energy to heal his wounded soul. He was horrified to realize that he had harmed her in the ways that he had been harmed. In his depleted energetic state, he was like a hungry animal seeking food with no awareness of the consequences of his actions.

After the soul retrieval, Phoebe felt much stronger and clearer. The self-abusive act of hitting herself in the head had ceased. The sense that she was bad and intrinsically dirty was for the most part gone.

Frequently energetic forms repeat the same cycle of abuse going back many generations. This is particularly true in families with a history of incest. Fortunately, through a shamanic healing the spirits can retrieve the energy that flows into the perpetrator, heal it, and bring it back to the client. The spirits also do healings for the perpetrator and all of the others, going back several generations. When you do a healing for one person you heal all that went before and all who will come after. Only after I began to do shamanic healings could I fully grasp the meaning and power of this statement.

There are many permutations involved in the exchange of energy. Rebecca, whose alcoholic father had sexually abused her, came to see me for help with her own addictions. When I began the journey into her dreambody, I found her surrounded by a cloud of grayish-brown energy. The density of the cloud reminded me of the black ink sprayed by an octopus in battle. Nearby I saw her sister who energetically looked like Swiss cheese, with grayish-brown energy racing through her flowing through their mother and in turn to the grandmother going back several generations. In the current generation Rebecca's sister seemed to be the spoke for this energetic darkness, but the cloud extended out to cover the other siblings, Rebecca included. I did a healing in dreamtime for Rebecca, for her sisters, her mother, and their ancestors.

Because the spirits removed and transformed the energetic sludge, it was possible to provide healing and relief for those who were no longer incarnate as well as to alter the negative energetic flow still in operation. Of course, a person has to be open to receive this healing energy. In Rebecca's case I had expected most of the healing work would be on her relationship with the father. But the mother's inherited dark energy had pulled a man to her who had been abused and who would in turn abuse her children. Soul loss from both sides of the family provided fertile ground for addictions to thrive.

I am sure that many of you know families that seem to be enshrouded in darkness and experience great misfortune and struggle. Still, invariably, there is at least one in the family who makes it out of the morass into a happy, productive life. I have pondered this situation and have come to understand that each of us has an inner strength to stand up and prevail over negative forces. Negative energy feeds off of fear and hopelessness. Yet if one turns to face the shadow or darkness, rather than hide from or remain stuck in its power, gradually one can be free of this energy. Psychological and shamanic work can greatly facilitate this process; however, it is essential that each person is actively involved in his or her own healing.

War

War plays a role in this cycle of ongoing abuse. Those exposed to the horror and trauma of war usually experience soul loss. In fact when I have done shamanic healings for those who have been in battle, I invariably find hundreds of lost soul parts energetically frozen in various states of torture and pain on the battlefield belonging to all who fought. Given the extent of soul loss, the energy of the killing and torture is easily taken in. Most who have experienced war try to bury the memories deep within the psyche. Repeated nightmares are the way some release this energy; others experience unexplained outbursts of rage; still others walk around emotionally dead, barely able to connect on any intimate level. Some spend their lives on the street or at the VA hospital unable to cope with the continual assault of images of death and dismemberment. While some release this violent energy by directing it toward others, still others try to rid themselves of the trauma by re-experiencing it through novels and movies or by re-enlisting in the military.

A poignant sequence in the film *The Deer Hunter* illustrates this point. A prisoner of war, played by Christopher Walken, was forced to play Russian roulette with other prisoners of war in Viet Nam. The prisoners sat in a circle with a gun containing one bullet. Each had to point the gun at his head and fire and then pass the gun on. One was sure to die. After witnessing death through this torture, but surviving himself, Walken's character lived in a dissociated, empty state. He wandered the back streets of Saigon until he found a betting house where Russian roulette was played. Walken's character was so driven to re-experience his trauma that he stayed on after the war, living a drug addicted, dissociated life and repeatedly playing this game in what Freud called repetition compulsion. Finally, Walken's character meets his death in a crowded gaming room as his friend, played by Robert DeNiro, who had come to bring him home, looks on in horror.

Not uncommonly refugees who have fled violent war-torn countries come to America only to die horrific deaths at the hands of fellow refugees or family members. My belief is that much of the violence and abuse that is inflicted upon others is the result of images and experiences of war, stored energetically that are waiting for an opportunity to be released through reenactment. It is important to understand that once one has been exposed to and taken in violent energy, there needs to be an energetic release of this energy to be free of it. Both shamanism and psychotherapy can help with this process. Shamanic healings can release the traumatic energy and bring back the lost soul essence. A psychotherapist can bear witness to the traumatic experiences and offer insight, understanding, and a re-framing that can help free the survivor of the guilt and shame that usually accompanies war.

Battered Women and Children

Other aspects of this dynamic can be observed with battered women and children. Usually the victim has intense connection and even loyalty to the batterer. Only deep work in therapy weakens these bonds. The general population frequently questions why a woman does not leave a batterer. Often they think she is responsible for her own abuse because she stayed. Those of us who work with an abused and battered population know how difficult leaving can be. Yet it is sometimes challenging to find the correct words and concepts to explain why people do not leave, or, in the case of abused children, why they do not tell. The unconscious process that draws people to re-experience their most traumatic moments, while hoping that they will receive some form of acceptance or absolution from their abusers, is difficult to explain. There are economic factors and the increasingly realistic fear of murder if one does leave. But there are other reasons as well. There is the belief that one is bad or somehow responsible for and deserving of the abuse, a belief that has an energetic base and is defined as an introject. In addition there is hope that the batterer will change; that he will be kind and loving and that through these actions the victim will be purged of her badness—as if only the batterer can take away the badness. Others' kindness and love are nice, but these do not change the core negative belief about the self. This negative self-conviction more than likely stems back to childhood and is based on a pattern of similar interaction with key figures in early life. Battered children often become battered or battering adults.

Working with Energy

A man I will call Peter came to me for shamanic work in the later part of his life. His father had physically and sexually abused him as a child. Throughout his entire life he had struggled with issues related to the abuse. He was angry, verbally abusive and on occasion, physically abusive to his own sons. He was obsessed with sex and frequently cheated on his wife. He worked hard to heal himself, spending most of his adult life in psychoanalysis, but despite his hard work, his wife and children left him as a result of his out-of-control behavior. In more recent years Peter has been in self-help groups and tried other alternative approaches to healing. Still the pain and the rage dominated his life. Peter had also struggled with the notion that he must be seen as successful in the eyes of the world in order to consider himself a decent human being. He felt his parents had been unable to accept him or give him love; this, coupled with the abuse, left him feeling he was intrinsically bad and had in some way caused the abuse. Even though he had had years of treatment and was successful in his profession, he could feel acceptable only if he felt adored by another. This fed his constant need for approving sexual partners.

Initially I did an extraction for Peter, removing the energy blocks or intrusions in the body and around his energy field. It is important to do an extraction before doing a soul retrieval, in order to make room for essence energy to return. I do not touch the body during an extraction. Rather I work with my power animals and spirit guides to psychically and energetically remove the intrusions. By moving my own energy out of the way, the guides can work through me. I am in a trance state even though my eyes are open, and I can carry on a conversation.

During the extraction, I saw a large, dark, bloody creature around Peter's heart chakra. This creature extended to Peter's throat and his solar plexus and was strongly entrenched. Finally I could feel it leave. There also was a cobweb-like energy around Peter's energy body and his groin area. My power animal told me that this energy belonged to his father and had kept Peter energetically bound to his father. One spirit guide took this energy and began to heal it, sensing we would encounter the father during the soul retrieval part of the healing.

There were several parts to the soul retrieval. While journeying, I found Peter when he was four or five years old. His father was sexually and physically abusing him. I could see a part of little Peter watching from above, floating in space near the ceiling. I saw that during Peter's absence from his physical body, his father's rageful energy entered him and resided around the groin area of Peter's body. When Peter was a teenager, his father tried to sexually abuse him. Peter was now as large as his father and hit his father repeatedly. I saw this occur and observed Peter trying to rid himself of his father's rageful energy in this attack. Needless to say, one does not rid negative or unwanted energy through violence. Later in the soul retrieval process we visited the land of the dead. Peter's father was found to be totally depleted energetically, his essence largely gone. My power animals and I took him to an island that was warm and sunny. First we took the gray energy removed from Peter and healed it by turning it into light energy. Then we gave this energy back to the father, healing him in the process. This enabled the father to ask forgiveness from all the parts of Peter that had been retrieved. The father told Peter he had loved him, and that Peter had in no way caused the abuse.

For Peter the most powerful part of the shamanic healing was in the extraction and removal of his father's energy. Over the next few weeks, he experienced major walls come down. Peter realized he had spent his entire life seeking approval from others to make up for the lack of acceptance he felt from his parents and from himself. He had been unable to welcome the soul parts back fully. He could not believe that anyone would want to be with him, not even parts of himself. With his father's energy gone, he began to experience his own essence energy emerge. Peter was sad to realize that his whole life had been an attempt to win external approval so that he could prove to his father, even after his father's death, that he was a decent human being.

Many in our culture do not understand why people cannot just put traumatic experiences behind them and get on with their lives. They do not yet understand the energy pull that binds a person to the trauma and the abusers. Yet many who voice this view were themselves mesmerized by the O. J. Simpson case. Mr. Simpson is rich and famous and had everything that many dream of having, a successful career and a beautiful wife. Mr. Simpson and Nicole Brown allegedly had a battering relationship that went on for years. When Ms. Brown tried to walk away and lead her own life, she was killed. This case fascinated the nation because the trial brought to personal and public consciousness what everyone struggles with in the deep recesses of the heart, what many of us have tried to suppress—our own feelings of jealousy, possessiveness, and anger and the fear of them flying out of control. How does one become so obsessed by another that unspeakable things occur resulting in physical harm to the one he loves most?

Reports of domestic violence are growing among all class and racial groups at alarming rates. There needs to be a dialogue about the rage that causes one to abuse another, to learn about the pain and suffering that triggers rage and to understand the accompanying, unbearable shame. We need to explore the factors within our society that foster this level of rage. There are many who know that rage and know how close they have come to killing someone they once loved and now want to possess. My client, Peter, knows that rage. He has lived it both as a victim of rage and a perpetrator of rage.

The origins of rage are extremely complex and are deeply embedded within societal policies and customs. From a shamanic perspective rage occurs as a result of disconnection from both one's true nature and the unifying and healing energies of the universe, as well as taking in another's rageful energy after soul loss. Not until I began doing healings for others and could *see* the layers of energy surrounding and flowing through my clients did I came to a new understanding of the sources of rage, abuse and murder. Now I have a deeper level of compassion for those who harm and are harmed.

Doing shamanic work has helped me both to *see* and to comprehend how energy is exchanged. The intuitive wisdom that led Winnicot and others to define theories about how we take in psychic parts of others is, in fact, correct. We do take in energetic parts of others just as we give away energetic parts of ourselves. Many of the feelings that we carry with us from our earliest years may be energy we have absorbed from our parents. As I struggled to understand more about how energy exchange works, my guides directed me to the ancient metaphysical practices of the East that have illuminated this issue for centuries.

Chapter 7
CHAKRAS AND ENERGY CORDS

Once when I asked my spirit guides what I should learn next, they showed me a human form floating horizontally in space with energy pouring in and out of the body. Some of the energy streams were small and faint while others were strongly embedded in the body appearing as a beautiful cylinder flower with energy flowing out of the center. The guides taught me how to feel the energy and to listen to what the energy had to tell me. Some of the energy streams flow out to other people from the body while some streams in. My guides showed me the ways we all communicate through energy cords and chakras and told me this is what I needed to learn next.

There are seven major chakras, 40 secondary ones, and, according to traditional writings, 88,000 in all which leaves scarcely a point on the body that is not open for the reception, transformation, or transferal of energy.[11] The chakra system, an ancient metaphysical system originating in India, ties the complexities of the universe to the intricacies of the human existence. When the chakras are open and flowing freely, one feels strong, energized, powerful, and at peace. Blockages are common in the chakras resulting in energy being stuck in different parts of the body. Yoga, Tai Chi, and Qigong are helpful practices in keeping the chakras open and flowing. Energy workers specialize in healing cords and opening blocked chakras.[12]

Often when I am *seeing* on another level, I find energy cords connecting the client to others. These cords flow out of the different chakras and are intensified the more intimate one is with another. Energetic cords are firmly established with one's parents. These cords serve as the avenue for all feelings to flow. Feelings of abandonment or, conversely, being invaded flow through the energy cords, as do feelings of love and care. Through the energy cords we send out our projections and take in the energy of others. People are often drawn to one another based on an energetic frequency that is similar and flows through the energy cords providing an avenue for growth and the re-working of old patterns.

Psychological and Developmental Components

As I began to study the chakra system, I discovered that each of the major chakras has unique functions that correspond to psychological developmental theory. I find it fascinating to discover how the link between these ancient practices of shamanism and the chakra system interfaces with current psychological thought. For instance, if a parent had difficulties in her life that resulted in blocked or malfunctioning chakras, her blocked energy may be transferred to her child along energy cords resulting in developmental difficulties at the same age that the parent experienced problems. A parent, fearful about leaving home and starting school as a child, who has not worked through and resolved the issues, may re-activate this fear when her child starts school. This blocked energy pulsates "looking" for an avenue for release. Through the energy flowing back and forth between the parent and child, the mother's pulsating energy flows through the energy cords right into the child, which can result in the child experiencing fear about starting school.

While working in a psychiatric hospital with adolescents in the late 1980's, I saw a number of young women who had been sexually abused. I was surprised to discover their mothers had been sexually abused at the same age the daughters were. In some cases the mothers' incidents of abuse had been repressed, not coming to conscious memory until the daughter disclosed her own abuse. Often the mother was aware of the abuse, but had felt too ashamed to confront what had happened, pushing the feelings under the surface. I did not do a formal study of this phenomenon, but in my caseload of patients there was not one exception. I was curious why this was true. Once I learned about energy flowing through cords from one person to the next, it made intuitive sense how this happened.

The first of the seven major chakras, the root chakra, which is located at the base of the spine, is associated with the solid aspects of the body such as the bones, teeth and blood. Our grounding to the physical plane flows from this area. Psychologically the first chakra is connected to our sense of trust, the first of Erik Erikson's stages of psychological development.[13] Those traumatized at birth or in the first year of life struggle with feeling comfortable and grounded in the body. Abuse and neglect at any point in life may result in difficulty with trust and feeling safe in the body causing one to leave the body through dissociating. Grounding exercises are extremely important for problems in this area.

This was particularly true for Heather, who often became flooded with memories of extreme sexual, physical, emotional, and ritual abuse. Heather had multiple personalities. One personality became psychotic when too many memories flooded her system. In the early years of our work before I had learned about shamanism, she was given Stellazine, an anti-psychotic medication with unpleasant side effects. It was supposed to diminish the psychotic thinking. During one such episode after I began working with energy, I decided to try a meditation to see if this might stabilize her. I asked her to concentrate on her breathing and to experience her breath going from the top of her head down through her spine and legs to the base of her feet. We worked with her breath until she was calmer; then I asked her to send the irrational thoughts she was experiencing down this same path through her feet and into the earth. As she was doing this, I asked my power animals and guides to help in pulling the irrational thoughts out of the body. After a few breaths, she reported feeling calm and clear. I then asked her to imagine pulling light from above into the top of her head, spreading this healing energy throughout the same path. The psychotic thinking that had been present for three days was gone. Initially she looked a bit dazed, but as she continued to breath, she experienced her mind as returning to a place of clarity. She spoke coherently and experienced tremendous relief.

The flooding of traumatic memories resulted in fragmentation of Heather's psyche; she experienced increased dissociation with little grounding in her body. The goal of the meditation was to bring the fragmented energy down into the body so that it could be released into the earth and then to bring in healing energy through the body to help ground her. In order to do this, it was important for the breath to flow to the root chakra at the base of the spine and then down the legs. Not all clients have the ability to focus their breath when they are in this level of psychological distress. Thus it is important for the therapist to attune her breath to her client's and gradually help the client to move her breath through the body to the base of the spine.

The second chakra is located between the base of the spine and the navel and includes the abdomen, genitals, hips, and lower back. It is the source of creativity, emotions, and sexuality. It corresponds to Erickson's developmental stage of autonomy that occurs around one and one half to three years of age, more commonly known as the "terrible twos." I frequently find energy leaks flowing from this chakra to one of the parents. The parent unconsciously tries to feed off the creative energy of the child while also attempting to control the child's freedom, creativity, sexuality, and autonomy.

Creativity and sexuality are extremely powerful themes in the American culture and these themes resonate deep within our being. Emotions are also stored in this area. Not surprisingly, frequent blockages and energy drains are common in the second chakra resulting in an inability to create and have fun, sexual obsessions or repression, or frequent illness in the abdomen and sexual organs. Problems in this area frequently stem from the second year of life when one is struggling to forge an independent identity while remaining connected and loved. The tension between connection and independence is present in all intimate relationships and thus blockages or problems can occur when there is an imbalance in this area.

Sally came to see me for reoccurring problems with intimate relationships. Whenever anger erupted in relationships, she became fearful, prone to panic attacks, and had an impulse to leave the relationship precipitously. I have studied with Tenzin Wygal Rinpoche, a Tibetan Buddhist Lama, and a master in the Bon tradition of Tibetan healing. He taught workshop participants a soul retrieval practice utilizing the deity, Sherab Chamma, a goddess of divine love and compassion. In this practice I led Sally on a guided meditation. By doing a simple chant, Sherab Chamma was invited to come and be with Sally. Once Sally felt Sherab Chamma to be with her, Sherab Chamma escorted Sally to her earliest or strongest memory of having been afraid or panicked. Soon Sally began to see a little girl with blond curly hair around the age of two or three. Her head was being smashed against the ground and large hands were around her throat, choking her. Before the little girl lost consciousness, she looked up and saw her mother's face. Sherab Chamma picked up little Sally, did a healing for her and brought her back to live inside of Sally.

Sally began to remember other incidences of abuse as a young child. This explained why it was so challenging for her to feel safe around anger in intimacy. Through energy work and shamanic journeys, we discovered that much of the trauma was still stored in Sally's body. The three chakras that were most impacted were the fifth, second, and root chakra. Sally had endured chronic intestinal problems and lower back pain her entire life and had unexplained pain in various parts of her body. She also had lost several of her teeth due to the trauma. Although the abdomen area was not directly assaulted, the first and second chakras were impacted because of Sally's age as were issues of trust and safety in intimate relationships. Sally began to do tonal chants to strengthen each of the impacted chakras and envisioned each chakra vibrating in the respective light of the chakra—red for the root chakra, orange for the second chakra, and blue for the fifth chakra. From my work with Sally I realized that physical problems in the body could point us to the age of a traumatic occurrence and to the type of injury that the body sustained.

Above the navel is the third chakra commonly referred to as the solar plexus. It is the source of power and will. The owning of power involves taking charge of life and living from a place of truth in relation to one's life path. It corresponds to Erikson's stage of initiative in the third and fourth year of life. Malfunctions in this area are manifest by eating disorders, ulcers, and other digestive problems or by difficulty in taking control of life or, conversely, by trying to force one's will on others. Many, especially women and cultural minorities, have difficulty in owning their full power because of societal myths and expectations as well as political and economic structures. Cultural expectations force many men to take charge by pushing their will on others even when this goes against aspects of their basic nature. Getting this chakra in balance may entail going against cultural norms. Many parents unconsciously pull energy from this chakra in an attempt to weaken the child's will and to strengthen their own. Once an unbalanced flow of energy is established, it is easy for others to plug into this imbalance. A child whose mother drained energy from the solar plexus is at risk of finding others who siphon her energy and attempt to control her.

Janice has a history of eating disorders. She can go for months barely eating and then within a week's time gain ten pounds from overeating. Janice is beautiful and a talented artist yet is lacking in any sense of her own worth and talents. She has had several relationships with men who are critical and overbearing. By the time each relationship ends, Janice is anorexic from lack of eating, appearing as if the life force has been sucked out of her. When I did a soul retrieval for her, I saw energy being drawn out of her third chakra by her domineering father. On closer look I saw that he was energetically weak. It appeared that an overly critical mother had drained much of his energy from him. To compensate for this, he was overly aggressive and unconsciously pulled the energy from his daughter at her will center. He left behind his feelings of failure and low self-esteem. Since Janice's father had opened a leak in her solar plexus, others with a similar vibration to her father could siphon energy from the same leak. When Janice attempted to fight back, she overate to restore her strength, but if she did not have the energy to fight, she literally began to disappear.

During the soul retrieval for Janice, the Garuda came with his sword and cut the flow of energy from Janice to her father and others. The Iguana came and sealed the leak in the chakra with his tongue. Then with the help of my guides I removed the energy of her father and the other men who taken energy from Janice, and did a healing for this energy before returning it to her father and the others. Upon returning the energy, I retrieved parts of Janice's soul essence that had been taken by her father and each of the men. After the soul retrieval, Janice felt empowered in ways that she had not before.

The fourth chakra is the heart chakra, the center of love and loving feelings. Most of us have experienced the joy of love flowing from this area. There is both a physical and spiritual feeling that emanates from our being when this chakra is fully open. Most have also felt pain in the area of the heart when there has been a loss of this loving connection. If the loss is a permanent one, the pain can be excruciating.

In intimate and familial relationships the energy cords that flow between people can be quite open with part of one person's energy flowing into the other and vice versa. When this flow stops through death or some form of separation, there is a void; some feel that part of them is missing. Some find it so painful that they are unable to eat, sleep, or function in a normal way. Many report feeling a pain that begins at the heart chakra and radiates throughout the body. Others cannot tolerate the thought of this pain and stay in unhealthy relationships to avoid it. As we know, most survive this ordeal and go on to love again.

Some so fear the pain of a broken heart that they block their energy from freely flowing resulting in limited or distant relationships. A child that is repeatedly hurt and lacks nurturing often begins to seal over the heart chakra at an early age. These children grow up to have a difficult time being in intimate relationships. It is not uncommon to find parts of another's energy blocking the chakras. In one healing I found a manhole cover that is used to cover an opening to the sewer and underground wiring in the street, blocking the heart chakra. When I removed the cover, I found the father's sadness buried in his daughter's heart chakra. When I told the client what I had found, she said she had always been aware that she carried her father's pain for him and was relieved to have this awareness validated. Fortunately, we were able to remove the father's energy, heal it, and return it to him.

Problems with the heart chakra are expressed through depression, low self-esteem, fear of intimacy, and isolation. Physically they manifest by problems of the heart and lungs, most notably asthma, circulation problems, and immune system deficiency. Developmentally the fourth chakra corresponds to Freud's oedipal stage around five to seven years of age when issues of intimacy, sexuality, and boundaries predominate and Erikson's stage in young adulthood that focuses on intimacy and isolation.

Issues and problems that are unresolved in childhood resurface at corresponding developmental ages in adolescence and adulthood. For instance issues of trust and safety come up again in early adolescence and early adulthood right when major transitions are occurring. Thus problem areas have a chance to be highlighted and worked through as one matures and develops.

The fifth chakra is in the area of the throat, neck, and shoulders; it is related to communication and the expression of oneself. Blockages in this area commonly extend to other areas. For example, one cannot speak the truth of the heart if there is blockage in the throat chakras. There are blockages in the fifth chakra when one exhibits difficulty speaking, listening, or telling the truth. It is important to watch the extremes. Some speak incessantly, do not listen, gossip, and are judgmental. Others have difficulty articulating their feelings, keep secrets, have little trust, and are easily shamed. TMJ, chronic problems with the throat, ears, and mouth or stiffness in the neck and shoulders all speak to problems in the fifth chakra.

When I worked with Allison, I discovered that there was shredded bamboo in her throat chakra. Allison looked at me in disbelief when I relayed this to her. Sheepishly she confessed that in her adolescence she was obsessed with killing herself by swallowing bamboo shoots, shredding her esophagus, and internally bleeding to death. She had no idea where that idea came from or even why she wanted to die. When I journeyed further on this, I learned that this was a past life memory. As a young maiden in Asia in the 16th century, she had fallen in love and had become pregnant. Since early childhood, she had been promised in marriage to another. When her father found out that she was pregnant, he insisted that she kill herself by swallowing bamboo, which she did. The pain of this past lifetime was so strong that it had leaked into this one. Allison spent her adolescence in a shy, isolated state fixated on a torturous death. Often blocks in the chakras are related to past life traumas that are "looking" for an avenue of release.

Developmentally the fifth chakra corresponds to Erikson's stage of industry or inferiority that occurs in the pre-teen years around eight to twelve. During the pre-teen years, a child should begin to find his or her voice and to feel a level of confidence in one's place in the world. Many girls experience this as a period of great self-expression and agency. It has been well documented by Carol Gilligan[14] that many girls lose this voice in adolescence, like Allison did, as a result of the internalization of societal expectations of the female role. Boys, on the other hand, tend to demonstrate a continual expansion of their voice as they go through adolescence into young adulthood. There are many possible pitfalls for both males and females as they struggle to find expression throughout the life span.

The sixth chakra is found between the eyebrows at the top of the nose and is commonly referred to as the third eye. It is given this name as it is the source of intuition, of seeing both this reality and realities beyond this plane in deeper and different ways. This chakra is extremely underutilized in western cultures. When I shift consciousness for shamanic journeys, I concentrate on the third eye and feel a sensation in this area that signifies that my consciousness has been altered. I can literally feel the energy move up and out. I am then privy to a plethora of information and images. Jung might consider this the gateway to the collective unconscious.

With the exception of Carl Jung, there is little in mainstream psychological literature that addresses the development of psychic abilities. In recent years there has been a growing interest in women's psychological development with women's intuitive and empathic abilities highlighted as strengths that women possess. In my opinion, it is not that women are inherently more intuitive or empathic than men, rather they are more in touch with the natural forces of the universe through menstrual cycles, and the bearing, nursing, and nurturing of children. These functions alter a woman's energetic frequency encouraging greater attunement to the intuitive. Through industrialization, most men have lost their attunement to the natural forces around them; they no longer look to the sky to predict the weather or know when it is time for a herd of buffalo to be moving through. Men have been encouraged to put their energies into the rational and scientific, thereby cutting off key aspects of their being and narrowing their frequency range. Some have so many thoughts and beliefs in the mental body, the third layer of the auric body, that they block access to the astral layer, the gateway to other realms of knowing.

Blockages in the third eye are manifest by insensitivity, difficulty remembering dreams, or difficulty visualizing. Problems with one's vision may also stem from blockage in this area. The denial of another's reality and insistence on being right are also hallmarks of the sixth chakra being out of balance. An excessively open third eye may cause hallucinations, obsessions, and delusions as well as headaches and difficulty in concentrating. Sleep problems such as insomnia and nightmares are also associated with the sixth chakra. By now my clients are used to me moving my hand in various motions or working with crystals as they talk. When I work with someone who has a headache or appears delusional or manic, I take my hand and direct it to the third eye. I then move it in a counter clockwise position to close the third eye down a bit and bring the client back into balance.

Behind the sixth chakra is the pineal gland. In many eastern spiritual traditions it is considered the gateway to joy. For some the pineal gland has become calcified resulting in depression, anxiety, and fear. Envisioning it opening like a lotus can revitalize it. In journeys I *see* the pineal gland as being the passageway from the 6th chakra to the 7th. When this area is open, there can be a true flow of energy, insight, and connection with the divine and other realms of reality. Interestingly when I looked up pineal gland in the American Heritage Dictionary, it was said to be a "small glandlike body of uncertain function found in the brain."

The seventh chakra, located at the top of the head in the newborn's "soft spot" in the cerebral cortex, is the area where many spiritual practices believe the soul essence enters and exits the body. Its function is to govern intelligence, information processing, and spiritual transcendence. Many report experiencing religious or spiritual encounters with God or the Tao from this area of the body. It is as if the soul merges with the infinite producing calm, joy, and peace. When the seventh chakra is open and functioning well, there is an ability to understand on both an intellectual and spiritual level and to integrate the two for a higher level of awareness. Problems in this area are manifest by a lack of curiosity and an inability to think for oneself. Adherence to other's ideas or a general sense of disinterest and confusion prevail. There is an overall sluggishness and a sense of being stuck. In the spiritual realm one may follow a religious practice with blind obedience with little real connection to God. One can quote the Bible without practicing the teachings of the Bible in daily life. For others there is a void in the area of the spiritual; one may be an atheist or agnostic.

In the ten years I have worked shamanically, I have yet to find someone with a closed seventh chakra. I would be surprised if someone who was closed to the spiritual would elect to come to see me. Conversely I have encountered clients whose seventh chakra is quite open with energy rushing out of their head, but there is little grounding in the lower chakras. Because we are human animals, we need to work with the instinctual parts of our being. Shamanism works with power animals to help us with our grounding and with the instinctual aspects of who we are. Health problems can result if we do not stay fully in our bodies.

There is a circular process between the chakras and psychological functioning. Energy cords flow from the chakra of one person to another, exchanging energy and setting the stage for psychological issues to emerge. Many psychologists are vaguely aware of this process without having words or theories to fully explain how this works. Leading scholars on women's psychological development[15] have introduced the concept of the circular exchange of empathy between women. They have suggested that a woman's core self structure is based on being in relationship with others. They put forth that there is an empathic flow of energy that goes back and forth between a mother and her daughter and from one good friend to another. Although they do not discuss how empathic energy flows between people, they do discuss that it is circular in nature with a *knowing* that flows back and forth.

Energy cords that flow from the chakras are the avenue for empathic and loving energy to be exchanged. Since we operate on a frequency level much like a radio band, the attunement of energy frequencies maintains the circular flow of empathy between people. When one member of the energetic exchange shifts frequencies, there is a break in the quality of the attunement. Almost all of us have experienced relationships where there has been a shift in intimacy. There still may be closeness, but the level of empathic connection is different. The relationship is not as it used to be; yet there is no ostensible reason why. People grow and change at different rates sometimes making it difficult to stay empathetically attuned at the same level that initially drew them together. Most couples struggle with periods of feeling out of tune over the course of their relationship.

Energetic patterns between people may become stuck or rigidified. The circular flow of energy becomes blocked stunting growth. We all know couples that bicker over the same little things driving each other crazy, yet are unable to let go of their harmful exchange. Sometimes the energy flows in only one direction with one person dominating the relationship while the other withdraws, feeling powerless. When the energy cords are used as pathways for destructive or harmful patterns, psychological and physical problems may develop.

Underlying issues and concerns may be communicated along energy cords resulting in a child living her parent's issues, sometimes causing her to feel that she does not have a right to her own life. If a parent operates from a place of fear, there is a tendency to control the child energetically. Often I find clients enshrouded in the fearful energy of their parents with energy drained from their bodies to their parents along the energy cords. I have had clients tell me they could not dream of making a change in their lives because of what it would do to their parents. When issues are explored from a rational place, they agree it makes sense to make the change, but in their gut they do not feel it is possible. Often clients have told me that I do not seem to understand that there is no choice. Energetically they live in their parents' sphere and literally do not feel free to make their own choices. They believe that something horrible will happen if they try to break this bond—a horrible ripping away, which will leave them empty. The fear of this emptiness is the result of having had their energy drained away.

The Healing of Energy Cords

In psychotherapy healing takes place in a cathartic moment when the client both understands the issues and feels an emotional, energetic release. For those ready to make a change, this therapeutic process can occur quite quickly. For others stuck in old patterns, it can be a long arduous time before the client experiences a cathartic moment that frees up his or her energy. In shamanic work the energetic release happens quickly. However, if a client does not understand the issues involved, old beliefs or thought forms can pull the energy back resulting in only temporary relief. Combining psychotherapy with shamanic work can deepen and speed the healing process.

Jessica, a bright, sensitive, and caring young woman who plans to have a career as an alternative health care practitioner, came for a healing and to learn more about shamanism. She had wonderful, warm energy that drew people to her. Jessica was experiencing a great deal of illness and was prone to chronic infections. She reported that she frequently felt off-center and exhausted. Western medicine had been unable to restore her to well-being. I began the healing by working energetically around Jessica's body. While in a light trance I ran my hands over her energy field. Guided by my spirit helpers, I discovered there were clouds around the fourth and fifth chakras and a block of wood stuck in the sixth one. Grotesque white worms were crawling around the lower three chakras. After these things were extracted energetically from her energy field, I balanced the chakras by moving my hands above each chakra in a clockwise manner. I was surprised to find so many blockages on such an open person.

When I did the soul retrieval, I discovered why. The father was drawing energy from the second chakra, her sister from the third one and her mother from the fourth and fifth. Her boyfriend was pulling energy from the sixth. Jessica had such wonderful energy that those who were near to her were unconsciously pulling energy from her. This left her depleted and prone to continual illness and infection. In the journey Jessica's and my power animals severed the energy cords between Jessica and each corresponding family member. The power animals healed each end of the cords for both Jessica and the family member. Severing the cords did not sever the relationships; it merely stopped the flow of energy out of Jessica. This process is analogous to cutting the umbilical cord. A person can stop the flow of one-sided energy on her own by being clear about boundaries and keeping herself grounded and energetically protected. Since we do not think of others draining our energy, we rarely consider protecting ourselves.

After stopping the one-sided flow of energy from Jessica to her family members, the energy that had been drained from Jessica was taken from the various family members and healed by spirit guides before returning it to her. The energy that had been removed from Jessica's energy field and chakras was transformed into healing energy that was carried by spirit guides to each family member. Each received a power animal to help in the integration of this energy. When healed energy is sent back to an unsuspecting family member, his or her essence decides whether or not to receive this energy. It took quite a bit of time to do this work. Jessica reported feeling exhausted afterward and slept a great deal for several days. She then felt much stronger with increased energy and clearer boundaries.

Energy drains can manifest in a variety of ways. In addition to energy being pulled through the energy cords, another's energy may be stuck to the energy body at various places along the energy body causing problems in these areas. During healings I have *seen* the energy form of another person holding on around the neck of a client. The client is literally carrying the energy of another around and is weighted down as a result blocking the free flow of energy. Stiff shoulders and neck plus difficulty in speaking what is in the heart are associated with this type of energy drain. In extreme cases a person may be energetically enshrouded in another person's energy to the extent that the person literally feels controlled by the other. An extraction can remove the other person's energy. Each time energy is removed, a healing is done for the energy before sending it back to the person to whom it belongs. This can occur even if the person is no longer on the physical plane. Fortunately spirit guides and power animals know how to find the right person wherever he or she may be.

When there is a mutual interactive flow of energy between people, it can be a positive exchange. Yet as we know, our relationships are seldom simple or static. Much of the complexity in our relationships is transmitted energetically. A clearer understanding of the various dimensions present in the on-going flow of energy between individuals is explored by examining the relationship between therapist and client.

Transference and Countertransference in Psychotherapy
The psychotherapeutic relationship is a complex and sometimes controversial relationship. Many grow and heal as a result of this relationship, while others struggle to make sense of it. This relationship has many facets, probably none more mystifying than the phenomenon of transference/countertransference. It is in this aspect of the relationship that unspoken and often unconscious dynamics are brought to light. The initial avenue for expression of these dynamics is through energy cords that develop between therapist and client. Those who have been in long-term therapy are familiar with the power of the bond between client and therapist and the uncanny way in which the client's deepest issues seem to rise to the surface within the safety and containment of the therapeutic relationship. Often the therapist takes on the face of unresolved issues. If a client fears being taken over and controlled by another, the therapist may be viewed as threatening and invasive; whereas if a client fears abandonment, the therapist may be perceived as rejecting and distant.

Often unresolved dynamics in the client's life are projected onto the therapist. For instance, a client, who lives under the watchful eye of a jealous mother who expresses hurt whenever her daughter forms a close relationship, may assume the therapist feels upset when the client finds a new boyfriend. Given this assumption, the client does not mention this relationship in therapy and over time feels anger at the therapist for *not allowing* her to talk about the relationship. The therapist may sense the client's anger but have no idea why.

Transference also develops when key mannerisms or ways of speaking remind the client of an important person in her life. An arch of the eyebrow can be reminiscent of Aunt Mary. If Aunt Mary is a beloved figure, then the therapist will be perceived in that light, but if Aunt Mary is a critical force in the client's life, then the therapist who lifts her eyebrow may be perceived as judgmental even if she is not.

These projections might just sit there if it were not for the flow of these projections through the energy cords to the therapist. Often, quite unwittingly, the therapist is pulled to act out the client's projection, even when it involves behavior that is quite uncharacteristic for the therapist.

For example, Jack came into therapy with me to work on career issues. Jack's father was quite successful in his career, traveled a great deal, and spent most of his weekends on business golf dates. His mother was quite busy in civic affairs and often accompanied her husband on business trips leaving Jack at home with his older sister. Jack successfully buried any feelings of abandonment or neglect by pushing them out of conscious awareness. As the therapy went along, he became concerned that I would abandon or reject him in some way. He did not mention his fear to me. These concerns persisted even though I had never missed an appointment except for scheduled vacations. Unbeknownst to me, Jack feared I would never return when I was away on vacation. He was embarrassed to express this concern as he was surprised and confused he was feeling this way.

Finally Jack's intense feelings of abandonment came into the open when I did not have time to reschedule his appointment after a Monday holiday. Usually I discussed rescheduling a week or two in advance to ensure he had an appointment, but this time I forgot. Jack was much more upset than I imagined. Then it became clear why I had forgotten to save a space for him. The energy in the room around abandonment was so strong that it had to come out into the open. Through the energy cords that had developed between us, Jack was pulling me to do something that felt like abandonment so these feelings could be addressed.

When a client is unable to give voice to an issue, there is a strong energetic pull to bring this issue to light so it can be resolved. In this incident, because I forgot to save a time for Jack, his feelings of abandonment were forced out into the open. With the issue of abandonment in the open we began work on this problem and quickly saw that his fear of rejection and abandonment that stemmed from his childhood had prevented him from taking risks and living up to his potential in his chosen field.

There are several key relationships in which energy cords and energetic bonds develop. Commonly we project issues with our parents onto friends and lovers. There is a constant pull to bring unresolved issues into the open, which is why close relationship can be so challenging. If problems are not addressed when they first arise, distance and disconnection are the likely outcome often followed by some form of acting out so that the problem can be aired. It is often difficult to tell at first glance if an interpersonal problem is really about the stated conflict or if there are layers of projection interlaced in the equation. In addition, it is common for one person to take on another's projection, as energetically this type of projection is familiar and it fits. The actual taking in of these projections is called projective identification, meaning that one identifies and resonates with the projection. In psychotherapy aspects of this dynamic are commonly called countertransference.

Countertransference develops when the therapist is having a reaction to the client based on the therapist's unresolved issue. Frequently this is activated by a client's projection through an energetic exchange flowing back and forth along the energy cords. Although therapists try to keep their own issues out of the treatment, maintaining a stance of professional neutrality, feelings and reactions flow through the energy cords. Ideally a therapist listens patiently and steadfastly as she works to understand the basis for a client's projection, feeling personally unaffected by what the client is saying. For example, when a client insisted that I was always angry with her, yet I was clear I harbored no feelings of anger towards the client, then it was easy for me to explore the origins of this belief with the client. I helped the client to consider that the feelings of anger in the room may be the client's own unexpressed anger or may come from her experience of having a parent or other key persons in her life frequently angry with her.

At other times I found that I can become embroiled in what is called a transference/countertransference dance. The essence of the energy or message being projected resonates within; it finds a home. For instance, Rachael asserted that I was stingy and withholding, which was reminiscent of what my mother used to say about me as a child. I was aware that I had developed a stance of being a bit withholding to protect myself from my energy being drawn away or, simply put, from feeling smothered by my mother. Nonetheless, the accusation that I was stingy and withholding left me feeling hurt and shamed as it did when I was a child. Energetically I pulled back and, in fact, became withholding. Rachael felt this and responded to it. I denied that I had pulled back, truly believing that this was no longer a problem for me. I said the right things and stayed focused on Rachael's feelings. But the "right" words were lost on Rachael by the shift of energy in the room.

Invariably this type of impasse impacts the therapy. It is impacted because the power of the unspoken energy in the room is denied, in the belief that words can alter what is felt. When I was accused of being stingy and withholding, I energetically retreated into myself for protection as I did with my mother because it meant that my mother wanted more from me than I wanted to give. The energy around this issue was in the room between Rachael and me. Rachael could feel this and felt confused or even a bit betrayed by my assertion that nothing had changed when in fact energetically the relationship felt quite different. This was a tricky problem, as I, as well as all therapists, need to keep our issues out of the room, yet it is humanly impossible not to get triggered or drawn in by clients. In this incidence I acknowledged that upon reflection, I felt myself pull back some and then shifted back to how this made Rachael feel that her words had that impact. If I had not been able to make this acknowledgment, Rachael's trust in me and what was happening between us would have been compromised.

A plethora of articles and books have been written on the psychological transference/countertransference issue as it is at the heart of the therapeutic relationship. The vast majority of these books and articles discuss situations similar to the two examples cited. Psychological theory understands that there is an energetic exchange flowing back and forth, but it does not take it further by naming it. What has been missing from psychological theory is a framework that includes the energetic reality of existence.

Aspects of the transference/countertransference dynamic exist in other important and intimate relationships. Many people hurt those they care about most by acting out unresolved issues in uncharacteristic ways. This happens as a result of the energetic pull to bring unexpressed issues to light. In the previous chapter the pull for trauma victims to release stored and blocked energy from the body by some form of re-enactment was explored. This same dynamic applies to small everyday traumas and hurts. It also happens when one or both people deny what they are really feeling even though the energy around these feelings is palpable. Often we choose people to be in our lives who help to awaken our unresolved issues while at the same time we are helping them to wake up. Many people form partnerships based on a mutual fit of each person's unresolved issues. Often we hear someone say that she thought she was marrying someone very different from her father, but in reality her father and husband feel emotionally the same. This is not a bad thing but an opportunity for growth and transformation.

How energy is taken in and exchanged may appear complex. An awareness of this process is the first step in sorting it out. The next step lies in giving oneself permission to pay attention to energy and to acknowledge shifts in the energetic flow. This process is similar to paying attention to one's feelings. The two processes are intermingled in many ways. After one has a better understanding of what is happening with one's energy and energy body, it is then possible to find ways of releasing, rechanneling and recharging one's energy. This often leads to a greater understanding of the psychological issues involved.

Chapter 8
THE DREAMBODY

I began to ponder where dissociated parts really go and how the journeyer is able to find soul parts that belong to the right person. There must be millions of lost soul parts floating around untethered. The landscape should be cluttered with so many lost soul fragments that it should be virtually impossible to find anyone, yet this is rarely the case. Usually I am led directly to a scene, which contains the lost soul part of the client, her guides, and other essence beings who are directly connected to the client and her healing. As I journey on these questions, I am directed to understand more about the dreambody and the various frequency bands on which we operate.

Although the dreambody is a concept new to many in the West, discussion of the dreambody is one of the cornerstones of ancient healing traditions used by the Tibetans, the Chinese, and the ancient metaphysical traditions of India. The most vivid imagery of the dreambody for Christians is that of Jesus ascending into the heavens surrounded by a vibrant light body.

The Workings of the Dreambody

Through my own shamanic journeying and work with clients, I have come to conceptualize the dreambody in the following way. Each of us is an essence or soul that carries an awareness of our purpose and place in the universe; some refer to this understanding of the soul as the "higher self" or the "over soul." Within the soul are the energy and physical bodies and the psyche, which contains our conscious and unconscious processes. All of these are vibrationally housed in the dreambody and operate on differing frequency bands.

Today our main method of communication comes via frequency bands through our televisions, telephones, radios, and the Internet. On many levels it makes sense that we also operate on vibrational or frequency bands and have the potential for greater levels of understanding and communication through working with our dreambodies.

The dreambody is holographic, moving in and out of the physical and auric body and vibrational field, housing all of the frequency bands of a person's experiences, both of this life and of past lives. Past life experiences and extremely traumatic events are at the outer edges of the dreambody, a faint vibrational tone, which can go unnoticed throughout a lifetime. Yet this tone can be brought to conscious levels through various therapeutic techniques such as hypnosis and shamanic journeying. There are hundreds of thousands of tiny vibrational threads that connect these vibrational tones to our major frequency bands, which are also housed in the dreambody. When I retrieve lost parts of the soul for someone else, I travel into his or her dreambody and am led by guides to the outer vibrational edge of the dreambody to retrieve the lost soul fragments. These lost soul fragments appear as images in my mind as the story of what happened to cause the soul loss unfolds before me.

Each of us has a major frequency band on which we most commonly operate analogous to what psychologists call the ego or conscious processes. Within this major frequency band, varying frequency waves contain different aspects of the self as well as some parts of the unconscious process. For most these waves are within a proximate range providing a sense of internal congruence. When we are with certain people or engaged in specific activities such as work or play, one frequency wave tends to dominate over others. Most of us have had the experience of meeting another person and immediately feeling connected and attuned. We feel this way because we operate on a similar frequency wave. Conversely at other times we meet people to whom we have difficulty connecting. Hard as we try, it feels like a struggle to find something in common or to feel comfortable and at ease. We literally are out of tune with these individuals. It is especially painful if a child is born to parents with whom there is little attunement. Some find they experience intense mood swings or are drawn to radically different people and activities. In these incidences, the frequency bands are disparate and these individuals tend to feel fragmented. A major goal of psychotherapy is to help clients to feel internally congruent by strengthening the core ego structure. This strengthening produces a wider and stronger frequency band.

The frequency band of an individual's dreambody is fluid and has the capacity to change. When an unconscious memory surfaces to consciousness, it widens the frequency band and range of conscious processes. When one member of a couple grows and changes, her frequency band is altered and the couple may no longer feel as if they communicate or connect in the same way. Most couples struggle throughout the years with staying attuned to each other as each grows and changes. Other couples, fearful of becoming estranged, unconsciously choose not to grow so as to remain attuned to one another.

Those who fear growth and change operate on fairly narrow frequency bands and feel quite constricted; whereas others who are willing to challenge themselves and push themselves to grow function on wide frequency bands. These individuals both feel and are perceived as being quite expansive. When one does shamanic journeying, the operating frequency band is expanded, allowing connection and understanding of a variety of experiences on multi-levels. The more one journeys, the further one can extend the frequency range in which she travels. Energetically we operate in a way that is remarkably similar to our telecommunications system.

Memory is stored on differing frequency waves. The more we use or retrieve certain memories, the stronger these frequencies become, allowing us to access more obscure memories. Gradually these frequencies blend into the major frequency band. Similar experiences that operate on the same frequency can be collapsed into one memory. When adults reminiscence about their childhood, they do not remember every event, rather there are clips that carry the affect of a certain period. I went to a recent high school reunion in Indiana where several people brought pictures of our childhood. There were 12 of us who were best friends from elementary school through high school, so the pictures covered a wide range of ages. Each of us had the experience of drawing a total blank when looking at some of the pictures. We all recognized each other, but each of us selectively remembered different events. "Oh here is a picture of a slumber party at Gail's house," said Linda. I looked at the picture and remembered nothing of this event even though I was in the picture. There were other pictures where I described the event in great detail and others were vague or hazy about it.

Different memories with similar emotional content sometimes collapse into one memory, which accounts for why many of us appear to have selective memory. For example, a person may look back fondly on childhood Christmases, feeling warm and aglow with the closeness that was felt.

A sibling may remember some Christmases in which there was strife and rancor, which was not at all pleasant or warm. Both experiences are true and valid, yet for each of these siblings the memory that is most easily accessed is the one that resonates affectively with her experience of being in the family. Each can usually access the memories that the other puts forth—the warm times and the times filled with conflict and drama—but it is not what first comes to mind.

Teachings from Dreamtime

The dreambody is the vehicle in which we gather knowledge and wisdom from other realms, allowing us to connect to information from both the past and future. The dreambody fits like a hood over the body, attaching at the solar plexus in front and the kidneys in back. The dreambody can detach and travel to different realms. We learn new things via the journeys our dreambody takes while we are asleep. I perceive the dream state to contain various levels of dreams. Some dreams re-work the day-to-day events and upsets of our lives; sometimes images from the last thing we saw on TV or at the movies appear in our dreams. Other dreams deal with deep issues in our psyches that are archetypal in nature. These archetypes are part of the collective unconscious, a common frequency or vibrational level to which we all have access. Yet the images we derive from these archetypes are uniquely ours based on our vast experiences that are energetically stored in the dreambody. I believe that our common connection to the collective unconscious is one of the sources of our capacity for empathy.

The third level of dreams is when the dreambody detaches and takes us to meet with teachers and guides in other realms. The week before September 11, 2001, I had the same dream every night. I was in an elegant office building. I was floating up the stairs doing energy work with my hands while people were coming down the stairs. We all smiled at one another. Those I passed did not seem to think that what I was doing with my hands was strange. In the dream I asked what this dream meant. Repeatedly I heard—as if a mantra—"move the energy, there are many layers." Later when I watched the CBS Special on September 11th, which had been filmed by cameramen working with the New York Fire Department that morning, I realized that I had been in the World Trade Center in the reoccurring dream. My teachers had brought me in dreamtime to begin the work that I was soon to do.

I awoke on the morning of September 11th in a bad mood. I attributed this to going back to work, although I rarely feel in a bad mood about going to work so it felt a bit unusual. I had been on vacation and had not turned on the TV for almost two weeks. Around eight a.m. I heard a voice in my head suggest that I turn on the TV as something may have happened in the world, but I ignored the voice, as I did not feel like having the TV on. By quarter of nine, my phone began to ring with friends and clients telling me to turn on the television. My son was living in Manhattan and had jury duty on Canal Street, a few blocks from the carnage. I tried to phone him on his cell phone and at home; there was dead silence. By this time my body was vibrating with the pain and tension. The Pentagon was on fire; then the first tower collapsed. I kept trying to find Josh. I went upstairs to e-mail him when the phone rang. Josh told me he was OK.

In the afternoon I did a meditation with one of my clients to pray for everyone. In the meditation I traveled in my dreambody to the World Trade Center and saw the area enveloped in incredible blue light with many healing and helping spirits trying to help folks cross over. On closer examination I saw that there was massive confusion. Souls wandered dazed and confused, unable to see all of the help that was there for them. To complicate matters, there had been massive soul loss. Many were unclear if they were dead or just out of their bodies. I witnessed souls whose bodies had died communicating with souls who were separated from living bodies. I helped a few people cross over and a few vibrationally reconnect with their bodies, but the task seemed quite daunting.

That night Linda Crane came to me in dreamtime. Linda was the shamanic healer from Gloucester who had helped me on my path and with whom I had become a good friend. She died July of 2000 from breast cancer. I had adopted her two cats and, Emile, her eldest cat sleeps nestled against my body all night. When Linda first came to me, she asked for cakes and surprisedly I had some prepared for her. We ate and talked and then she said, "I want to show you how to help people cross over with the massive confusion many are experiencing regarding whether they are dead or alive." Linda surrounded me in blue light and told me to stand with my arms out, inviting souls to come to me. The souls were to walk through me and as I experienced them move through me, I would be able to tell if they were still attached to a body or if their body had died. I had guides on both my right and left sides assist the souls as they passed through. The souls, whose bodies that had died, went to the right. They were led to their protectors and deceased family and friends to help them cross over. Guides on the left assisted those who had left their bodies during the trauma find vibrational threads, which enabled them to reconnect to their bodies. Although I dozed off and on during the night, each time I regained awareness, I experienced the flow of energy through my body as souls passed through.

Early the next morning I met with a group of friends to meditate and to pray for peace and for everyone impacted by this crisis. Again I found myself in blue light with beings passing through my body. I was heartened to see that there were many people doing the same practice. During the day I met with clients. There was stunned disbelief, a need for clients to tell where they were when they heard and the initial impact the attack had on them. Most, myself included, seemed disconnected from their center, a sense of ungroundness. I spoke with Josh often. Each time a building that surrounded the trade center collapsed, it sounded like another attack. This coupled with numerous bomb threats and rumors left him shaken. Each time I paused to breathe, meditate, or be still I experienced the souls passing through. That night when I went to bed, the souls passing through intensified.

That Saturday I did a workshop for therapists who want to learn how to integrate shamanism into their psychotherapy practices. This is an on-going group and I had already prepared a focus for the day, which I promptly discarded. It was time to teach global shamanism and psychopomp—the practice of assisting the dead to the other side. The energy in the workshop was scattered. We began the session with a meditation; it took all of my energy and focus to ground the energy in the room. It was apparent that the attack had profoundly impacted all of our nervous systems and that none of us was fully in his or her body. After an initial journey to gather information regarding the meaning and significance of the attack, I taught them the practice that Linda had taught me in the dream state the night of the September 11th. Several were skeptical that they could do this practice. I told them to journey to the World Trade Center, allow spirit to guide them, and see what transpired. All had powerful journeys. Each made contact with someone who had died and assisted them in passing over. A common theme was taking the deceased to their loved ones to say good-bye before they crossed over.

I believe that a global shift in consciousness is occurring regarding the understanding of our place in the universe. Our collective vibrational levels are rising as is evidenced in the cultural opening to the spiritual and the paranormal. The immense popularity of the Star Wars series, The Lord of the Rings and The Matrix trilogies speak to our fascination with other realms of reality and with the energetic forces of good and evil. This shift is taking place in the dream state.

We are learning new information as we sleep, just as I was taught the above practices as I slept. When information we receive in our dreams appears in the culture as a new idea it immediately makes sense to us. Conversely we put into the culture what we learn. I think thoughts that would have never entered my mind ten years ago. When I cautiously share these thoughts with others, expecting that they will think that I have gone mad, I am met with understanding and relief that someone else is having these same thoughts. When I first shared with a colleague with whom I had gone to graduate school that I was studying with the Bomoh and learning to journey and work with energy, her response was, "Great, I've been really reading a lot about past lives. Can you do journeys into past lives?" I replied that I could and then we were engrossed in sharing all of the things that we had been thinking and doing in the past few years. We were both surprised that the other was exploring the spiritual realm as neither of us had given an inkling that the other one was predisposed to such interests.

When one journeys, the dreambody detaches from the body as it travels to other realms. I began journeying before I knew about the dreambody and found that, the more I journeyed, the more I experienced pain in my neck, upper back and shoulders. I later learned that I was not properly reattaching the dreambody and thus was putting a strain on my neuromuscular system. One reattaches the dreambody by simply rubbing the solar plexus and the back above the waist at the kidneys. One can also focus the mind's energy to make sure that it has reattached.

Energetic Frequencies: Our Mode of Operation

When I journey for others, I am now aware that I travel into their dreambodies and connect with their various frequency bands. This explains why I do not encounter lost soul fragments wandering about that have no connection to the client. A lost soul part or entity does, on occasion, enter a frequency band within the dreambody accounting for all sorts of problems and distress, but this part can be removed by an extraction or depossession. Usually these energy fragments enter the dreambody when a traumatic event occurs resulting in soul loss; the marauding soul parts are usually connected in some way to the trauma.

I invite people to bring significant others to their healing ceremonies; sometimes there are three or four people in attendance. Before we begin, I ask them to stay open to what they might see or experience as we all direct our attention and energies to the healing of their friend. Usually these people have had no formal training in journeying; yet, it is common for us to have similar images or sensations. This is because we are all entering the client's dreambody and are tuning into the same frequencies. We all have the capacity to still our minds and connect to the wealth of information that is around us.

Sometimes I am surprised by what I find in my journeys and question whether I should share the images with the client. Usually, however, the client verifies the information. I had seen Jennifer for six years as a psychotherapy client before doing a soul retrieval. I assumed that in that six-year period I had heard most of the major stories in her life and would not be surprised by what I saw. In the journey I saw a car chase. As the scene unfolded, I saw the police chasing a car in which Jennifer was riding. The man she was with was drunk and speeding. The car spun out of control and crashed. Jennifer was sobbing hysterically as the police approached the car. When I shared the scene with Jennifer, her face turned pale and she said, "You really saw that? I never told you about it as it was so horrible that I didn't want to think about it or talk about it." We did not talk about it further, but I did return to her the healed part of her soul that was left at the crash.

Each day we experience periods in which we visit different frequency bands within our dreambody. It is commonly called daydreaming. Psychologists term it dissociation. When we leave conscious awareness, we go into a different frequency band within the dreambody. There are many levels to this experience. Often when reading a book, a thought can trigger me and I am off somewhere, unaware of the words that fly by on the page in front of me. There can be pleasant triggers that cause us to tap long ago memories and soon we find ourselves reliving a special experience. There are other triggers, a smell, a tone of voice, or an image on a movie screen that brings panic and a sense of fear or danger. These triggers tend to awaken vibrational threads to parts of us with whom we have lost contact. As a result of the many and varied frequencies that make us who we are, each of us has a reality that is uniquely ours.

The vibrational threads in the dreambody carry images and senses from our past experiences, which intermingle with and impact the present. Our projections flow from this place. Sometimes we meet a person who feels vaguely familiar, reminding us of someone we know. Images are activated imbuing the new person with affect and memories of the past causing the new person's individual attributes to dim while she absorbs the energy of the projection. Usually this is an unconscious process and thus we are unaware as to why we are experiencing such strong feelings about a person that we have just met.

People process their experiences in differing ways and create new and individualized meaning to their reality based on all the associated images and fragments that are stored. When groups of people are asked to witness the same event and then recount what has happened, invariably no two people report seeing exactly the same thing. The same experience can resonate differently within each person and a whole array of associated images and sensations mix in with the current experience. All of us have had arguments with friends or family in which no one could come to an agreement on what was said or what really happened. Many relationships have ended or have been severely damaged as a result of an inability to agree upon the *truth*. When we are able to accept the other person's version of the story not as truth but as the other person's *experience*, our relationships flow in an easier manner. Within the field of psychology, there is a theoretical camp called constructionism, which focuses on this phenomenon and conducts therapy by honoring the unique perspective of the client without judging it as abnormal.

There are more profound levels on the continuum of dissociation. Some report not being in the body or only partially being in the body when confronted with an actual terrifying encounter or a situation that triggers a memory of this encounter. During these periods of being out of the body, one has left the normal operating range and is at the outer edges of the dreambody. In most incidences, when the threat is over, the energy essence returns to the physical body and to the normal operating frequency. Sometimes if the situation is particularly terrifying, a part of the soul's essence will go to the outer edges of the dreambody and stay there. In this case the soul fragment will need to be retrieved for one to feel whole.

At times the essence part stays in the dreambody as a separate split-off part housed in a different frequency band that can gradually be brought back into consciousness and into the normal frequency realm of the person. This is what takes place in psychotherapy. As the client works with stories and images, a wider range of affect and memories begin to emerge. The differing vibrational levels become somewhat blended. The dream life of the client becomes rich with images from the split-off frequency band and a host of new feelings emerge. There is a tug in the body, in dreamtime and in one's deepest feelings, which pull these sealed off parts into the conscious mind. In therapy we talk of cathartic moments when feelings and images come together in such a coherently powerful way that there is a break-through that alters a person's perspective and way of being in the world. This breakthrough or catharsis has cognitive, affective and energetic components and usually results in a shift in the vibrational or frequency level. With the integration of a lost or split-off memory or essence part, there is a clarity or understanding that allows the person to be more uniquely who she is and find a sense of wholeness heretofore unexperienced.

If a child was quite young when intense and repeated abuse occurred, the fragmentation may be extreme enough to warrant the creation of separate and distinct personalities. The psychic structure of a child is not fully formed until around four to five years of age. If there is too much fragmentation, there is no core structure to hold the personality together. Arnold Mindell[16] described the dreambody as... *a collection of energy vortices held together by the total personality.* If the personality is not formed, it cannot hold these energy vortices or fragments together. Thus the development of different personalities is very adaptive creating energy bands around the psychic structure holding it in place. If this were not to occur, the fragmentation could be severe enough to result in a psychotic state from which it would be difficult to heal. These different personalities are housed in the dreambody on different frequency waves but are fluid and travel back and forth fully occupying the body.

When there has been intense trauma, there is also the possibility for delusional thoughts to occur. Many times it is difficult for a child to believe that the person she loves, trusts and depends upon has betrayed and abused her. Thus, a child may dissociate, go into the dreambody and try to make some sense of what has happened to her. In this process one can weave a new version of what has happened which removes the one who is loved from direct responsibility for the torture. The terror and fear from the experience is carried into the dreambody so that the fear and terror become part of the new story. Energetically, the new version takes on its own life and is as real to the person as if it had actually happened. Sometimes the newly created reality is less rigidly held. At a later time, when the survival of the child is not dependent upon the abuser, this version will start to feel less real and she will be able to understand in a clearer way what actually happened to her. Again this process is necessary for the day-to-day survival of the person. This is not a lie but a way that our psyche and energy system has of adapting so that it can survive. At times these thought forms are quite fanciful and can be recognized as delusional. Sometimes the new thought forms make sense and are taken as the truth. Herein lies some of the confusion and controversy in the false memory debate.

The dreambody also contains threads that connect us to our various past lives. Many times we find experiences that awaken us to feelings, smells and experiences that happened long ago. Sometimes images from these lives intermingle with current reality further blurring our understanding of what is occurring in this life. I have found that some clients' "delusional" accounts are actually past life experiences that affectively, and occasionally literally, match the traumatic experience that they had. On a soul or energy essence level these past life experiences are as important to heal and bring back as current experiences of soul loss.

Often people come into this lifetime with soul loss from a previous lifetime. In an attempt to heal, conditions may be set in motion to recreate affectively and energetically the experience they had that resulted in the soul loss. One who was hanged in a previous life and had part of the soul essence lost in that lifetime, may have chronic sore throats, difficulty breathing, or trouble expressing what is really felt. Images of hanging and bodily experiences of being choked or having the neck broken may litter the dream state, yet there is lack of clarity as to why this imagery is there. Another may be born into an abusive family in which there is physical violence and actual attempts at strangulation, which literally recreates the terror of the hanging. Some spend a lifetime searching for a part of them that is missing, never feeling whole or content.

Sometimes these past life threads are awakened if we are in close relationship to one with whom we have unfinished business. One woman came to see me reporting that although she knew that her father had not abused her, she felt as if he had. Carol felt fearful of him and did not want to be alone with him. Carol had raised this concern with him on several occasions and felt that his open, caring non-defensive way of responding to her did not fit with one who had been abusive. Nor did she, her mother, or sisters have any memory of abuse having taken place. We explored the many ways in which emotional incest can feel like physical incest, yet this did not seem to fit what she was feeling either. When I did a journey and soul retrieval, I found that the abuse had occurred in another lifetime and that they were together to heal these old wounds. In the journey I saw that her father, an invading soldier in the 14th century in mid-Europe, had raped and murdered her. It was part of the spoils of victory at that time in history to do such things. Since I do a healing for all of the people I encounter in these situations, both Carol and her father received a healing from this trauma. Two days later Carol's father called her reporting that two days ago he felt this incredible burden lift from his being and that he felt better than he could ever remember feeling. Carol, shocked that he had felt the impact of the healing, went on to tell him about the past life soul retrieval and the origins of her fear of him.

Fortunately there are positive past life threads as well. Frequently we meet someone and feel an immediate connection as if we have always known this person. There is such sweetness when we encounter our former lover or family member. Many of our closest connections we have known before.

An understanding of the dreambody both enhances and expands on our perception as to how we operate and the vast untapped potential we have, while also challenging many firmly held beliefs. Those of us who work shamanically know the power of the connection with spirit guides, power animals, and the various levels of non–ordinary reality. Yet for most that have been educated in the West, the notion that we exist on frequency bands and can travel to different realms is truly fanciful. It is through our dreambodies, however, that we process and make sense of all the information that comes to us from the culture in which we live. Vibrational frequencies are created in the dreambody that house the images, which flood our psyches from the culture. Thus each of us carries not only all of the vibrational frequencies of our many lifetimes, but also create new frequencies to incorporate the images and senses that flow to us daily.

PART III

VIOLENCE WITHIN: VIOLENCE WITHOUT

Americans are continually bombarded with violent images from the media. A cross fertilization process occurs in which our inner images create those that glare back at us from our television sets and those coming back at us from the screen inflame the psyche. Violence can take many forms. Abusive words and acts of humiliation scar the soul and psyche as much as physical wounds. When hateful words and physical assaults are combined, the results are devastating. Violence to the soul is a major cause of our most serious emotional problems. It is both the cause of soul loss and the result of it. As a society we are governed by a set of beliefs that keep us shackled to a hierarchical system based on individualism and greed. We have lost touch with the mysteries around us and our innate individual power and abilities to heal others and ourselves.

Shamanic work opens us to the wisdom around and within us, offering a path to healing on both an individual and societal level. The psyche, physical body, and spirit are viewed as interconnected entities, powerfully impacted by society and the natural forces around us. Much of our suffering, anxiety, and alienation flows from a lack of awareness of the extent of our interconnection. We struggle inwardly with our aloneness by running from one addiction to the next to bind the emptiness we feel. Through the vividness of clients' stories, the complexities of our interconnections and interactions become apparent.

Chapter 9
DISCONNECTION FROM SPIRIT:
OUR CULTURAL HERITAGE

Gasping for breath between sobs, the woman across from me spoke in a childlike manner as she struggled to put words to the unbearable images that flooded her mind and tortured her body. Slowly she gave voice to the images of violence and torture, of her young body being held down with arms bound over her head as she was raped and sodomized. Bravely she described the smells and re-experienced both the longing and fear of death as she lay crushed and suffocated by his large, disgusting body.

The words and painful expression of affect of clients who have endured extreme and horrific abuse have tormented me for years, resulting in a compulsion to understand the propensity of people to harm one another. Since I was a young child, I have been unwilling to accept that there are those among us whose basic nature is evil. I cling to the belief, that if given a choice, man would operate from a place of goodness. I believe those committing evil acts do so as the result of having been broken or harmed in some fundamental way.

When I went to live in Borneo at the age of 22, I was struck by how kind and open hearted the people were. There was a sweet genuineness that had been missing in the American culture that I had known. Shortly after we arrived, first Martin Luther King, then Robert Kennedy were murdered. A fellow teacher asked why it is that people in my country like to shoot others in the head. Her words caught me up short, as if I had been kicked in the stomach. Violence has been such a part of the American culture that I never really questioned its origins. The people in Matu worried about our returning to America, fearful that we would be harmed. We had brought a battery-powered radio to Matu, which kept us in touch with the American Armed Service Station in Viet Nam. We sat riveted to the radio as the Tet Offensive was enacted before our ears. Since our house was a gathering place, we were asked to translate the radio telecasts to all that gathered. The people of the village could not comprehend why Americans were in a foreign country fighting a war between two opposing groups. The clarity and common sense approach to their questions highlighted the absurdity of the war. They spoke of it not in the rhetoric of two opposing political perspectives but from the heart about the senseless loss of life. They shared with us how much they would resent America if our government came to fight in their country. The often-repeated phrase, as if a mantra, was "they have no right to do this; they have no right to be there." This was followed with pleas for us to stay with them rather than return home to have Bob be drafted to fight.

During school vacations we traveled to Bangkok, Hong Kong, and Singapore. The streets overflowed with soldiers on leave, stoned and dazed with a hollow deadness emanating from their being. The stark contrast between their experiences and ours was heart wrenching; while we experienced the best of man, they lived an unimaginable hell. Unfortunately, during this time I held considerable disdain for anyone who would be willing to fight in such a war. It took several years of reflection and the power of the movie, *Coming Home*, for me to grasp that this had been a class war. The educated middle and upper classes had the luxury of seeking deferments, such as Bob had done, or even the funds to go to Canada if all else failed. The working class had no option but to serve when they were drafted or to go to jail and forever be branded a coward.

When I returned to the United States, I became active in the anti-war movement. As the protests intensified in number, so did the violence against the protesters. Once police chased us on horses from the Boston Common down narrow alleyways on the streets of Beacon Hill. We searched for an opening to escape being trampled. While Bob participated in a non-violent protest against the war with fellow divinity school students, he was beaten and jailed. After students at Jackson State and Kent State were killed, the character of our country was called into question. For many of us the right to free speech had been taken away. The myth that we lived in a free country had been shattered.

The 1970's were a difficult time for many of us. As the nation struggled to end the war and find a level of normalcy, many, feeling defeated and spent, turned to drugs and alcohol to numb the pain of the last few years.

The issues were too complex to sort through at such close range. I retreated to graduate school to study psychology, hoping to find answers regarding the nature of man, still devoting much of my time to change the divisions in our country that were based on race, class, and gender.

As my anger at my government's disdain and maltreatment of its own people grew, I became involved with left political groups that wanted to change the very fabric and organization of America. All too often discussions on how to rid society of classism, racism, and sexism ended with talk of an armed struggle being the only viable option for true change. Most of us believed that the wealthy corporations who controlled the infrastructure of both parties were too entrenched and powerful to relinquish control through peaceful elections. The same people who offered armed struggle as a solution had been staunchly against the Viet Nam War and were kind, considerate people. It was heart wrenching to grasp the extent to which violence as a solution to problems was entrenched in our beings, part of our collective vibrational frequency. I am still hopeful that the teachings of some of the great pacifists, such as the Dalai Lama, Martin Luther King, and Gandhi will find a way to alter this mindset.

From a shamanic perspective, the increase in violence stems from a deepening disconnection from spirit, each other, and the spirit in all of the natural forces of the planet; it stems from forgetting that we are all one and part of a greater whole. One of the greatest gifts of my opening to a shamanic path has been the ability to connect with the spirits that reside in all aspects of our environment and in the universe at large. I never feel alone or unprotected since being introduced to the power and love of these spirit beings. Each of us carries a cellular memory of our sense of connectedness; it is why we long for that wonderful feeling of being in love and feeling deeply connected to another. The pain caused by disconnection to the wonderful energy around us leads to a deadening and eroding of the soul resulting in soul or essence loss. Many lead their lives feeling empty and alone, even when surrounded by others; this emptiness often brings depression and rage at the lack of meaningful connection.

Violence in the United States

The United States is the most violent country in the industrialized world. We pride ourselves on our military preparedness, frequently failing to see the link between interpersonal and societal violence. In 1991 the Senate Judiciary Committee released a report affirming this assertion stating that the United States "is the most violent and self destructive nation on the earth." The report found Americans killing, raping, and robbing one another at alarming rates far surpassing all other countries that keep crime statistics.[17] Our military budget is more than the next fifteen countries combined. This disturbing report is in many ways not surprising as the United States has a frequency of violence that runs through the core from its inception. Struggling to escape tyranny and oppression, some of those who migrated to North America from Europe believed they had the right to kill, conquer, and corral the people who had long inhabited this continent. These early settlers reenacted the violence that they were trying to escape and had most likely endured. Some of the pioneers who came to North America not only destroyed the lives and culture of the Native Americans but also broke the sacred trust that had been established with the natural forces of the land. The violation of the sacredness of another's way of life continued through the kidnapping and enslavement of Africans.

We come to understand the rules, beliefs, and structures of our lives by being taught as children. One of the most important lessons learned from my two years in the Peace Corps is that reality is a creation of the culture in which one lives. We often accept a belief or custom as the truth or the only way to do something solely because we were taught it. When I first went to live in Borneo, everything I did was a source of great amusement and wonder to the people who lived there, and everything they did was curious and disorienting to me. In Matu, for instance, everyone ate with his or her hands. To them, it seemed quite absurd attempting to place food on tiny prongs, navigating this instrument into the mouth without spilling—especially when eating with one's hands worked so well. When I first began eating with my hands, food would be all over my face and hands, sometimes extending into my hair, until, finally, I learned the art of eating gracefully in this most natural manner.

The Dualistic and Expansive Mind
Much of what we think is a result of our cultural perspective—our collective thought forms. In the United States the intellectual underpinnings are dualistic in nature. These underpinnings stem from Cartesian and Newtonian thought and have a concreteness that I found missing in Matu. For example, in the United States we are taught that Columbus discovered America. It is true that he alerted Europe to the existence of the North American continent. Yet it is also true that North America was the Native American's home. There are many stories and perspectives, many different truths that make up our early history. When we are able to hold the complexities of

situations, we can perceive many levels that go beyond a black and white analysis. It is through this black and white or dualistic thinking that the divisions that lead to violence are born. A person or racial group may be portrayed as good or evil, our enemy, or our friend. With these black and white distinctions we lose the complexity and heart of the person or group.

The Buddhist speak of two minds; there is mind with a small "m" that is dualistic in nature and then there is Mind with a big "M" that is expansive and spacious and has the potential to comprehend all.

In psychology there is a school of thought called constructionism, which acknowledges that reality is uniquely constructed by each of us and that there can be multiple realities existing simultaneously. When a therapist works with a couple or a family, it is folly to try to ascertain the truth of a situation. What is important is to try to create perspective that allows for several truths to flourish without judgment regarding which is best. It is only through hearing and accepting another's reality, even if we disagree with it, that we come to truly know each other. I find this practice also works with individuals. Many people endure great suffering from an either/ or perspective. "If I had a different boss, I would like my job." Once a client can grasp that there are many factors that go into a situation, there is a widening in the heart and mind to envision change. If George can understand that there are several factors that go into his unhappiness at work, he then has the power to make some changes. His projected view of his boss may hold him back from taking the risks that could increase his happiness at work. His boss may be difficult, but there is much that George can do to make the situation better. I find that most clients are relieved to discover the freedom and non-judgment that comes from an Expansive Mind perspective and strive to shift their thinking. When we step out of a right and wrong perspective, we glimpse the possibilities for change, our hearts soften, and we feel compassion for others.

The cultivation of the Expansive Mind is necessary if we are to find peace and a cessation to the cycles of violence. For some time I had been feeling that some form of disaster was coming to the United States. I could feel it in my bones and got messages in my journeys. For several years I was told by various guides that if America did not shift some of its policies and practices that were harmful to all people in the world that a disaster would occur to awaken us to our need for change. First President Bush refused to sign the Kyoto Accords—going against the rest of the world by choosing business practices over halting environmental destruction. Next we walked out of the meeting in South Africa on racism. I worried that my country's flagrant arrogance was drawing negative energy to us. We already consume an obscene amount of the world's resources and are the major polluters on the planet; it felt that it was only time before energetically we drew a vicious attack to ourselves.

Thus when the attacks of September 11, 2001 came, I was deeply saddened and shaken to my core. But I was not surprised. I sincerely hoped that as well as bringing this country together in common grief and compassion that this attack would herald a dialogue on issues—that we could ask why it was that some people so hated us that they were willing to give their lives to assert that hate. I had hoped that in this time of grief and shock that we could employ an Expansive Mind. President Bush quickly shut down any hopes of this dialogue by asserting that "you either stand with us or are on the side of the terrorists, the evil doers." He used this attack to take away rights of his own civilians and to perpetrate war on those that he determined to be evil—furthering dualistic thinking, violence, fear, and disconnection.

Journalists who dared to ask the questions that might lead to a more expansive debate were silenced. Nine months after the attack there was considerable controversy at Harvard University over the commencement address by Zayed Yasin, a graduating student of Moslem faith. Zayed's goal was to defend the word "jihad" as a symbol of peaceful struggle while condemning the terrorists' actions and use of this word to further its cause.[18] The fear in learning another meaning to a word that had come to symbolize evil was palpable for some. Fear keeps us stuck in dualistic thinking and prevents us from making the leaps necessary to truly understand the many levels of an existing problem.

The Interplay between Societal and Interpersonal Violence

Our psychic structures are quite complex; there are many layers that weave in and out of our conscious and unconscious mind intermingling with the rich images stored in the dreambody. The layers that comprise the psychic structure come from one's genetic make-up, environmental and family influences, spiritual, cultural and national beliefs, and past life influences. All of these forces intermingle with each other to produce a unique blend that makes each of us different. Yet there is much that is shared.

Americans share a common history with accompanying myths and symbols and a common way of thinking and processing reality. There are three key concepts that are imprinted into our psyches. One is the value that we place on individualism. The second is the belief that we are all equal and that anyone can make it in America. The third belief is that our country and way of doing things is better than anyone else and because of this we have the right to do what ever we want. These beliefs or myths have an enormous impact on how we feel about ourselves and on how we conduct our lives.

A hallmark of our cultural identity is that of the rugged individual. We admire and emulate cultural icons such as John Wayne, General George Patton, and Teddy Roosevelt. The press praised Jacqueline Kennedy for not crying at her husband's funeral heralding her for the positive example that she set. The mental health profession labels people who appear too interconnected as co-dependent and enablers. We question why half of all marriages end in divorce without considering the burden that we place on ourselves by honoring family and marriage while the culture encourages us to be independent and self-sufficient. In the United States, one out of every four households has just one person living in it.[19] This not only fosters a sense of isolation and disconnection, but also contributes to environmental waste. Our educational system evaluates individual performance and fosters competition. It does not encourage collective problem solving—a skill that is needed in most workplace situations.

There are cultures in the world in which community and a collective mind is encouraged over individualism. In Matu a person would never live alone and most rarely spend time alone. On my first return visit to Matu, I had been visiting friends in the village and wanted to go back to where I was staying to take a nap. I was escorted back to my room by two of my former students who did not want me to walk alone. The friends with whom I was traveling had gone to visit another village and had not yet returned. My former students insisted on staying with me until my traveling companions came back as they did not want me to be alone. They told me to nap and sat on the edge of the bed while I slept. Of course this level of connection and protection probably feels extreme to most of us, yet our level of independence seems strange and unnatural to them. There are cultures in which a blend of these two stances is the norm, where family and community concerns are often considered over individual needs, but individual expression is also encouraged.

As a society we fail to grasp the extent to which our drive towards being independent and self-sufficient is the result of culture and not reflective of our true nature. Many who suffer from depression do so as a result of feeling alone and unseen. There are those with whom I work who need to be part of a community in order to heal fully. Each lived such a lonely and disconnected childhood. It seems next to impossible to heal the level of pain they feel without the holding of a loving, supportive community. If, as a child, one grew up feeling alone and unloved and this state continued into adulthood, the pain can be profound. We search for true love, in hopes that this level of connection will heal our wounds. We do not realize that our need for connection extends beyond what one person can give; we have lost sight of the healing power of community and of our connection to the natural forces around us. The burden that we place on each other in hoping that another will meet all of our needs while we struggle to remain independent is huge. The disappointment we feel when our relationships fail to work often results in despair, depression, and rage. Few of us have the community of friends to help us through difficult times.

Another shared belief is that we live in a free society where all people are equal. The adage that anyone can make it in America is strongly embedded in the American psyche. The fact that we are not all born into the same economic condition, nor do we all have the same intellectual or physical abilities is overlooked, providing the rationale for those that are more advantaged feeling little sense of responsibility or concern for those less fortunate. The disdain we display for the poor, homeless, and mentally ill is part of the cultural mindset.

The belief that we are all equal and that anyone can make it in America carries with it heavy psychic burdens. Those who are not successful experience an incredible sense of failure and frustration. These feelings of inadequacy can result in depression and despair. Many live their lives feeling less than others, tied to deadening jobs from which they see no escape. Having been told "anyone can make it in America," they blame themselves for their failures. Some cope with these feelings by turning to drugs and alcohol; others spend hours numbing themselves in front of their television, living a vicarious existence through the stars that come to represent all that one might be. Nancy Carlsson-Paige, mother of actor Matt Damon, relayed her fears and concerns about her son becoming a star in her local paper, *Cambridge Chronicle*.[20] She described watching how people treat Matt as if he is different from the rest of us, imbued with a sense of power when, in reality, the power lies in the hands of image-makers who create symbols for the masses to emulate and adore. Matt's mother pondered about the long term effects on her son from carrying this symbolic role.

For some there is rage that the belief that we are all equal is a lie. Many know they are not perceived as equal to the millionaire who lives on the other side of town. They do not feel free as they are defined by their class, gender, or race and by expectations of others. When I first began work as a therapist, I was a counselor for nine elementary schools. I soon discovered that a child was labeled a success or a failure by the end of the second grade, and, from that point on, a subtle tracking began to steer each child into the college track or the trades.

Americans live in a society in which the upper and upper middle class is seen as better than the working class, in which men are viewed as more competent and powerful than women, and in which Caucasians are believed to be superior to all other racial groups. For our society to function, as it is presently constituted, there needs to be a working class to do the menial, repetitive jobs that support the wealthy and their enterprises. A key aspect of a capitalist economy is that there be unemployment so workers will accept the wages they are given. Yet those who are not able to find a job or who are underemployed feel like a failure for conditions inherent in the system. There is a simmering rage often erupting in violence for those seeing the contradictions between the myth and reality. Those who do not see the contradictions experience a quiet despair, a sense of failure, and often depression. This despair and frustration sometimes leads to violence as well.

A third unifying belief is that American lives and way of living have more value than those outside the country and, because of this, we have the right to do whatever we wish to those we view as inferior to us. How many times have dubious political stances been justified as "being in our national self interest." George W Bush's attack on Iraq in 2003 is an example of this. Americans are horrified to think that six million men, women, and children of Jewish ancestry were exterminated more than sixty years ago. Yet the belief that *German lives and way of life have more value than others and because of this we have the right to do whatever we wish to those we view as inferior or different* was in the psychic structure of the German people and laid the groundwork for this incredible atrocity. This belief also was in the psychic structure of those who felt justified in destroying the Nation of the North American Indian, yet many Americans look on this destruction with pride, not horror. It is within this mindset that the right to act violently has its roots. Since we still honor and celebrate how our nation came to be, this belief influences how we view others and how we act.

Acting violently can take a variety of forms. It can harm the spirit as well as the body. The culture in the United States is increasingly becoming more violent, both in the staggering number of violent acts and the horrific manner in which these acts are committed. It is also evident in the lack of tolerance for opposing views. There are subtle forms of violence, as well, illustrated by calls for more prisons and less support for the poor and infirm. There is less willingness to understand why a person acts in a certain way and more of a tendency to blame, a product of the dualistic mind. The tendency to judge and blame without understanding greatly affects our sense of safety and trust, for if we judge and blame others, our fear is that others do the same to us. We guard our backs, developing a defensive posture, which blocks us from loving and accepting others and ultimately ourselves. Since we are so preoccupied defending ourselves, it is difficult to understand and to heal the negative or wounded aspects of our personality.

The belief that we are all equal contrasts with the belief that as a nation we are better than others around the world and as a result can do whatever we want. The belief that our country is superior to others lays the groundwork for all types of dichotomous categories and is, of course, the basis for racism and war. This filters down into our psyche as we struggle with feelings of inferiority and superiority. The more we feel less than others on a personal level, the greater the tendency for us to believe we are superior to people we do not even know. There are subtle dichotomous categories that exist such as "thin is better than fat," "young is better than old" and "wisdom based upon intellect is better than intuitive wisdom." As a result, each of us struggles with the notion that we are better than or less than someone else. A national anxiety exists that focuses on comparisons, preventing each individual from simply being who she is. Again, the dualistic mind severely limits us and brings great suffering to the soul.

The media upholds the myths of our culture, further pushing us to deny our own reality. Through the media we are told who to be, how to act, and we are given the frame and structure of our reality. These guidelines limit the possibilities of what we can know and who we can be. Those who stretch the limits of these guidelines or who have experiences outside of conventional reality worry that, at best, they will be marginalized and, at worst, thought to be crazy. Through the media some of our most violent fantasies are played out, all too often spilling over into real life enactment. The media both shapes and numbs us while also igniting and bringing to consciousness the more base, and, at times, more wonderful aspects of our being.

I cannot begin to count the number of hours spent with psychotherapy clients who struggle to overcome feelings of inadequacy or a sense of being abnormal for not wanting to do what is expected of them. Many want emotionally fulfilling jobs and the desire to live a life shaped by their spiritual and ethical beliefs, but fear being seen as a failure if they are not wealthy or successful by cultural standards. Those believing they cannot be who they truly are do not feel free. Others feel a sense of frustration and alienation and do not know why. In a conversation with my generation X son, Josh, and his friend, Sara, they spoke of the lack of spiritual focus and sense of purpose that grip their generation.

"Your generation had the Viet Nam War and a belief that you could change society for the better," Sara said. "The media targeted us as their market and told us who we are, what is cool, and what we need to do to be successful. The legacy of our generation is that we have been brainwashed to be consumers and to find our identity through consumption. We have no generational soul, no purpose, just an underlying anxiety that we are supposed to be succeeding, but there is no meaning behind what we are doing."

There are other psychic burdens that go into maintaining these societal beliefs or myths, for maintaining the myths requires that certain aspects of reality are denied, resulting in more damage to the soul. If we buy into the myth that we are better than others, it is very difficult to own or look at the negative aspects of our personality and actions, as we are busy struggling to be perfect.

If we are to believe we are the chosen ones, the ones who are culturally and morally superior, our emotional and spiritual connection to everyone and everything is denied. We lose sight of being the same as a starving child in Brazil or a sick and deformed old man in Bangladesh or, for that matter, the same as an ant we might squelch on the floor. Aspects of our humanity are diminished by thinking ourselves better and more entitled than others, all the while being plagued with feelings of inadequacy. We struggle constantly with this duality, the duality of superiority and inferiority. It is a challenge to allow each of us to be who we are, respecting and honoring our differences without flaunting our accomplishments or feeling like a failure for our weaknesses. Many are haunted with a drive to be perfect at all times, unable to admit and work with our foibles.

The denial of the painful or negative aspects of our being leads to the shadow or unknown and unintegrated side of our nature being pushed down. Confronting our demons is painful, as we fear the shame and judgment that comes in acknowledging that we are not perfect. Weeks and sometimes months are spent with each psychotherapy client getting to a place of trusting that I will not judge them for what they perceive to be the shameful and bad aspects of their being. Often these feelings are so painful that they are not brought to consciousness but rather are projected onto another. Lizza felt as a child that she was less intelligent and capable than her siblings even though she is quite talented artistically. The feelings of inadequacy that Lizza experienced as a child are expressed when she puts down others that she feels are less competent than she. Lizza would not need to put anyone down if she were not trying to compensate for feeling deficient in some way.

Others may become the receptacle for parts of ourselves that we cannot accept and acknowledge. Whenever I listen to a client rant about the negative aspects of someone close to them, I suspect these issues are at the core of what the client needs to be dealing with herself. When Jane is angry with her partner for not being more assertive and successful in the world, I hypothesize that, on some level, she is upset with herself for these same reasons. Helping her to own her power in the world and to feel good about herself will decrease the focus on what her partner is or is not doing as she will be doing what she needs to do for herself. If Carl complains that his partner is selfish and inconsiderate, I may understand this to be a statement of Carl's unmet or denied needs. I also may suspect he is struggling with the little kid inside who wants to get his own way and be taken care of. If I can help Carl accept and acknowledge his needs, then he, in turn, can be more accepting of his partner's needs. In our culture it is often considered a sign of weakness to acknowledge that one has needs and is not strong and independent. Thus these needs are pushed down to become an unintegrated shadow that literally follows us around, waiting to pop out in a negative way when it is triggered by another's needs.

As a society we project the shadow aspects of our culture onto others. Each year there is a new group to carry negative feelings. Young Afro-American males carry our rage for the injustices in society and are feared for their expression of our anger and frustration. Pregnant teenagers symbolize our declining morals, seemingly, as if teenagers stopped having babies then all of our social ills will evaporate. Welfare mothers bear the brunt of the shame for the apparent millions given to the very rich in the form of tax breaks and corporate gifts. Those of Arabian descent are being targeted for the fear and vulnerability we feel as a result of the acts of a few misguided souls.

The shadow or negative aspects of our personalities can find common, almost socially acceptable, avenues for expression in society as well. We cheat on our income taxes, partners, and exams. Initially, when President Clinton was accused of shady land deals or infidelity, most were either disinterested or unperturbed as these alleged behaviors are commonplace in our culture. We develop ways of rationalizing our behavior so that it is acceptable, and we do this for our leaders and pop icons as well. We adopt the paradigm that the end justifies the means. We deny the power of our actions. The price for our denial is difficulty in trusting on the most fundamental levels. As a result of our inability to trust, we become untrustworthy. We create ways of protecting ourselves and justify striking first as a part of this protection. We live in fear and act out of fear. This fear was apparent in President Bush's stance against Iraq in 2003 and his call to war. This fear is concretized with violent and horrific images at our local cinema and on our television sets. This imagery lives within each of us; it is with us in the dream state. Fear, with its accompanying violent imagery, affects our level of safety and our willingness to form community. It is played out within the family unit with domestic abuse being a national disease. It is at the root of many of our psychological disorders.

It is difficult to know if violence within the psyche and within the home creates societal violence, or if the violence of war and greed in the greater society so damage the soul that violence is manifest on the personal level. I believe it is circular in nature with images of societal trauma inflaming the personal consciousness and the personal response impacting the societal reaction. The tension between our desire to deny the violent nature of our society while living within it, coupled with the tension of wanting to believe we are better than others, (while all the time fearing we are not), results in a sado-masochistic underpinning to our collective unconscious. All too many of us live either the role of victim or perpetrator in our attempt to submit to or control our fear of violence and inferiority.

Soul Loss as a Result and Cause of Violence
From the shamanic perspective, the violence caused by our sense of disconnection creates havoc producing soul loss. Issues of trust, abandonment, profound feelings of loneliness, and emptiness are at the root of much of our mental and emotional anguish. They are the underlying causes of the addictions and obsessions that haunt Americans, which force millions to turn to drugs, alcohol, food, work, exercise, shopping, and sex to mention but a few of our most common addictions. We spend hundreds of hours in front of our televisions, numbing our souls, keeping ourselves company and cementing a collective reality fueled from the images and messages on the screen.

From a shamanic perspective we suffer from massive soul loss as a result of our lack of connection to one another, to the natural forces of the planet and from the trauma and violence that is a daily part of our lives. As

I spend more time with the natural elements of the earth, gaining wisdom from the trees, rocks, and plants, I experience such a rush of pleasure from feeling the oneness with all that exists. The power of the awareness of our interconnectedness with all that exists sustains me and allows me to be present as I bear witness to the pain in the lives of others. With this awareness the need for any sort of hierarchy, be it man over man or man over nature, diminishes.

Shamanism honors the harmonious interdependence of all beings and creatures that inhabit the earth. Spiritual energy exists in every fabric of the planet. Modern western and some eastern cultures have moved away from an awareness of the spiritual interconnection of all things towards a paradigm in which man reigns supreme. Accompanying this mindset is a struggle to determine which man, which cultural group is dominant over all the others. The perspective of human hegemony is beginning to shift as a result of the environmental movement. There is an increasing awareness that our survival and the survival of the planet are inextricably linked. Through the increasingly frequent occurrence of natural disasters, we are humbled.

Many who practice the ancient healing arts know the incredible power and wisdom that resides in the natural forces. These healers know how to work with these powerful forces for healing and transformation. Over the eons, shamans from a variety of cultures have conducted rituals and ceremonies that have the potential to impact the weather or improve the production of crops. Gradually our awareness of this wisdom is creeping into the dominant culture. *The Boston Globe*[21] cited in its earth week section that "torrential rains fell over the burning rain forests and savanna of northern Brazil just hours after two native shamans conducted an ancient ritual intended to end the region's worst drought on record." The shamans had been flown in by the government and performed the ritual on a dried-up riverbank.

The plants and trees outside our doors are waiting to help us in our healing. The foundation of the Bomoh's healing practice lies in his partnership with the spirits of the plants he uses. When I first became aware of the spiritual energies in plants, I went into the woods to find a plant that would be my spirit plant. I ran my hands over a number of plants until I found one plant, the Indian Paint Brush, which caused my hands to vibrate with incredible energy. I began journeying to the plant just as one would to any spirit guide to ask for guidance. I was thrilled when I returned home to find the Indian Paint Brush lived in a tiny area of my yard. I began working with the plant on a daily basis. The next spring I was delighted to find that the

Indian Paint Brush had sprung up all over my yard greatly increasing the amount of energy it had to give me.

I had a similar experience in finding my spirit tree, the oak. I went into the woods and asked for my spirit tree to make itself known to me. As I walked by an oak tree, my jaw began to vibrate and throb. I walked over to the tree and leaned against it and asked it if it were my spirit tree. As I did this, I experienced my energy go down to the roots, intermingling with the oak tree's vibrant energy. I have several oak trees with which I work. Whenever I feel tired or depleted, I go lean against one of these trees, sending my energy down into the root and then drawing up into me the powerful energy of this ancient wise being.

Through a journey to the oak, I have come to understand that trees are our vibrational connection to ancient knowledge stored in the core of the earth. Large ancient trees with roots growing deep into the center of the earth connect us vibrationally to millions of years of information. Each time we destroy these ancient wonders we are breaking our connection with this knowledge. When I go to Borneo and witness the on-going destruction of the ancient rain forest, my whole being aches at the tremendous loss that is occurring. Simultaneously I am encouraged by the global awareness of our need to protect the great resources that have been so carelessly exploited.

Daily I am heartened by the amount of healing energy that is available to us. Even though we live in a time of violence and disconnection, there is the potential for positive transformation for both our planet and ourselves. An initial step in this process is to identify those aspects of our society that harm the soul and to understand the role societal violence plays in our most common psychological disorders. There are generations of harmful interactions born from broken souls and negative and destructive thought forms that need altering if we are truly to be free and whole. Great change and healing can occur when we broaden our conception of what is possible, cultivate an Expansive Mind, and stretch ourselves to understand the many levels on which all is interconnected. We are all one—we are not free or safe until everyone on the planet is free and safe.

Chapter 10
SOUL LOSS AND DISCONNECTION:
THE FOUNDATION FOR PSYCHOLOGICAL DISORDERS

They glide down the runway with a sense of power and poise that most women can only dream of possessing. Clothes frame their lithe, long bodies. They are deemed the most beautiful women in the world and are paid hundreds of thousands of dollars a year to stay thin. Their images are air brushed to remove all flaws. They create an illusion of perfection that even the models themselves cannot re-create in reality. Many men hold these women to be the ideal to which all other women are compared. Girls and women, hoping to be like these sleek models, often engage in a very dangerous and sometimes deadly battle with food in order to emulate them.

Addictions and Obsessions

Eating disorders can be linked easily to the power of the culture and media to shape the psyche in self-destructive ways. Invariably when I turn on one of the morning news programs, there is a segment on exercise and how to get the "abs" hard. The exercise teacher has a perfect body. She teaches the television audience firming and toning exercises through instructing the female anchor, who also has a perfect body. Many of us feel defeated and inferior while we observe a form of perfection that we can only dream of achieving.

Eating disorders, clinically known as anorexia nervosa and bulimia, afflict millions.[22] The fascination and obsession with thinness haunts many throughout the life span. Those who are unable to starve themselves frequently engage in binge eating; forcing themselves to vomit, use laxatives and/or exercise obsessively so as to lose weight. Many die each year as a result of complications due to these life-threatening disorders.

There are a number of theories as to the origins of eating disorders. One is our society's pre-occupation with being thin. Implied in this pre-occupation is that one is most valued for her outer appearance. Many women and girls feel inferior if they are not thin and beautiful, and more and more males share this belief regarding their own self worth.

Another popular theory is that teenagers, who are pressured to be good, smart, popular, thin, and beautiful crumbled under these expectations. Feeling that who they are is overshadowed by who they are supposed to be, they mirror this feeling by becoming outwardly invisible just as they feel inwardly unseen. Others who feel bereft and invalidated stuff themselves to quiet their pain. Some allow their bodies to become enlarged, protecting them from the outside world. Others attempt to purge themselves by throwing-up their pain. For all food becomes an obsession, a pre-occupation blocking out the noise of the world, the pain in the heart, and the emptiness in the soul.

More recently, eating disorders also have been linked to sexual abuse. The body is seen as an instrument of betrayal. There is a desire to alter the body, to punish it, to make it so undesirable that no one would want to touch it again. Some become dangerously thin, denying their emerging sexuality hoping to appear as a child. Others become unhealthily obese, symbolically wearing a sign that says **Keep Away**.

In shamanic terms, eating disorders are the result of the loss of part of the soul. The pain and emptiness is so great that the obsession with food, the life force of the body, is used as a weapon in which to deal with this void. Some try to fill the abyss; others try to merge with it. For all too many it is a long silent suicide as a result of violence to the soul. Lily came to see me in her early twenties out of desperation, aware that her life would soon be over if she did not get a handle on her eating disorder. She had struggled with anorexia, sometimes to the brink of death, since early adolescence. Lily was an only child from a highly intellectual family in which the mind was valued above the creative and emotional realms. There was scant emotional holding; the only attention she received stemmed from her school performance. Lily was raped by a neighborhood boy four years her elder when she was ten. After the rape, she lost her ability to concentrate and her grades suffered. Lily never told her parents of the rape, feeling much too much shame to even utter what had happened. Her shame was experienced on a daily basis as her parents chided and ridiculed her for her poor school performance. At the onset of her menses, Lily stopped eating, furious at her body for bringing her to womanhood and the shame the blood represented to her. The rape had been brutal and Lily had bled considerably. When Lily decided not to eat, she experienced some degree of control over her life, a sense of control that was absent from all other aspects of her life including her own emotional states. An added perk to barely eating was that the monthly flow of blood ceased. Throughout her adolescence, she was in one hospital after another as she continued to hover at life threatening weights. She never told any of her therapists about the rape; the shame was too great. Her parents, successful professionals, attended to her just enough to deflect awareness that their icy and harsh connection to Lily was part of the problem.

When Lily came to see me for psychotherapy, I was the first therapist that she had chosen for herself; her mother had picked all of the others. After several months of therapy, Lily felt safe enough to tell me of the rape and to begin to paint a picture of the emotional void in which she had grown up. I began to talk to her about soul loss and energy intrusions. Soon she felt ready to receive an extraction and soul retrieval. When I first began to do the extraction work, a panther appeared as a power animal and a beautiful older woman in a flowing white robe appeared. When I asked her who she was, she said that her name was Isabella and that she was Lily's great-grandmother. As I began to run my hands over Lily's energy body, it was strikingly devoid of energy, a sense of total depletion was present. There was a leak in her third chakra flowing to her mother; it seems that from a very early age her mother had been pulling on her will center, taking Lily's energy to use as hers. Her mother's energy sat squarely over her heart and throat chakras, repressing any expression of what was in the heart. The energy of Lily's rapist and her father's energy were around her second chakra, blocking the development of her emotions, creativity and sexuality. With the help and direction of my guides, I removed these energies and did a healing for the energies that belonged to her parents and the rapist. Then my guides sent back the healed energies to each of them. I then channeled in light energy from the spirit world to hold the space so that she would be protected as I did the soul retrieval.

The spirit guide, Isabella, led the panther, my guides and myself to a dark room where a baby was lying in the crib. On closer look we could see that little Lily was about 8 months old, lying still and lifeless with her eyes wide open staring blankly into space. It was clear that a major part of Lily had left at this young age due to a lack of love and nurturing. There was a look in her eyes of a failure-to-thrive baby. Throughout her twenty-three years of life she had struggled with whether to live or die. An African woman appeared dressed in a colorful flowing gown holding a ball of pure light energy. Umanda, a spirit guide and spirit healer, had been caring for Lily's detached soul part, teaching her and loving her. Isabella held little Lily as Umanda blew the ball of light energy into Lily. Little Lily's eyes brighten as she looked around and smiled broadly as she nestled into the arms of her great-grandmother.

Next Lily's panther took us to the scene in which the older boy in the neighborhood raped Lily. They were inside a tree house. Another boy in the neighborhood had removed the ladder so that Lily had no escape, a feeling that has haunted her her entire life. I could sense the fear and confusion emanating from Lily and then I watched as she floated out of her body onto a tree limb outside of the tree house. From there she peered into the window as she watched the boy rape and sodomize her with a gleeful and sadistic look in his eye. Ten-year old Lily had stayed on the tree branch for all of these years, too terrified to move for fear of more harm. Panther climbed the tree and brought Lily down to the ground where Isabella, little Lily, Umanda, and I and several of my guides greeted her. We all did a healing for her by pulling off the energy of the rapist and then placing her in a cleansing spring after which we enveloped her in healing blue light.

The last part of the soul retrieval involved traveling to find the mother who had taken Lily's energy from her solar plexus. We found the mother sitting at her desk in a large law firm in which she was a partner. My guides carried the mother's healed energy from the extraction work, knowing that we would travel to meet the mother to retrieve the energy that she had pulled out of Lily. One of my guides, Hekate, and Lily's guide, Isabella, entered the office carrying the energy ball that is the mother's healed energy. Isabella spoke to the higher self of her granddaughter, acknowledging the painful and difficult life that she has had. The mother had blocked from consciousness a rape that she had experienced by an older brother at a similar age to Lily. She dealt with this experience by closing her heart to others and by putting all of her energy into intellectual and professional pursuits.

Lily's mother had married a man similarly driven and cut off from his emotions. They had not intended to have children, but when confronted with a pregnancy they half-heartedly decided to have Lily. When Lily was born there was a tug on the mother's heart to experience her love for Lily, but this opening began to bring in the pain of the past and she shut it down. The closing of her heart took more will than she had. Consequently she unwittingly drew some of Lily's energy from her third chakra leaving Lily depleted and unable to adequately fight for her own survival. The mother was presented with her healed energy, which had been used to block any expression of Lily's heart. The mother unconsciously needed to do this to insure that Lily would not awaken in her the pain of her own abuse. This block was so formidable that Lily knew that she could never speak of her own rape to her mother or to anyone one else for that matter. The mother was mesmerized by the pure ball of light energy that was her own energy and happily traded it for the release of the part of Lily that she held deep within her. The mother was not told of her own rape as that was to come to her in time, but she was told that Lily needed her energy back if she were to fight to stay alive and that she needed her mother's love and support to do this. On the soul level the mother accepted this.

After the three soul parts, the panther, and two spirit guides were blown into Lily, she was told of all that had transpired. Learning that her mother had had a similar experience to her helped to explain why her mother had been unable to connect with her. This understanding allowed an opening for a powerful release of feelings. Where there had been anger and bitterness toward her mother, there now was compassion and a willingness to forge a connection with her. In the weeks that followed, Lily and her mother made more of an effort to spend time together. Lily spoke of feeling that her great-grandmother, Isabella, was guiding them in their connection. As the connection with the mother grew, so did Lily's ability to feed herself. She had her will back along with a strong infant self and a healed ten-year old. Lily was well on her way to reclaiming control of her life.

Eating disorders are but one of many addictions to which people turn to numb their pain and fill the emptiness that is at their core. The addiction one chooses comes, in part, from a person's genetic make-up, from environmental influences and culturally sanctioned rituals. Those that come from alcoholic families tend to choose drugs and alcohol to numb their pain as the energy of this addiction is in the air. In Lily's case, the desire to erase the painful trigger of the sight of blood, coupled with a life long struggle around living, made starving herself the logical addiction to choose.

The addiction one chooses is often dictated by what the culture deems permissible. In the fifties and sixties smoke-filled cocktail parties were the culturally acceptable ways of entertaining and unwinding after a long stress-filled workday. If one were still tense, sleeping pills and anti-anxiety medications were prescribed. It was easy to slip unnoticed into one or more of these culturally sanctioned addictions. As we now know, cigarettes, alcohol, sleeping pills and Valium are extremely addictive, both physiologically and psychologically. The seventies and eighties brought cocaine and marijuana into mainstream culture. For decades heroin and, more recently, crack co-caine have been the chosen numbing tool for the oppressed and disenfran-chised and are now fashionable among all levels of society. Many that strive to be upwardly mobile and physically fit find themselves addicted to work and exercise. Others become obsessed with love and sex in hope that if they merge with another, somehow they will be whole, the void erased.

Unfortunately these addictions have just made things worse. Instead of alleviating the pain and filling the emptiness, people fall into greater despair engulfed in an energetic cloud of grayness that has imprisoned them. Addictions are one of the main causes of violence. People steal, cheat, maim, and murder to support their habits. They abuse and murder those they purport to love when they feel they cannot control and possess their love object. Much is written about the destructive power of addictions, yet we are cajoled to "just say no" to temptation, to walk away as if it were an easy thing to do. Yet those who have experienced the pain and emptiness that comes from being separated from core aspects of self understand the need to fill the void and ease the suffering.

From the shamanic perspective everything on the planet is imbued with energy and spirit. We are all part of the same whole. In most western countries man is perceived to be the superior being on the planet. Plants, animals, water, natural resources and land are thought to be for the service of man—not living beings with whom we are intimately connected. In-stead of a worldview that man dominates the planet, shamanism sees a co-operative, mutually dependent relationship. Before one builds a house in cultures that practice shamanism, the land is asked if it is all right for the house to be built and if there are things that need to be done so that the relationship can be mutually supportive. When a tree is cut or an animal killed, thanks are given to the tree or animal for sacrificing its life. This reverence naturally carries over to how people treat each other. There is a sense of the power and beauty in our interconnection that breeds respect for everything and everyone that is encountered. In the awareness of our interconnection there is a peace and wholeness. Without it, there is an emp-tiness—a void.

In the United States we have lost our sense of oneness with the planet and with the spiritual energy that abides everywhere. This spiritual energy in no way diminishes or contradicts the teaching of the major religions, rather it enhances and enlivens them by placing God or the Tao in every-thing. This loss of awareness of the spiritual interconnection of all things has led to an existential despair that results in alienation and disconnection.

There is rage resulting from this disconnection. Some express this rage out-wardly towards others. They yell obscenities as they drive, stab their co-workers in the back, or abuse their spouses and children. Others turn to addictions to push down feelings of anger and frustration that want to spill out.

A Shamanic Approach to Healing Addictions

Shamanism offers a way of understanding and treating addictions that may seem foreign to some. Many that practice shamanism believe that there is an addiction spirit that enters the energy field of a person. This spirit can come from a family member through energy cords or simply by being ab-sorbed into the field. It can also come from the energy field of one who is recovering from an addiction or from one who has died. The addiction spirit exists as an energetic form of its own, a shadowy entity that hangs like a cloud in the energy body eventually creating its own vibrational layer in the dreambody. The notion that there are spirits roaming around entering people's energy fields is a bizarre concept to the western mind. We do not think of our fundamental being as energy that can split off. When energy splits off, it can go to a variety of places including into the energy field of another. Conversely when we have energy voids, split-off energy from oth-ers can enter our field. This happens most frequently within families and with others with whom we are intimately connected.

This is quite consistent with the notion that there is an addiction gene, a physiological link between one generation and the next. When energy comes from one to another, there is a change in the physiology of the per-son receiving the energy. On one level we understand this. In AA members are strongly encouraged to cut their ties with those who are actively drink-ing. Initially the newcomers are not integrated into general meetings, as there is fear and anxiety in being around those who have recently stopped drinking. This fear exists on a somatic level that includes the physiological and energetic even though this fear is not consciously articulated. Members who have many years of sobriety under their belts are called on to lead newcomer meetings.

In shamanism there are ways of removing these addiction spirits. My teacher works with the power of intention. The Bomoh gave me prayers written in an ancient script that have been used for many hundreds of years. I do not know what these writings say, but they are powerful and effective in removing the addiction spirit from the energy field. I was told by the Bomoh to write these prayers on leaves that I put into water that has been blessed by my spirit guides. Then the leaves are placed on a person's forehead and solar plexus.

The most important part of this entire ceremony is the intention that I hold and the intention that the person wishing to rid herself of addictions holds. I am to journey to be with the addiction spirit and, with the help of my guides, assist the addiction spirit in leaving, receiving a healing and finding its proper home. The person wishing to rid oneself of the addiction must concentrate on letting this energy go. After the addiction spirit leaves the energy field, it is necessary to bring in healing energy or lost soul parts to fill the energetic void left by the removal of the addiction spirit. This ceremony will not work unless the person is willing to release this energy or she will just call the energy back to her, pushing the new energy out.

Meredith came to me to stop smoking cigarettes. She had tried to quit several times before. She used the patch and hypnosis but had never been able to stop. First I did a soul retrieval for her to bring in more of her own energy and to help her to connect to her spirit guides. Meredith worked with these energies for a couple of months before she felt that she was ready to let the cigarettes go. We explored what the cigarettes meant to her. Meredith acknowledged that cigarettes were her best friend—a source of comfort and relaxation. After the soul retrieval she began to feel that the cigarettes were controlling her. They took on a negative connotation in her life.

During the ceremony to remove the addiction spirit, I applied the prayers to her forehead and abdomen and then did energy work over Meredith's body searching for the addiction spirit. Not surprisingly it was located around her heart and throat chakra. This being entered her field from her father who also smoked. The being that Meredith later named Tradlindada was firmly entrenched. I thanked Tradlindada for helping Meredith through some very difficult times in her life and asked her if I could help her return to her place of origin. Initially Tradlindada was resistant, but as my guides surrounded her, bringing her glimpses of the light on the other side, she loosened her hold on the lungs. I then was able to lift Tradlindada off as my guides took her to the other side. Then I saw a beautiful goddess floating nearby who said that she had come to be a healing and guiding presence in Meredith's life and to protect her field from the entry of any other addiction spirits. Together we filled Meredith's lungs with healing blue light.

After this ceremony, Meredith gave up cigarettes with ease. She reported having no urge to smoke and did not experience the painful period of physically withdrawing from cigarettes as she had in the past. Five years later she was still cigarette free.

Psychologically it is very difficult to give up an addiction; thus much psychological work must be done in preparation for this ceremony. But as we know, there is also a physical side to the addiction. This ceremony can aid in the removal of the energy that is housed within the energy system on a physiological level. It is necessary to abstain from the addictive behavior after the shamanic work as one does not want to invite the spirit to return. This is consistent with the philosophy of AA.

There are many routes to relief from addiction that come from a variety of traditions throughout the world. Different plants and herbs that purify and tone the body are helpful in healing from addictions. Acupuncture also has proven quite effective in removing the addictive energy or spirit from the energy system and in keeping the body calm as it goes through withdrawal. The common thread throughout these various traditions comes from altering the energy body and the energy field.

The importance of community in healing addictions cannot be stressed enough. The various self-help movements, spawned from the model developed by Alcoholics Anonymous, has been extremely helpful in providing both community and a link to a spiritual system. Shamanic practices are not intended to replace existing models but to aid and enhance them. Both shamanism and most self-help models stress the importance of the spiritual in healing, a concept that is slowly coming into acceptance in mainstream treatments.

Anxiety, Phobias and Depression

There are those who find that they cannot relax into their bodies. They run from one thing to the next, terrified of being alone or being with themselves. They live with a pressure in their chest that at times leaves them gasping for breath. Some fear they are having a heart attack; others worry that they are going mad. They may feel dizzy or faint. At times they feel as if they are not embodied and eerily watch themselves from a corner of the room, shaking in terror. Others become so frightened that they will not leave home. Some become obsessed with order and cleanliness and develop rituals that bind them together. Many have difficulty sleeping. Most turn to addictive behaviors to quell the anxiety. Those who do not turn to addictions struggle to get through each day living in a state of constant agitation.

Panic disorder, obsessive-compulsive disorder, and agoraphobia are some of the diagnostic categories that are given for various manifestations of anxiety. For years I have believed that anxiety was caused by a struggle between feelings and memories that want to emerge into consciousness being pushed down by protective defense mechanisms that believe that the system will not survive the remembering or re-experiencing of that which wants to come into consciousness. Medications and desensitizing one to stimulus that provokes anxiety or compulsive behaviors are the usual methods of treating anxiety. While these treatments are quite effective in controlling anxiety, they rarely get to the underlying cause of the anxiety, which results in symptoms manifesting in other ways. In the case of medications there are side effects that can result in a sense of detachment or numbing. Some of the medications are habit forming and addictive.

There are many causes for anxiety states. Shamanically I find that a young child can absorb the anxiety state of a parent. Sometimes this anxiety state is passed on for generations if no intervention is made. All of us can most likely remember experiences when we are in the presence of one so anxious that we begin to feel uncomfortable and anxious ourselves. Martha's mother was so anxious that when Martha was a small child, she absorbed this energy into her field, leaving Martha in a state of constant anxiety. When I did energy work for Martha, I found her enveloped in a cloud of static energy belonging to her mother. When I removed the energy, healed it and sent it back to her mother, Martha felt a calm that she had never experienced. In this incidence the healing was a straightforward one.

Ralph had also absorbed his father's anxious energy, but in this case it was paired with negative statements. Ralph's father was so concerned about his ability to do things correctly that he projected this onto Ralph, telling him that he was always doing everything wrong, that he would never amount to anything. Ralph took in the negative beliefs about himself as strongly as he had his father's anxiety. He began to adopt compulsive behaviors to try to control and contain the anxiety. If he made sure that everything in his room was properly organized and neat, then perhaps this would please and calm his father. By the time that Ralph was an adult, his need to have everything organized and neat was so strongly developed that Ralph had difficulty leaving the house for fear that something was left undone.

In working with Ralph the mere removal of the anxious energy was not enough to significantly alter his emotional state. Ralph would find some immediate relief from the energy work but in a day or two the symptoms were back. We began to work on the negative beliefs by identifying where the voice originated and if it was a voice that he needed to keep. Initially there was great fear that if he let go of the voices nothing would be there and that he would disintegrate. We did a soul retrieval and brought back three lost soul parts and several helping guides, which helped him to feel more whole and enabled him to begin to relinquish the negative beliefs. As we explored each negative belief that he had about himself, I would pull it from his field and bring in light and energy from my guides and his. Thus we adopted a pattern of doing energy work and talk therapy simultaneously, pulling out energy spurs of negativity as Ralph was ready to release them.

Sometimes anxiety states are the result of severe trauma that has not been fully processed and integrated. Helen's childhood was devoid of emotional nurturance and care. Helen's description of her mother led me to believe that she was psychotic or schizophrenic. When Helen was a small child, her mother would tie her to her bed at night and lock the door, leaving her there for ten to twelve hours. Helen would frequently soil herself after such a long wait. Her mother would then engage in an obsessive cleansing ritual, which was sexually intrusive and sadistic. This is just one example of the bizarre and inappropriate behaviors that Helen's mother inflicted on her.

Helen's energy is frequently so anxious that when I travel into her energy field, I see and experience differing bands of energy swirling around untethered. Each has its own color and frequency wave. It is as if the energy swirls are trying to locate a home—a frequency band in which to safely resonate. There is no container or organizing context to ground Helen in this anxious state, just as there was no container in her childhood. There is no energetic form to hold her as the abuse began before the ego was fully formed, leaving her without a major frequency band around which to organize. No wonder Helen often feels as if she will die or dissolve into a million pieces.

With the help of my guides, we created an energetic container by placing her inside a large energy ball that was filled with blue light. Then I called in a column of light to run through the center of her being and began connecting the untethered energy frequencies to this light column. I also gave her one of the Bomoh's prayers to drink that is designed to help one reconstitute after intense fragmentation. I put the prayer into a sacred bowl of water and then blew into the water, imbuing it with spirit energy and then gave it to her to drink. Within a few moments Helen returned to a state of equilibrium. This calm only lasted a day or two as the primary traumas connected to the anxiety and fragmentation have not been fully processed emotionally and released. It is essential that at least thematic aspects of the trauma be brought to conscious and worked with psychologically for complete relief to occur. As the memories of the abuse are brought to consciousness memory and integrated into the core of the psyche, a major frequency band begins to form. Unfortunately there is no short cut in working with and digesting our most painful experiences and feelings.

As in Helen's case there are situations in which it appears as if there never was a container to bind the energy of the person. The outer edges of the energy field are quite thin and porous with the person's energy swirling around in a free-floating manner. The loving, containing environment, which parents and caregivers are supposed to provide for their offspring, appears to have been missing since the first year of life. The need for an energetic container is felt to be so great that the person may experience herself as incredibly needy. She may feel as if she can never be soothed or comforted. As a result a depressed, isolated existence may feel more manageable as the depressive energy can offer a gray, cloudy container. Often the depressive state feels better than the uncontained anxiety. For others the dark abyss of depression can be terrifying. There is a fear that one will never emerge from this dark hole.

Vibrational Threads and the Dreambody

Depression and anxiety are opposite poles of the same continuum. Both of these states occur when there is soul or essence loss. Again I return to the dreambody to better understand how this works. There are parts of our essence energy that have strayed from the core part of our being; they remain connected by a vibrational thread. Sometimes these parts were lost in other lifetimes, and thus we were born without them. More often they were lost during our childhood in this lifetime. Frequently these lost parts utilize the vibrational threads to find ways to bring to consciousness the pain of the lost energy essence through experiences that re-create, vibrationally and affectively, the trauma of the lost soul parts, be they from this lifetime or past lives.

Sometimes a person has to keep repeating similar experiences until the conscious mind is ready to confront what has been lost. This is similar to Freud's repetition compulsion. The vibrational thread flows through varied experiences over time. These threads float through the holographic membrane of the dreambody into our dreams and our various senses of smell, light, sound, and touch into our conscious mind. Sometimes there is so much pain attached to these essence energy fragments that one is pulled into deep despair and depression, unclear as to the source of this pain. Affectively and vibrationally one re-experiences the soul wrenching pain from long ago. Energetically it is difficult to move, to eat, or to be social.

Before I fully understood that there are vibrational threads connecting us to affectively similar occurrences, I would ponder why it was that two people could experience a similar event in which one would bounce back from it while another would become so distressed that she would become essentially non-functional. The ties or lack of ties to previous traumas clearly impact the response to a given event. This was found to be true during the Viet Nam War as soldiers who experienced intense bouts of Post-traumatic Stress Disorder were more likely to have had traumatic experiences in child-hood than those who did not have a trauma history.

These vibrational threads can pull us to past terrifying experiences that make us incredibly anxious. Sometimes we are haunted by so called irrational fears. Hard as we may try we can find no reason to explain why we are terrified of heights or why certain noises cause hair to stand up on our skin while everyone else remains calm. These fears are the result of prior experiences to which we are connected that are split off and unintegrated. Things that trigger affective or vibrational memories can result in panic, fear, and anxiety.

Our culture affords us with many opportunities to re-connect with these vibrational threads. The media is ripe with violent images and tales of betrayal. At the cinema and on our television sets we are haunted, terrified and titillated. Many times these images awaken memories stored within our cellular being. All too frequently we find ourselves re-enacting these hidden experiences as a way to bring them to conscious reality with the unthought wish that, through the re-enactment of the trauma, we can rid our energetic being of these painful feelings. Some re-enact the trauma on themselves in self-abusing behaviors; others re-enact the horror they experienced on others, unfortunately passing this unseemly energy on to someone else.

There are many forces within our culture that are subtle and less dramatic that result in soul loss and disconnection from the self. Alice Miller[23] stated that the major cause of depression is caused by the loss of one's true self. This loss needs to be viewed literally as well as figuratively given our understanding of the energetic nature of our being. It is because of soul loss that we are vulnerable to intrusive energies and mind-numbing addictions. The pressure in our society to be successful and acceptable to the dominant culture results in many of us working much too hard, striving to outdo our nearest competitor and earn the admiration of our superiors.

All too many of us find that we live a public life filled with expectations and obligations with very little attention paid to our inner lives and to those things that feed and nurture our hearts and souls. Many have reported over the years that there are competing voices within the mind; a true center within seems lacking. There are those within the American culture who spend a great deal of time in fantasy, creating scenarios that engender good feelings, or pretending to be the characters seen on television. Others are so driven by the *shoulds* that the inner voice that comes from the heart scarcely can be heard. Not only are we disconnected from each other and the natural forces around us, but we are also disconnected from ourselves, from our true essence.

A Shamanic Healing for Anxiety and Depression
Shamanic work can help to alleviate the anxiety and depression that people feel by removing unwanted energy and bringing back parts of the soul essence that has been split off. Frequently people wear the anxious energy of others or have it housed in a chakra or other parts of the body. When I first worked with Jean, she presented herself as quite anxious with a depressive core. I assessed if there was any unwanted energy around or in the body and to see if there were energy blocks that prohibited the free flow of energy. I did this by running my hands above the body to feel energy blocks or leaks. My spirit guides directed me to the part of the body and energy field that I was to work and explained the significance of what was there. I experienced their wisdom arising in my mind and felt their energy work through my body as together we pulled out the energy that did not belong.

There was a cloak of another's energy around Jean's shoulders, neck and heart. My spirit guides told me that this energy belonged to her mother, and I was to remove it. One of my spirit guides took the mother's energy, did a healing for it, with the knowledge that we would be working with the mother's energy during the soul retrieval. Underneath this cloak I discovered considerable blockage between the heart and throat chakras that effectively prevented Jean from having access to what she felt or the expression of these feelings. There was also an absence of vital energy in the lower chakras, which signified that Jean was not fully grounded in the body. There were blockages in these areas as well, including a leak in her first chakra. Her mother seemed to have drawn off energy via the energy chord of the first or root chakra. Jean was living with significant blockage around the heart and lungs, a mantel of depressive, anxious energy around her shoulders and little sense of being grounded or housed within the body. It was no wonder that she felt quite anxious and depressed.

During the soul retrieval a woman who was Jean's spirit guide led me. She had flowing red hair and a magnificent green cape and carried herself with calm and grace. We went to a small room that was dark. In the room I saw an infant Jean gaze out through the bars of her crib. Her mother was sitting next to her shaking and sobbing. Her father had been killed in the Viet Nam War three weeks before Jean was born. Throughout the pregnancy her mother had been extremely fearful and anxious, sensing intuitively that she would never see her husband again. Jean's mother was so distraught that she was unable to adequately care for Jean, let alone bond with her. As Jean's mother sat there, I saw energetically the flow of energy from Jean to her mother; it emanated from her root chakra and tried to forge a connection in order to give her mother enough energy to connect with her. In despair I saw tiny Jean turn away; she looked forlorn and bereft. Then I witnessed part of her essence energy leave the body to go live with her spirit guide. With this departure I saw Jean's remaining energy lose form and swirl around uncontained. Next to the crib I saw a buffalo.

First we did a healing for Jean's mother with the energy that was removed during the energy healing. We closed off the energy cord from which energy flowed from Jean to her mother. At that moment the essence energy of Jean's father appeared. He blessed them both and offered his love and support. Jean's energy was strong and vibrant as she had been living and learning with her spirit guide. The essence energy of the mother, father, and daughter embraced before the mother's energy was sent to be with her in ordinary reality. Then I brought back the core part of Jean's essence that had left in the first weeks of life, her spirit guide, and the buffalo as a power animal to help her in grounding to the physical plane. Jean's spirit guide told me that Jean's life task is that of a teacher. This would become apparent to her as she became more in touch with her core essence. Previously Jean's anxiety had been so debilitating that she could scarcely hold down a menial job; thus, the thought that she could have the calm and presence to teach others was thrilling to her.

After the healing, Jean's eyes were clear and focused. She could feel her breath move calmly through her body, a sensation that she had never experienced. The anxiety had lifted and for the first time in her life she felt hope for the future.

Jean had been depressed and anxious since her infancy when part of her core essence left and her mother's grieving energy entered her body. Because Jean's mother had been unable to bond with her as a result of her grief, Jean had no energetic container to bind the anxiety and sadness that had flowed from Jean's mother to her. Jean's mother in no way wanted to harm Jean; it was an unfortunate by-product of war, a by-product that brought years of suffering for both of them.

Soon after the soul retrieval, Jean enrolled in graduate school to become an art teacher. For years she had struggled to release the considerable creative energy that had been blocked from expression. Now her paintings flowed through her, as did her emerging sense of self.

Chapter 11
PSYCHOSIS, RITUAL ABUSE, AND
EXTREME TRAUMA TO THE SOUL

Images of decapitation and dismemberment are at the centerpiece of horror movies and haunt the psyches of those who have faced mortal combat in war. We try to deny that these atrocities happen and push them out of our minds, yet these images creep into our dreams and as flashes before our eyes at times when we least expect them. Sensational crimes both horrify and mesmerize us and remind us that unimaginable abuse does in fact occur. We pray those acts are an anomaly and desperately want to believe that stories of ritual abuse are the product of overactive imaginations.

As a psychologist I have sat with a number of clients who have relayed horrific occurrences that literally took my breath away and left me nauseous. The psychological community is at odds as to how to understand and work with those who bring us these stories. There are some that view these clients as delusional or psychotic. Others believe that clients are encouraged to tell such tales by therapists who take great interest in these stories, thereby re-enforcing the client's desire for attention. Still others argue that unskilled therapists, at a loss for how to interpret and work with their client's pain, suggest that horrible things must have happened to them and encourage the development of dramatic and bizarre stories.

There are those of us who do not wish to hear the re-telling of torturous occurrences, yet find our clients' accounts to be, if not credible, at least symbolic of incredible psychic pain. Many therapists simply sit while their clients tell their stories and help them sort through the meaning that the story has for them, not being invested in the veracity of the story. Others fervently believe the experiences that their clients describe are true and push their clients to seek legal prosecution as a way of healing their wounds. As I better understand the workings of the dreambody and vibrational threads, I believe that the exact truth in ordinary reality is somewhat illusive while the feelings and symbols carry powerful meaning for the client that needs to be understood, processed, and released.

In spite of the confusion regarding the accuracy of stories of torture and mayhem, there are many thousands of people who live each day with images of unspeakable acts captivating their minds. People, who re-experience the pain of these images in their bodies, struggle with them in their nightmares and live each day in fear of the images becoming real in their daily lives. All one needs to do is watch the news or go to a movie to have these fears substantiated. There is a circular loop in which the images from the culture feed the psyche and the psyche drives the images that appear in the culture.

The Face of Trauma

Torture and abuse of one individual by another is unfortunately all too common. Some children are fondled by adults or spanked in ways that are clearly abusive. (Some would argue that all forms of physical punishment are abusive.) Some children have been molested or raped by a neighbor or stranger passing through. Other children are raped often by the same family member. Sometimes several family members abuse the same child, or the abuse takes place with the knowledge of adults in the family. All too frequently physical torture accompanies the sexual abuse. Some are tied and gagged; others have painful objects inserted into various orifices of the body. One woman reported enduring a reoccurring ritual in which she would be tied up by a caregiver, who then inserted large sharp objects in every orifice of the body. Some have reported being burned, stuffed in closets, and locked in basements. Others report witnessing horrific torture of others in group settings. They tell of being asked to participate in the torture of others. First they are told that if they do not torture others, it will be done to them. When this fails to get them to be torturers, they are told that if they do not torture one person, several people will be tortured. Some have reported being buried alive. There are other stories too gruesome to relay.

Some clients with extreme abuse histories become obsessed, on some level, with the images of the violence they have experienced. Often, initially there is not a conscious awareness of the abuse, but a desire to recreate the abuse—to re-experience it by re-enacting it in a variety of ways. Some find avenues for release in the form of writing or drawing about it, unclear from where the images flow. Many compulsively watch violence and horror at the movies and on TV. Sometimes the client ties herself up, locks herself in the basement or inserts objects in the body in the manner that was done to her as a child. Others draw people to them who will re-enact the abuse upon them. It is believed that the vast majority, if not all, of prostitutes were sexually abused as children or young adolescents. Some perpetrate on others that which was done to them in hopes of obtaining some power and control over what has happened while also trying to rid the body and psyche of the energy and images that continually haunt them.

A client told me that she has a vivid memory of the day in which she knew that she needed to decide if she was going to be a serial killer or be good. She decided to be good; to live her life totally thinking of others, all the while aware that the murderous rage lay just beneath the surface. Others do not make this decision; they become numb and icy cold as they slip into the role of perpetrator.

Some deal with their abuse by becoming addicts and mental patients, so shattered that they cannot cope. It is easier to believe that they have a disease or addiction than to entertain the possibilities of what they have endured. They are haunted with images, smells and voices of the abuse. They wander around seeming delusional and paranoid, labeled as psychotic so no one bothers to take their ramblings seriously. They rock to soothe themselves and shuffle along stoned on prescribed medications, alcohol, or street drugs. Many of us cross to the other side of the street when we see them approach. Still others live in a shell unable to talk or connect with the outside world, fearful that if they venture out they will shatter into a million pieces.

Through working in the dreambody I have come to gain a greater understanding of what occurs in the soul and psyche of those who have been shattered by traumatic events. I worked with Judy who, as a child, was raped and battered by her father as her mother ignored what was happening. Judy functioned very well in her day to day life but frequently dissociated in sessions, sometimes being far away, unable to talk for ten or fifteen minutes. One day after Judy had been silent, in a dissociated state for quite a while and would not respond to my questions, I asked if I could journey into her dreambody. I would never enter a client's dreambody without her permission. She nodded. I went inside and found a young child hiding in a closet. The little girl was a young Judy. The adult Judy had vacated her body and was not even conscious of being in the closet. I talked to young Judy for a bit in dreamtime then told her that I wanted to speak directly with the part of her that was hiding in the closet. I told her that I was going to leave dreamtime and wanted to speak with her in ordinary reality. As I started to speak out loud with her, a young child's voice responded, continuing the conversation we were having in non-ordinary reality, detailing her fears and feelings after having experienced being raped and beaten. This allowed Judy to come back into the room to hear the story of this split-off part and to begin the process of re-integrating the frightened child into her. This part was the first of 13 different personalities to emerge.

If a person has experienced multiple traumas and/or has been neglected and dismissed as a child, there is the potential for fragmentation of the psyche and the soul essence. Many of these fragments live in the dreambody out of the reach of the conscious mind as was the case with Judy. A person may experience these fragments as intrusive thoughts or as flashbacks. This becomes complex, for sometimes if there has been a great deal of soul loss with a large part of the essence energy living at the outer edges of the dreambody, there is room for part of the soul essence or spirit of another being to slip into the body. When this happens, it might feel like an intrusive thought, or it could feel like what one might imagine it would be like to have been programmed through political torture or cult abuse. Judy's father told her that he was beating and raping her because she was bad and that he was trying to force the devil out of her. That aspect of Judy's father had its own frequency band. It occupied the space that little Judy was in when she left her body during the abuse. Judy came to believe that at her core she was bad.

Judy was a beautiful person, an excellent mother, and had received community awards for her service and dedication. Still Judy believed she was bad. If I tried to counter this belief, she hit herself in the head—as her father had hit her. Judy had great fear that if she ever said out loud that she was not bad, that horrible things would happen to her. Her father's programming, whether intended or not, was quite rooted in her psyche. At times Judy felt as if she were going crazy when she heard her father's angry voice in her head. In psychological terminology, this interloper is called a perpetrating alter, meaning that the energy and voice of Judy's father is within her psychic structure.

I have found in both those with multiple personalities and those who have been programmed through political torture or cult abuse that it is possible to remove or extract the programming or perpetrating alter. It is a very difficult and complicated process because frequently, the frequency of the perpetrating energy is wrapped around and through other frequency bands like the wires in an electronic device. The father's energy had joined with an alter, named Ryan, that believed that it was his job to protect Judy and her different parts. He protected them by seeing that Judy adhered to the beliefs and statements of the father. If she did not, he abused her. I formed a therapeutic relationship with Ryan and over the course of several years convinced him to lessen his abusive stance to the system all the while praising him for his commendable job of protecting her. It took time to convince Judy and Ryan that the message of the father was not correct and could be removed. For years Judy held onto her father's voice as the truth until finally one day she was able to say that she was OK, that she wasn't bad. With that shift in consciousness it was possible to pull the father's energy out using a crystal. It was not possible to remove the father's energy until Judy no longer believed his words to be true. Her mind would have just pulled the father's energy back.

There are different ways to remove the frequency of the alien energy. One method is to travel with my guides into the dreambody, locate the frequency on which the interloper resides and surround it in healing light. Sometimes the alien energy is lost and is quite relieved to be led back to where it belongs, but more often it is reluctant to leave, being deeply entrenched and intertwined and in some incidences harming the host when threatened with removal. Sometimes I take this being into my own body by psychically pulling the entity into me or pull it into a crystal that I am holding. I then transform the entity by surrounding it with light and compassion. With the help of my guides, they pull the entity out through my feet. My guides do a healing for the entity and then escort the alien energy to its proper home. I think of this method as a modified version of the Buddhist practice of Tonglen in which you breath in the suffering of others and breathe out love and compassion.

Care and protection must be taken to protect the client and myself during this process. I always begin by putting both of us in protective light and calling in all of our guides. I have stones that are wrapped in prayers that offer protection. There is also a ritual that I do involving incense, which protects my energy field. I have a number of guides whose main purpose is protection; they step in front of me and surround me when I am threatened or I go inside them. My energy can be quite ferocious when I am inside my crocodile. I received the crocodile spirit through a ceremony of transmission with the Bomoh that involved my swimming in water that crocodiles inhabit. At the time of the ceremony I was unaware that there were crocodiles in the water. There is something to be said for not always getting the translation right.

On one of my trips to study with the Bomoh, he gave me a powerful prayer used in removing interloping energy or entities. This method may sound strange, but is both easy and effective and does not take the energetic toll that the previous methods do. I ask the client to bring me a white bed sheet; then I write a prayer on the top of the sheet. I cover her body with the sheet with the written prayer over her head. I then put a copy of the prayer into water and spray the energy of the prayer onto and around the client. I sit next to the client and wait as the energy begins to float out of the client. Frequently we see the same energy leaving at the same time. Strange as this may sound, it has been remarkably powerful and effective in releasing the interloping energy. As with all of the rituals, the client must be willing to have the energy leave or the mind will call the energy or a similar energy back a few weeks later. This prayer can be used to rid the body of all sorts of energies. My dear friend, Patti, had breast cancer as did her mother before her. Fearing that the cancer might be genetically transmitted, I used this prayer to remove the cancerous energy from her body and from the body of her daughter, who at the time was cancer free. So far both are doing well.

Psychosis and Posttraumatic Stress Disorder
Historically it has been difficult to know exactly what it is that pushes one over the line into madness. In western cultures there are those who believe that psychosis is a mental disorder that is incurable. It is thought to have a biological base, treatable and capable of being managed through medications, but not cured. From this perspective it is psychosis that causes one to believe that horrific things have happened to them; it is the psychosis speaking when tales of ritual abuse, torture and extreme abuse are relayed.

There are others who believe that many people that present as psychotic are actually in the throes of extreme phases of posttraumatic stress disorder. These clients may be delusional or experiencing hallucinations. They often are incapable of communicating to others in a coherent way. In these moments the psychic structure begins to fragment as memories or senses of the abuse flood and overwhelm the client.

From an energetic perspective a transitory psychotic state may occur when triggers from the culture and the environment interact with vibrational threads in the dreambody in such a way that the energy vortices, which hold the personality together, comes apart resulting in a disorganization of the psychic structure. In this disorganization other energies can enter resulting in disruption of normal bio-chemical functioning. Noted psychiatrist Bessel van der Kolf[24] has found that trauma does alter the physiological make-up of a person. Acupuncturists also have confirmed this. Several clients reported seeing their acupuncturists a few days after a soul retrieval and were told that their energy system or chi had been reorganized towards health and balance.

I have worked with clients who have extensive trauma histories, yet function well in their day-to-day life, who would lapse into a psychotic state when confronted with terrifying stimuli either from the external world or from within. In a psychotic state one loses touch with the reality of day-to-day life. Some hear voices or see bizarre and frightening images before their eyes. Some are told to do or say things that are incomprehensible. Sometimes it is impossible even to understand the words that are being uttered. They make no sense. Usually, however, if I listen carefully enough, there are key words and themes that alert me to the content and images with which the person is struggling. A person in a psychotic state frequently is unaware of what time it is, what day it is, or even where she is. Personal self-care stops; sleep is disrupted; any semblance of a normal routine is lost. Sometimes the psychotic state would last a few hours, sometimes a few days. With each one there was a different way to help them reconstitute.

When I have journeyed into the dreambody of clients in a psychotic state, there is total chaos. The power animals and spirit guides are in a panic running about in alarm, unsure of what to do. There is darkness, with energy spinning out of control. Sometimes I see different parts or aspects of the person screaming or crying while others curl up in a ball shaking in fear. Through working with my clients and my spirit helpers, we form a containing energy band in the dreambody around the edges of the energy that is spinning out of control. Gradually the band is tightened allowing less and less space for the energy to spin out of control. It is like an energetic straight jacket. Then, sometimes, it is possible, through the guidance of my helpers, to pull out some of the chaotic energy.

I worked with Frieda, who had several loosely formed personalities. One day she came to see me in a psychotic state. I journeyed into her dreambody and saw various alters fragment into more and more parts, until there were literally 50 to 60 soul fragments. With the help of spirit helpers, we formed the parts into four distinct "family" groupings based on their vibrational frequency level. Each of Frieda's power animals or spirit guides was assigned to one of the family units to provide an energetic band around them. Columns of light were sent down to each unit. By the time Frieda left my office, she was calmer and less agitated; by the next day the psychotic symptoms were gone. A week later she reported that she experienced her parts in four distinct groups. Previously she had felt quite fragmented. Frieda also reported feeling more depression and despair as there was calm. She had grown accustomed to the fragmentation and chaos, which held the darkness at bay. Yet it was the darkness that needed attention. She needed to understand what had happened to her so she could begin to heal.

Miriam Greenspan[25] discusses our culture's phobia around the dark emotions of pain and suffering, rage and hostility, grief and fear. She stresses the importance of allowing our clients and ourselves permission to be in and be with these powerful feelings. I concur with Ms. Greenspan that the only way to rid oneself of these feelings is to fully experience and learn from them. The dark emotions need to pass through us before they can be released.

I am saddened by our culture's inability to provide a container and support for the release of these feelings. In so-called "undeveloped countries" there is a community to hold and support one as they go through the dark emotions. The healers stay with the person they are healing until the work is finished. The work is not confined to a 50-minute hour. Thus when I suggest to a client that she needs to allow herself to be fully present to the depths of her pain, I am aware that I am asking her to do something that is incredibly difficult to do in this culture. There is not the support that is needed to face the pain from the kind of horrific abuse I am discussing now.

Power Animals and Spirit Guides

Shamanism offers a means of support and comfort for these dark emotions through contact with our spirit guides and power animals. Although it may be difficult to fully take in the concept of spirit guides and power animals, there is supportive, wise and loving energy around us—spiritual guidance that exists just for us. On one journey I was told that we alternate life times being spirit guides and being incarnate. Our guides and power animals actually become bored when we do not call upon them and drift away looking for something to do. Those clients who have had the most powerful results from their shamanic healings have been the ones who have been able to work with their guides in integrating the energy that has been given to them. Our guides can provide a sense of comfort and remind us that we are connected to energies much larger than we are.

Our spirit guides and power animals have a way of letting us know that they are present. Some report always knowing or sensing that they had protective energy around them. Most children are aware of these beings and are in active communication with them; their parents commonly refer to them as "imaginary friends." The highly popular comic strip, *Calvin and Hobbs*, was an example of a boy and his power animal. Others ask their guides for help, guidance, and protection and actively feel a response to this request. For those who need tangible proof of the existence of these protective beings, I suggest that power animals can be helpful in finding lost keys and securing parking places. Some find it easier to start working with them on this concrete level.

When I do shamanic work, the power animals and spirit guides do all the healing work. I am only the medium on the physical plane to transmit the energy. These power animals and spirit guides are essentially energy, but they take the form that they do because they carry the energy or "medicine" of what they represent. I have numerous power animals and spirit guides with whom I work. When different helpers appear for a healing, I am aware that their particular healing skills or "medicine" is what is needed to help the person with whom I am working; they provide a diagnostic function by their mere appearance. The more that I work with and trust my power animals and spirit guides, the deeper the level of work we are able to do together, and the greater the level of support and protection that I receive from them. When I work in the spirit realm, there is the possibility of encountering wonderful light beings just as it is possible to encounter some very dark energy. One is quite vulnerable if one is afraid as the fear is sensed just as animals sense fear in their prey. The only way that I can do the work I do is to trust that my guides will protect me and teach me what I need to know to handle any given situation.

Spirit Possession and Depossession

Spirit possession is considered a major cause of illness and suffering in indigenous cultures. It is believed that spirits from those who have lost their way in crossing over to the other side after death can inhabit the body of another. Usually these spirits are benign but clearly serve to confuse and disorient a person. Spirit possession happens when a person has had sufficient soul loss to allow a spirit to slip into the body. Sometimes the energy or spirit of a person who abuses another can slip into the body while the abuse is occurring. Those with multiple personalities often have an alter, or personality, who embodies the energy of the perpetrator as was the case with Judy. I have witnessed remarkable healings as a result of having these spirits removed. I often wonder if many people diagnosed as psychotic in western cultures actually suffer from spirit possession.

In some cultures curses are placed on people resulting in spirits entering the body. A curse was placed on a fellow Peace Corp volunteer who lived in Sabah, another state of Malaysia in Borneo. She had stopped shopping at a particular shop that was owned by a woman. Soon the volunteer began experiencing debilitating headaches causing her to writhe in pain unable to move. The local shopkeeper, known for practicing black magic, was seen near her house chanting. Another healer was called in to remove the curse and the volunteer was instantly healed.

The Bomoh is frequently called upon to remove spirits that were the result of curses by healers who have lost their way. I have wondered if suicide bombers have had curses or spells placed upon them. My greatest concern, if shamanism becomes more mainstream in the American culture, is that some people will take the incredible healing power that the universe has to offer and use it in destructive ways. Energy is neutral and can be used for either positive or negative purposes. The power of positive healing energy is more powerful than negative energy, but much harm can be done before the negative energy is brought back into balance.

Joyce came to see me for shamanic work. Joyce was an extremely bright and beautiful woman who had been diagnosed as psychotic. She was on high doses of anti-psychotic medication and was working with a therapist and several psychiatrists. Joyce had been sexually abused as a child and came from a family with a history of addictions. Joyce told me that she felt as if she were possessed; she truly believed that there was another energy force present within her that did not belong. I experienced Joyce as only being partially in her body. Her true essence seemed clouded by the strong medications she was taking.

First I did an extraction for Joyce. There was a black snake in her lower chakras extending up through the fifth chakra. The snake was difficult to remove; soon it became clear that it had strong spiritual powers. The energy of one of her abusers was around her second and third chakra sucking energy from her. While I did a soul retrieval for Joyce, she also journeyed. We had remarkably similar experiences.

Suspecting that I might encounter some hostile energy, I did the entire healing from inside one of my power animals—Bear. Most of my power animals and spirit guides were present for the healing. A creature immediately appeared. Given that I am working in the frequency realm, I first see faint wavy outlines that gradually come into greater form. The creature seemed witch-like and had a cackle. Inside the witch was a small child. Both appeared somewhat deranged. A battle ensued between the witch and my power animals. Finally one of my spirit guides, Quan Yin, put the witch in a container of light. There was a gorilla that was part of the struggle. I wondered if this might be a power animal for Joyce. We did a healing for the witch-like figure and the small child. I was told that the witch was the child's mother and had killed the child and herself in a psychotic state. The child was taken to the light. The gorilla went into the woods and brought out a baby.

Suddenly I heard crows outside my office window cawing loudly, which brought my focus back to ordinary reality. At the time my office was in the middle of the city so it was unusual to hear such a large and boisterous flock of crows. This alerted me to danger. When I returned to the journey, I saw my main spirit guide, the Garuda, jump the gorilla. Part of the spirit of the witch-like creature was inside of the gorilla. Another fight ensued. Some of my protectors appeared. Finally a snake entered the body of the gorilla and went up through the gorilla transforming it into a white crane.

While this part of the healing was occurring, Joyce journeyed. She had a snake enter her body and perform a dismemberment. From a shamanic perspective, a dismemberment is a gift from the spirits as your energy system is torn apart and reassembled in a healing way. After Joyce was dismembered pure white bones remained. A panther and a spirit guide emerged with a powerful message for Joyce.

Meanwhile in my journey, a panther came and retrieved the baby that the gorilla had been carrying. The baby embodied a major part of Joyce's essence, which had been lost since infancy. This loss of essence allowed space for the other energy or spirit to enter her body. There were two more soul parts retrieved that were related to her abuse as a child. Healings were done for both of these parts as well as her abusers. Then a spirit guide appeared who is a powerful symbol of feminine power, a warrior. This spirit guide is both a guide and a protector. Joyce saw the same spirit guide in her journey and had had her appear to her on several occasions in the past.

When I blew the soul parts, power animals, and spirit guide into Joyce, she felt fire flow through her body. She experienced the spirit who had possessed her leave her body. There was an amazing transformation. Joyce looked and felt like a different person. The haze was gone from her eyes, she looked clear, whole and fully embodied. We worked on some exercises for raising Joyce's frequency level so that other spirit energy would not come in.

Joyce and I saw similar things and had similar experiences on our journeys because we both tuned into the same frequency in her dreambody. The same spirit guides and power animals appeared to us both, as their medicine was needed to enact change and transformation for Joyce. Both of us saw and experienced a black snake dismember and transform the foreign energy or spirit into a different form. In Joyce's journey the energy changed into white bones, in my journey it changed into a white crane. The Bomoh taught that the energy or spirit with whom you do battle is always transformed into another form or spirit after it has been healed. He said that frequently these spirits become helpers or guides.

Although Joyce felt wonderful for a few days, over time some of the old feelings returned. Joyce began to lose some of the power and energy from the healing. We continued to meet periodically and do more healing work. Joyce worked hard with her power animals and spirit guides to integrate the healing energy that had returned and to keep out energy intrusions. In many ways her greatest struggle came in dealing with the negative messages from her psychotherapy team who did not believe that she could really change and be healed. Gradually Joyce weaned herself off the medication, even though her psychiatrist predicted disaster. She began to feel her power, strength and clarity return. Her creativity resurfaced, and she began to dance, paint, and write.

Although Joyce experienced immediate relief for a while, she still had to struggle with messages and voices that had plagued her in the past. There are powerful energetic imprintings and thought forms that can pull us back to old patterns and ways of being. All one has to do is to be in the energy field of one who represents or supports these old thought forms for this energetic pull to emerge. It is as if the frequencies reconnect. Joyce had several people in her life that supported the belief that she was psychotic and would always function in a somewhat marginal way. She also had some in her life that actively believed she could change. I believe that her ongoing trust and work with her spirit guides and power animals were key in her transformation.

Some ventures into the dreambody bode more challenge and difficulty. I worked with a woman named Pam, who had a history of ritual abuse and extreme torture. She also had a number of personalities and an extremely complicated and complex internal structure. Pam had undergone extensive programming. Whenever a program would be broken, a new, more virulent program would spring into being. It seemed as if her tormentors had been able to open or create their own frequency within the dreambody—

much like a computer virus. This frequency or energy force had a demonic quality and was capable of violent outbursts and destructive actions towards the body and towards others. This energy was quite dissimilar to the quieter, gentler nature of Pam's true essence. In dreamtime the programming appeared in the form of invading spirits, similar to what some cultures call spirit possession.

One day Pam came to see me with her therapist, Gail. Pam had experienced a situation which was terrifying to the child alters in her system. She was shaking in fear, barely able to speak. The three of us decided to do a journey to take the children to a place in non-ordinary reality where they felt safe. Journeying, or entering non-ordinary reality, to take the children to a safe place had proved helpful, calming, and reorganizing in the past.

As I began my journey, I witnessed the children running about screaming in terror. They felt as if something or someone was about to attack them. I gathered all of my power animals and spirit guides as well as all of Pam and Gail's spirit helpers. We formed a spirit corral around the running, frightened children until gradually, the children were in the middle of a circle with the spirit helpers encircling them. We began to climb up a mountain with the Garuda leading the way. Suddenly a large black creature appeared who strongly resembled Jabba the Hut from the *Star Wars Trilogy*. This large creature reached out and swallowed up the Garuda. Within 30 seconds of this occurring in the journey in dreamtime, Pam began to yell in a threatening voice and flail her arms about in my office. I asked Gail to try to contain her as I had to complete the journey. I could not leave my main spirit guide in the jowls of this creature. Several of my power animals, spirit guides, and I charged the creature while the Garuda applied pressure to the adrenal and pituitary glands from within the creature. One of my power animals worked on the third eye. Pam's arms began to flail more violently and the yelling increased. An angry male voice threatened to destroy the room and kill both Gail and myself. In dreamtime we lassoed the arms of the creature and tied them up. Within thirty seconds, Pam's arms were calm by her side, the flailing had ceased, but the threatening shouts in the room persisted, asking "what the fuck did you do to my arms, untie me this instant." In the journey we shot a dart into the creature's third eye, and the creature dissolved into a puddle; the Garuda stepped out of the puddle unharmed. Within thirty seconds Pam's energy shifted, she looked around confused and asked in her normal voice what had just happened. She had heard the yelling threats in her mind but was unaware that they were coming through her so that Gail and I could hear them. Mindful that the work was not finished, I returned to the journey. Fortunately I had presence of mind enough to remember the Bomoh's teaching that I needed to transform and heal this energy. The black puddle that had been the creature was changed into a beautiful rainbow butterfly. I then continued to take the children to their safe place in the mountains before ending the journey and coming back into the room.

I had not been sharing with Pam or Gail what was occurring in the journey as it was happening. Thus it was striking that the struggle that was ensuing in the journey in the dreambody was also being re-enacted in the room. It is not uncommon to be tricked or attacked in dreamtime while doing shamanic work for another. However, I had never before experienced the attack occurring in both dreamtime and in ordinary reality simultaneously. This, more than any other experience in my shamanic work, conveyed to me the existence of the dreambody, the ability to travel in another person's dreambody, and the ability to enact change in this realm that was immediately noticeable in ordinary reality. Through concerted effort my guides and I were able to subdue and transform the angry violent energy that had taken over Pam's body. Both Pam and I were exhausted after this experience and slept for several days. The Bomoh reported that he frequently becomes ill after this type of an experience, as the energy expended is considerable and sometimes the toxins of the dark energy impact the physical body.

For two months Pam felt calm and was aware of the rainbow butterfly being with her. Then the other energy reemerged, and she never saw the rainbow butterfly again. I am unclear as to why or how this energy rematerialized. I asked the Bomoh and he told me, "when you become more powerful you will be able to make the invading spirits stay away for good." This is no doubt true. There is still much for me to learn. I do believe that there must be a way to close off frequencies that pull in negative and destructive energy. Each time I journey on this question, I am told that the client has to work with her power animals and spirit guides for this to happen. The role of the therapist or healer is to bring the client to the place where she can own her own power and believe that change can come. For any healing to be effective, be it through shamanic work or psychotherapy, the client has to be actively involved in her own healing. The thought forms that we have can have a powerful effect on the work as does the energetic imprinting to which we are born. Pam found it difficult to believe that her helpers are powerful enough to keep away the demonic energy that has haunted her her entire life. This energy has been with her since she was a small child; it has always controlled her. The child parts of Pam could not imagine that they have the power to keep the demonic energy away. Although the adult part of Pam still struggles with this dark energy, she is able to control it and not act on its angry and destructive impulses.

Throughout my years of practice, I have worked intensely with a number of clients who are survivors of cult and ritual abuse. They all are extremely bright, which makes me wonder if only the bright survive this horrendous abuse or have the strength to make their way to treatment. It also raised the question as to whether bright children were chosen for experimentation in mind control in the fifties and early sixties. During the Iraqi War in 2003 a number of the cult survivors I see struggled mightily to hold down the voices within that urged them to commit violent acts. As I bore witness to their struggle and offered what I could to get them through this period, I also watched the war on Iraq unfold before my eyes. The trauma in the eyes of the Iraqi people, who have endured years of a brutal dictator and the terror of the onslaught of the most powerful military in the world, deeply saddened me. Young American soldiers, who bravely offered to risk their lives for their country, were not fully aware that they also had surrendered parts of their souls to the violence that unfolded before them. I write this book, in part, to bear witness to the indelible harm that violence does to the soul and psyche of both the victim and the perpetrator.

PART IV

THE ENERGETIC MATRIX

As my shamanic practice deepened, I noticed that some clients had powerful transformative experiences while others had some relief, but, after a few weeks, the old patterns returned. As I journeyed on this, I discovered the power of the mind to call back old beliefs and stuck patterns. I began to work with clients to identify negative beliefs and thought forms, which hold stagnate energy in place. This made a difference for some, but for others the healing energy seemed to evaporate over time.

I returned to study with the Bomoh and asked him about this problem. He gave me written ancient prayers that, when added to water or other forms of ritual, alter the vibrational field and allow for the release of negative energetic patterns and thought forms. For some of my clients, these prayers have been life altering. For others the debilitating energy was released only to be called back. As I journeyed more on this question, I learned that not only do our thought forms limit us, but also the energetic imprinting of our early upbringing. Each of us lives in our own energetic cocoon. We draw people and experiences to us that feel familiar energetically even though they may be harmful to us.

Like a complicated matrix, our thoughts hold the energy in place and the energetic imprinting pulls the thought forms near. It is through altering these powerful forces that real change can occur.

Chapter 12
THOUGHT FORMS AND THE CREATION OF REALITY

Once I did a journey to meet an ancestor who was a shamanic healer. I found myself in a sparse room with clay walls and an earth floor. A woman with solid hands and feet squatted over the body of an ill woman. The healer did not turn to look at me, but sensed my presence and began to speak. She was a powerful, beautiful woman who lived in Chile centuries ago. She told me that healing is much more difficult in my cultural and historical time period than in hers because of the many thought forms that have been created. She said, "These thought forms are so powerful that people believe them to be true. People in the American culture are not in touch with how energy works and is released, and they hold onto energy via their thoughts." She went on to say that if I am to be effective as a healer, I must come to understand the power of thought forms and how to help people energetically let go of them.

When I was a graduate student, it was important to declare a theoretical camp. Taking aspects of the different theories and developing one's own style was not in vogue. The choices were the analytical models, which explored unconscious processes, the systemic perspective that looked at the interconnections and interactions between people within families and organizations, and the cognitive-behavioral paradigm that worked with the rational aspects of mind and behavior. I managed to embrace two of the models and still be taken seriously; the one I did not pursue was cognitive-behavioral theory. At the time it seemed that there is so much more to who we are than what we think. On one level this is true, but our thoughts and beliefs are much more important than I ever could have imaged back then. Our thoughts and beliefs contain the energy of our unconscious process and influence our interpersonal exchanges just as the energy from our unconscious process shapes our thoughts and guides our interactions. Each of the major psychological theories is illuminated by an understanding of energy and is linked together through energy. Alone, each model is incapable of fully explaining how we function.

In the eighties and nineties the term post-modern dominated the intellectual landscape. The underlying tenet of this concept is that reality is a creation of the mind. There are no absolute truths. From a post-modern perspective psychotherapists enter into the world of the client without judgment or a preconceived notion of what is good for the client. I embraced post-modernism as it made sense to me. After living for two years in a radically different culture, it was apparent that there are no absolute truths; one's reality is a construction of culture, class, race, gender, and spiritual practice. My initial understanding of post-modernism was largely an intellectual one, bound by the confines of what I would allow my mind to consider.

Thought Forms as Energy

From journeys for others and in conversations with my guides, I have been able to see and experience the power of thoughts to create reality, which has brought a whole new meaning to my understanding of post-modernism. A man named Dylan came to see me who believed he had been abducted by aliens and had been channeling information from a far-off galaxy since he was a child. Over the past few years, he had experienced a number of losses and set backs and felt that he had lost his connection with this galaxy. As I listened to his story, I was aware that there were many factors in his life, which might cause soul loss and his ensuing problems. Although I attempted to remain neutral in my mind as to whether aliens had abducted him, in my heart I doubted it. Thus I was not prepared for what I saw and experienced during the shamanic healing.

During the soul retrieval, I traveled through darkness for some time and then found myself in a very strange place. It is difficult to describe, as it is not in my frame of reference. The images were not three dimensional but oddly linear; the beings were lacking any affective element but were in no way like Dr. Spock from Star Trek. Communication was telepathic; language was not used even among the beings there. After some confusion we were able to work together in a healing way that was positive for Dylan. After the journey, I began to describe what I had seen and experienced. Before I could put words to the images, Dylan said did it look like… and began to describe in vivid detail what I had just witnessed.

Afterward I began to ponder what had just happened. Did I travel to a far off galaxy or was Dylan's belief in this galaxy strong enough to create a frequency or reality that was readable when I journeyed into his dreambody? Either prospect seemed daunting. I journeyed to my guides who affirmed that this far-off galaxy was a thought form created by Dylan.

In this journey my guides showed me many things and beings that have been created by thought forms. They took me to the edge of hell. Protected by a thick membrane, I viewed a grayish brownish black energy vortex that sucked and devoured anyone or anything in its field while simultaneously spitting out energy. I was told that hell is both a reality and a thought form. The energy from people's collective thoughts has created hell. If a person believes she will go to hell, that is what she will experience immediately after death. If people quit believing in hell, the energy that creates it would dissipate and hell would cease to exist.

My guides then introduced me to positive energy forms that have been created. Mythological and historical figures such as Athena and Zeus, Joan of Ark and Sir Lancelot have an energetic frequency and are as real as you or I. Deities and religious icons have also been dreamed into being. While retrieving spirit guides and power animals for clients, I have met Jesus and Mary, Quan Yin and the Buddha, and a host of mythical deities such as the Geneshe and Hanumman. Our collective need for these archetypal entities has indeed created them and on a frequency level they exist, and can and do communicate with us. Demonic and terrifying creatures are also dreamed into being. I have encountered several vampires, wicked witches, and devouring monsters as I travel in the dreambodies of my clients.

Each of us exists within our own dreambody, yet has access via frequency waves to the collective unconscious that Jung so eloquently described. Certain images resonate vibrationally with our frequency and become part of our dreambody. Some people are haunted by the darker images of the psyche and pull negative illusions from the collective unconscious into the dreambody. Others who embrace a more Utopian perspective pull in the ethereal. Images from the collective unconscious flow back and forth among our individual dreambodies, which influence us individually and collectively and bring some images fully into conscious awareness while others that hold less resonance, recede.

My guides helped me to understand why Dylan had created the belief that aliens had abducted him. The collective unconscious houses several images of aliens that mirror differing affective states. Over the years the vibrational frequency related to aliens has strengthened to the extent that the existence of aliens is now part of the collective conscious of our culture. For many, aliens are real and abductions do occur. Some report terrifying encounters with aliens, others proclaim a positive, almost mystical, experience with these beings, while others' experiences are more mixed.

My guides showed me that Dylan had contact with spirit beings that channeled information to him. Dylan had never heard of spirit beings; thus he had limited choices as to how to interpret these events. He could deny that these encounters occurred, burying memory of them deep in his unconscious. He could fear that he was going crazy. But given the positive power he felt inside himself as a result of these encounters, Dylan adopted the only explanation that was available to him: that of being abducted by friendly aliens. Dylan's childhood lacked strong loving connections; thus the aliens were perceived as being void of emotions. During the journey for Dylan, I was told that he has powerful energy. Many of his recent problems stem from his not owning and working with this power. Dylan never had been given the support or understanding to recognize or develop his talents. Instead of utilizing the power that he was given by the spirit world, he created a reality that made him a passive recipient of these gifts.

A teenage woman came to see me with her mother, Janice, whom I had worked with before. Janice was quite open to working in the spirit world. Janice experienced her daughter, Holly, as psychic and wanted Holly to have a chance to explore this. In the course of our conversation Holly revealed that she occasionally saw a green being in her bedroom sitting on the bookshelf. She reported that she had never been afraid of this being but accepted it as a natural occurrence. Holly had never told her mother of this being, but it was clear that her mother's open acceptance of the spirit realm helped to make these visits natural and non-threatening.

Children often create new meaning and images out of events that they are unable to intellectually or emotionally understand. The creation of new thought forms becomes a reality in its own right often erasing the memory of what actually occurred. The new thought form, however, does carry the emotional content of the occurrence. Dylan's "alien visitors" made him feel special and powerful, but also mirrored the emotional vacuum that he experienced in his family. Without support he was unable to own the power he had to connect to the spirit world; thus he created a reality in which he was dependent on the "aliens" for connection.

Many are critical of "new age" teachings, as they are perceived as blaming the victim for his or her plight. Thus I want to stress that I do not blame Dylan for the creation of this thought form; rather I view it as a very inventive coping mechanism. Blame is a concept or negative thought form that is embedded in our culture and is one of the greatest roadblocks to establishing a climate for change and transformation. We all spend much too much energy trying to "be right" while fearing that we will be blamed or told we have done something wrong. Our beliefs provide a structure to contain our soul. Love, acceptance, and compassion are needed as a new container for change to truly occur; blame gets in the way of this. If Dylan had had the support that Holly has, his experience might have been radically different and he would not have needed to create a reality in which aliens abduct him.

The Power of Rigidified Thought Forms

Many of our thoughts come and go and are quite fluid. Others become rigidified thought forms that become energetic entities. When we become laden with rigid thought forms, our frequency range becomes dense and heavy, literally causing us to be rigid and sluggish.

These rigid thought forms come into being in a variety of ways. As with Dylan, sometimes one has a difficult or significant event occur that is outside of one's frame of reference, so new thought forms are created to make sense of the experience. Many thought forms are taught by family and society and are taken in as reality. Sometimes another's beliefs become embedded in our energy field and appear to be our thoughts. This causes confusion when the beliefs are counter to what we know to be true. I began elementary school in the fifties when racist views were quite prevalent. As a young child some of my most loving and protective caregivers were Afro-Americans. This produced a schism between what I was taught to believe and what I knew in my heart to be true and undoubtedly laid the foundation for my becoming a sixties activist.

Often ideas we have about our feelings become thought forms just as our thoughts can create feeling states. Many of the trauma survivors with whom I have worked live in the feeling state of the trauma and, understandably, project onto the present and future the reality of their childhood. Frieda had been horribly abused and by men in her childhood and, not surprisingly, had married an abusive man. She was invited to a party in which men would be present. Frieda felt terror at the thought of going as she assumed the men would be abusive. (Her feeling state created an erroneous thought form.) I worked with Frieda to understand that the terror, which she was experiencing belonged to her childhood, that it was just a feeling and not a fact. Frieda looked at me quizzically and asked, "You mean that feelings aren't fact?" I replied that they are not, that feelings are fluid and only become fact when our mind makes them fact. Frieda adopted a new mantra in which she repeated, "feelings are fluid, they are not fact." With this mantra firmly embedded, Frieda went to the party, talked to men, and had a good time.

Most of us experience life-transforming events that shatter our worldview and force us to create a new one. Often these events are more commonplace than visitations by spirits. Susie was six when her mother died of a cerebral hemorrhage. Susie could not image a worse thing happening than to have lost her mother. She believed that she must have done a horrible thing for this to occur. Susie searched her mind; the only thing she remembered doing was lying to her mother when asked if she ate all of the cookies. Unclear whether it was worse to have lied or to have eaten all the cookies, she stopped eating for fear of doing another bad thing that might result in her father's death. The belief that she was somehow responsible for her mother's death acted as a container for the unbearable pain she was feeling. Within this belief lay the premise that things do not happen randomly. Susie believed that if she had been good enough, she could have prevented her mother's death. Unfortunately Susie's created explanation for why her mother died resulted in her developing an eating disorder and compromising her health.

Many of our most rigidified thought forms are either taught to us at an early age by those closest to us or are absorbed from the culture in which we live. I can remember clearly a day in my twenties when I was working in the garden on my farm in New Hampshire. I looked up at the mountains around me, struck with the realization that there were two distinct voices in my head. One carried all of the messages and beliefs I had been taught throughout my life. The other was my true voice, containing what I really thought and believed. For a number of years these two voices had been at war. It took hard work and a self-imposed exile from television to distance myself from society's messages and sort out these voices. Ultimately I realized that my true voice arose from the wisdom and knowledge that is stored in the soul. Many of us go through life feeling that we are the only one that struggles to accept the dominant belief system and pushes what we really feel and think away. In my thirty plus years of doing psychotherapy, the vast majority of folks who have come to see me have struggled with the tension around what they were taught and what they believe to be true. Many fear coming to therapy, as they do not want to confront what they know is true in their heart.

Often the rigidly held thoughts and beliefs of parents or other significant people attach to the energy field or are stored in the body. When journeying for clients, I have found thought forms appearing like little spurs in the energy field or body. Thought forms that belong to others can become toxic when they are counter to the true path of the soul. Sometimes these spurs become energetically infected resulting in emotional or physical illness. These thought forms tend to manifest in an area of the body that corresponds developmentally to the belief. Jane was told that girls should not say what they really think but defer to the wisdom of males,—"men do not like little girls who know too much." This thought form became lodged in Jane's fifth chakra, which governs expression and is housed near the throat. It appeared as a cat fur ball that made it difficult for Jane to breathe when she talked, in effect silencing her.

The images and messages we receive from society, our families, and friends infiltrate the psyche and impact and influence our feelings. Our thoughts and beliefs give form and shape to the images that swirl around in our heads providing a container and often a mirror for our feeling, sometimes freezing us in rigid patterns of behavior, making change and growth a very difficult process. Sometimes our beliefs bring certain feelings into being. Fear is one of the best examples of how a belief can create a feeling state just as the feeling state can give birth to a belief. If we are taught that those who are different from us are dangerous, then we will feel fear when we encounter a person of a different race. When my son, Josh, was in high school, he was the only white boy on his basketball team. When the team visited other towns and walked down the street together, people with fear in their eyes scurried across the street to get away from them. If we believe that we are unsafe in a certain part of town, we will feel unsafe whether we are or not.

Conversely the feeling of fear can create beliefs and actions that energetically pull for the fear to be actualized. The fear of betrayal can cause one to strike preemptively by leaving a relationship. This sets into motion what one most feared—abandonment. Many divorcing couples fall prey to horror stories about what happened to a friend or a neighbor when they divorced. Out of fear of what they believe could happen, they empty out bank accounts, hire expensive lawyers, do things that are counter to who they are and end up hurting themselves, their children, and the person whom they once loved. By acting out of irrational fear they bring their worst nightmare to life and add energy to the belief that divorce is a nasty process.

The energy from negative thought forms often paralyzes us in stuck behaviors. Clients come into therapy struggling with negative beliefs about such things as their appearance, intellect, or creative abilities, which give a cognitive frame for feelings of inadequacy. Feelings of inadequacy often stem from childhood. A little boy, teased as a child because his ears were too big, sets in motion the belief that he is ugly. Another is told that she has no artistic talent because she could not color inside the lines. Another child carries a lifelong sense that she is stupid because she was the first one out of a spelling bee. Because these occurrences were painful and humiliating at the time, erroneous beliefs become firmly implanted, which, in turn, holds one back for fear of failure and further humiliation. When one does not live up to one's potential, depression often results.

Negative beliefs also act as self-fulfilling prophecies as a result of the energy attached to them. If the energy of the negative thought forms is strong enough, there is a tendency to manifest this energy in a concrete manner. Jim has applied for his dream job, for which he has spent years training, yet he fears he is not smart enough to do it. He is quite anxious when he goes to the job interview. His anxiety and self-doubting beliefs are in the room; the interviewer senses this and does not give him the job even though Jim's resume and recommendations are far superior to the other candidates.

Others draw people to them who verify their negative self-perception. Stacey is an attractive woman; many are drawn to her. She married a man who is critical of her slightest flaw, re-enforcing her negative self-image. Stacey's negative beliefs stem from the energy she introjected or took in from her mother. Her mother felt unattractive. This was constantly re-enforced by her father's negative comments to her mother. Stacey took in her mother's pain and adopted her mother's negative view of herself even though by most standards Stacey is considered quite beautiful. A combination of the energy introjected from her mother and the beliefs that she has attached to this energy propelled her to find a man who made her feel as her father had made her mother feel.

When I began to do shamanic work, I was struck with the ease with which some clients integrated the new soul parts and spirit guides. Others would feel relief for a month or two but then would begin to struggle anew with the same thoughts and feelings as before. Surprisingly, some reported that they did not feel like themselves—that they had grown used to feeling miserable and did not know who they were without this as their identity. Strong beliefs have their own vibrational frequency, some of which are powerful enough to push away the new energy and pull the old back. I found that clients who had had some therapy and had worked to understand their thoughts and feelings had an easier time relinquishing these old thought forms. Therapy weakens belief in negative thought forms, which diminishes the power of the frequency. Therapy also encourages the development of new possibilities and dreams, thereby creating a new frequency and home for the returned soul parts and guides.

Thought Forms as Protectors from Emotions

I have had great teachers throughout my life—most notably my clients. I have learned that beliefs were often put into place to protect the developing emotional state of the child. Some things were just too horrible for the child to endure and part of the child left, leaving behind a very defended ego state. I understood this intellectually, but it was not until I observed what happens in the auric body, that I fully "got it." There are seven layers to this energetic body. The first layer of the auric body is the physical, followed by the emotional body. The mental body is next. When one has endured a great deal of traumatic occurrences, the emotional body or the second layer tends to predominate. When this takes place, the cognitive structures of the mental body act as a container for feelings. Often the words and thoughts of the perpetrators energetically inhabit the mental body providing a negative container. It can be a long arduous process to replace these negative beliefs because of the energetic tie to the emotional state.

Beliefs or thoughts about why traumatic incidences occurred tend to function to hold the emotions of the trauma in place. If the belief system is challenged, the container for the emotional system is threatened and emotional chaos results. I have been struck throughout the years that the vast majority of clients with trauma histories initially believed that they were truly bad and deserved what happened to them. When I challenged this belief, and told them that they are good and undeserving of what happened to them, panic would come over their faces and I could observe the psychic structures begin to weaken. Some would yell at me, "I am too bad" and even begin to hit themselves or do other self-destructive acts.

In journeying for these clients, I discovered an energetic band around the emotional body created by thought forms in the mental body. There were vibrational threads linking the affect of the emotional body to thoughts that mirrored the affect. The negative beliefs about oneself provided a rationale for why those that they loved and depended upon would harm them in the ways that they did. Without these beliefs as a container for the powerful feelings of grief and abandonment housed in the emotional body, there was danger of fragmentation of the psyche resulting in psychotic states. Through the gradual release of the painful feelings, while simultaneously grounding one in ways that these old beliefs are not relevant to their current lives, help to lessen the hold these negative beliefs carry.

Sara had been abducted into a ring of child pornography when she was a child. There was a great deal of accompanying abuse and torture. When I first began working with Sara, she was in and out of psychiatric hospitals and struggled with intense programming that told her to kill herself if she began to remember. I began to work with Sara before I was introduced to shamanic work. Many of the more traditional means of dealing with programming such as hypnosis were minimally effective. Fortunately Sara responded very well to an integration of shamanic work and psychotherapy.

Sara began to claim her life after a shamanic depossession in which the torturous energy of her perpetrators, who had stalked her with images of death, was removed. Several helping guides plus the strong aspects of her essence were returned in the same healing. Over the next few years Sara's life shifted from one of survival to enjoyment and productivity. Two things she never dreamed possible were part of her life; she had a challenging and satisfying job and a stable and nurturing relationship. The suicidal feelings and energetic introjects of her perpetrators were gone, yet Sara was haunted by negative messages telling her that she would lose all that she had gained— that she had no right to be happy or successful. Sara worked hard with her guides and power animals to chase these messages away, but occasionally she would become overwhelmed by them. At other times she would be fine, the negative messages pleasantly gone.

As we worked with these pesky thought forms, I saw a vibrational thread connecting Sara to her abusive past. When certain triggers arose such as making a mistake at work, Sara felt the full force of these messages telling her that she was a failure and would never amount to anything. This thought form had grown out of a belief that she was shamed and contaminated by what had happened to her, condemning her to a life of failure and misery. At times the vibrational thread that carried the message became quite powerful and threatened to overcome Sara and the positive affirmations with which she had replaced them. A combination of medication, working with guides, doing energy work, and debunking the negative messages would cause them to recede, but the messages were never fully eliminated. Finally I was able to see and comprehend the role these messages had in containing the painful unhealed parts of the trauma that threatened to destroy Sara.

Sara had made the decision not to uncover all of the memories of her abuse. Through her years of hospitalizations, she had known others who had become shattered by the painful memories of past traumas and were unable to function in society. Sara feared this happening to her and chose instead to put her energy into enhancing and stabilizing her life. The difficulty, however, lay in the fact that the energy from the unresolved memories would become activated or triggered by emotionally similar situations. When this energy began to push up, causing anxiety, the old thought forms, paired with the affective state, would emerge and overtake Sara. This resulted in periods of high stress. The negative thought forms acted as a container for the anxious feelings. Instead of feeling the fear and pain associated with what had happened to her, she would focus on how bad she was for misspelling a name at work. Sara worried that she could lose her job and possibly become homeless. These worries were far out of proportion for what she had done. In doing so she translated the unresolved feelings of her abuse to a situation, which carried an element of the abuse. It seemed that any mistake, no matter how minor, would trigger feelings of destruction and loss. Rather than go into the memory of what had happened to her, it was safer to put the pain onto a situation in her current life. Even though Sara was aware that this was what she was doing, when she was in these states, she had difficulty accessing that knowledge. Gradually as the anxious feeling state would recede, the negative beliefs would fade away. A part of Sara initially had difficulty in developing care and compassion for what had happened to her and still believed that she was tainted and somehow responsible for what had occurred. This belief is common among survivors and keeps the negative messages in place and the experience of harm present. After much hard work, Sara is able to be aware of what is happening when the negative messages arise. As a result, the power that they once had is gone.

Many use their thoughts to keep their feelings at bay. In certain professions and strata of society, it is considered positive to do this. For these individuals most of their energy is in the mental body. The third layer of their auric body is large and dense, squishing the other layers into small bands. As a result of the density of this layer, it is difficult for these individuals to feel their emotions or be in touch with the various feelings in the physical body. The impenetrability of the mental body makes it difficult to access the upper four layers of the auric body, which are the gateway to the intuitive, the collective unconscious, agape love, and union with the divine. Given, however, that emotions are extremely powerful, they can break through the barrier created by the mind much like an exploding pressure cooker. When this occurs, one literally feels as if she is losing her mind.

Most live somewhere between being overwhelmed with feelings and blocking them from consciousness with thought forms. Yet all of us have thought forms that bring pain and suffering. Rick is a man of many talents and has the financial security to develop his talents. Yet he cannot enjoy his freedom or his gifts because he is haunted by the belief that he is less than others because he is not gainfully employed. When confronted with filling out forms stating his occupation, he is filled with shame and confusion for not having an outer identity. Rick carries the belief that one must have a title to be valued and overlooks all the ways in which he enhances other's lives. This belief mirrors the feeling he has had since he was a little boy: that he is inferior to others. Thus the belief keeps the feeling active and the feeling keeps the belief in place. Both the feeling and the belief must be worked with for Rick to be relieved of his distress.

When emotions that are paired with a thought form have been understood and healed, it is relatively easy to remove the thought forms energetically. An extraction can be done to pull them out or one can do a ritual such as writing the thought form down on a piece of paper and burning it. Meditation can also be a powerful tool in ridding the mind of unwanted thoughts.

The Practice of Non-attachment for the Healing of Rigidified Thought Forms
Buddhists have long believed that attachment brings suffering and that the mind[26] is the vehicle for attaching. From the time we are small children we believe if we just get a certain toy or are able to go to Disney World that we will be happy. If we do not get these things, then we are full of disappointment and sadness as a result of the belief that these things will make us happy. While we are preoccupied in our misery over our beliefs, we fail to be fully present in our lives and miss many things that have the potential to make us happy. As adults we still believe that if we buy a house, a new car, or go on a cruise then all will be fine. But after years of experience, most of us realize that these moments are fleeting.

Vipassana meditation, a form of Buddhist practice, helps us to understand the mind. This practice teaches one to focus on the breath. While focusing on the breath different thoughts usually float into the mind. One is to note the thought, then let it go and return to the breath. If a thought persists over time, then it is a signal to examine this thought at another time. The goal of this practice is to become mindful of what the mind is doing and to develop a sense of detachment to all the thoughts that race in and out of the mind. Jon Kabat-Zinn[27] popularized this ancient practice and brought meditation into hospitals throughout the country as part of stress reduction programs.

When I first began meditating, I was amazed to find how much my mind was full of self-centered thoughts that stemmed from beliefs about how I thought things should be. "It is my birthday. If I am not honored in the way I believe I should be, then I will be disappointed." From watching my mind, I discovered that my thoughts could create certain feelings. My mind could whip me into a frenzy over totally meaningless things in no time at all. From this I realized that I attached way too much importance to other's actions to make me happy or miserable. The less I had expectations about outcomes, the happier I became. I also had to face intense feelings of shame as I examined the thoughts in my mind. I was amazed at how easy it had been to rationalize my behavior or blame others.

After several years of meditating on a daily basis, I came to find—on occasion—the pure bliss that comes from having an empty mind. By emptying out all the thoughts that are stuck in the mental body of the auric field, it is possible to experience the joy that comes from connecting with divine love in the sixth and seventh layers of the auric body. I had been mediating for a number of years before I began shamanic journeying. I believe that I would have had difficulty entering into the realms of non-ordinary reality without my meditation practice. One journeys through exiting the astral or fourth layer of the auric body. Without learning to clear the thoughts in the mental body it is difficult to move onto the astral. People have come to me to learn to journey. Some have been unable to access non-ordinary reality because of all the thoughts in their mind that are stored in the mental body, blocking access to the astral. When I suggest that they first begin by meditating, I am often meant with disclaimers that they have tried meditation and have gotten nowhere. A wise Buddhist teacher once said that taming the mind is like taming a wild horse. When you first go to lasso the horse, it becomes wilder than before. When you are finally successful in corralling the horse, it begins to calm down and soon you have yourself a wonderful horse. By ridding one's mind of meaningless thoughts, beliefs, and worries, it is possible to find enough stillness to open to the infinite wisdom that is within us and around us.

There are cautions to using meditation as a tool for ridding the mind of unwanted thoughts. Thoughts and beliefs provide a container for powerful feelings that may be overwhelming if one were to experience the full force of her feelings. Some have tried to deal with the turmoil in their lives through meditation only to find that they have unleashed more than they can handle. Thus as one begins to mediate, it is good to have a teacher or a therapist to help with the feelings that may arise.

Healing through Transformational Thought

Just as self-destructive thoughts cause suffering and draw negative energy to us; affirmative thoughts can herald in positive outcomes and alter the affective state. The power of positive thinking has been part of many spiritual traditions. My father was a devotee of Norman Vincent Peale, a Christian minister, who wrote extensively on the power of positive thinking. His teachings have impacted hundreds of thousands. Many have attributed Michael Jordan's success as a basketball player to his belief that he could pull wins out of the hat with logic defying skill. The belief that he could do this was as important as the incredible talent that he possessed. Jordan's coach, Phil Jackson, a Buddhist, was said to have worked with Jordan and his team on staying in the moment and in believing that they could do anything.

Positive affirmations can work toward healing the negative thought forms and affective states of those in deep emotional distress. For those haunted by negative thoughts and terrifying feelings, it is important to create new beliefs to counter the destructive ones that keep the feelings contained. The first step is to realize that the thought is mirroring painful affect usually connected to the past. Liz had suffered horrific abuse as a child. After struggling for years with being overwhelmed with self-destructive thoughts and unbearable feelings, Liz constructed a plan to deal with the negative messages. When she began to experience the hurtful feelings and thoughts, Liz took a deep breath. Then on the out breath, she blew away the negative thought, replacing it with the following mantra: "this is an old thought form connected to my childhood. I am safe; I am loved." Although this technique did not fully eliminate the self-destructive thoughts, there was considerable relief.

One mother created a mantra for her young daughter, Tasha, who believed that she was bad and acted out these feelings of badness as children frequently do. The mother told her daughter to say, "I am a good girl" every time that she felt that she was a bad one. I had worked with Tasha for over a year uncovering the reasons that Tasha had grown to feel so badly about herself. Her parents and teachers at her school had tried a variety of things to alter her negative behavior and view of herself to no avail. Within a few weeks of repeating this mantra, Tasha proudly told me, " I no longer need to repeat the mantra as I now believe it." A few weeks later we stopped meeting; six months later I received a note from her mother stating that Tasha was happy and doing great. This was a powerful intervention, in part, because it came from the mother, but also because it changed the cognitive structure which positively impacted the feeling state.

The Bomoh's teachings derive from ancient teachings indigenous to Borneo and are also grounded in the Islamic Unani tradition. An important aspect of this teaching is in working with the power of the mind to heal. When one works shamanically, one must clear away one's energy and thoughts for the spirits to move through and then concentrate the power of the mind on the intention of the healing. The Bomoh is able to dissolve cancerous tumors by concentrating the full power of his mind combined with the energy of his spirit guides.

In the American culture there are many accounts of the power of prayer to heal and numerous incidences of people altering their lives through positive affirmations. Some who have fallen on hard times purport that this thinking blames them for their own misfortunate. Yet if we compassionately take the time to examine our thoughts and see those areas where we may be unconsciously blocking ourselves by holding onto self-defeating beliefs, powerful change can result. There are, to be sure, situations where external change and intervention is needed. We must constantly be mindful of the multitude of people who live in poverty and oppression.

Manifesting what you want with the power of the mind is the hallmark of many of the new age spiritual traditions. Manifestation can happen on both an individual and collective basis. In recent years we have witnessed the peaceful transformation of repressive regimes through the fall of communism in Eastern Europe and the Soviet Union and the end of Apartheid in South Africa. The people's collective desires to bring an end to repression was key. The Dalai Lama has requested that mindful concentration be focused towards the peaceful retreat of the Chinese from his homeland in Tibet. The Dalai Lama opposes the use of force to end the Chinese occupation of Tibet and looks to the dynamic work of Nelson Mandela in South Africa as a beacon for peaceful change. Before and during the War on Iraq in 2003, there were calls to pray for peace and for all of the leaders involved in the conflict. These appeals came through the Internet and suggested a time for all to pray together so as to magnify and intensify the power of each individual prayer. It is hoped that it had some impact on limiting the number of casualties from that war.

We have yet to fully explore the power of collective minds to enact change, but many believe it is one of our greatest untapped resources. Shirley

Andrews[28] reported that forty thousand years ago, the people of Atlantis were able to communicate telepathically. Groups of people gathered to focus the power of their collective minds on moving a large object such as a boulder. By Andrew's account, they were far more advanced than we in utilizing the energy that can be directed with the mind.

It is my hope that by collectively directing healing energy toward those who harm others, we may begin to eradicate poverty and oppression and bring peace to the planet. Currently our minds are infiltrated with numbing messages fed to us by the dominant culture subtly convincing us of our limitations, our lack of safety, and of the evil in others. From exploring the psyche and the mind through shamanic journeying, I have come to appreciate the vast amount of information available to us as well as the incredible potential to transform the destructive elements on our planet and heal the soul.

Chapter 13
Energetic Imprinting: Our Vibrational Home

On the day that Judy was to come to do a ceremony using the sacred prayers that the Bomoh had divined for her, a crow was sitting outside of her door waiting for her. All the way to my office, Crow accompanied her. When Judy arrived, she told me the story of the Crow. We looked up Crow's role and teaching in the Medicine Cards. It said that Crow is the keeper of the sacred mysteries. The next morning when I left my house to walk down to the ocean, a crow was sitting on a telephone wire a hundred yards ahead. In my mind I spoke to Crow and said, "If you are the keeper of the sacred mysteries, wait until I walk under you, then caw three times." As I walked under Crow sitting on the telephone line, he cawed three times and then flew off.

Ancient Prayers from the Bomoh

I have visited the Bomoh in Borneo three additional times since I received the transmission of the twelve guides and six protectors. During the next two visits, the Bomoh gave me further transmissions as well as sacred prayers that are ancient and have the power to alter the vibrational frequency of a person's energy field. They are written in Jawi, the Arabic script. It is unclear if the prayers come from the Islamic Unani tradition or are indigenous to Borneo, passed down by word of mouth for many centuries, and then written in Jawi when the Muslims arrived in Borneo in the 15th century. My guides believe that the majority of the prayers that I work with on a regular basis are indigenous to the Melanaus in Borneo; some are from the Unani tradition. I have received over forty of these prayers; some are quite sacred and are used to bring the soul into wholeness or to rid it of unwanted energies. Some are as frivolous as getting unwanted guests to leave or bringing back wayward husbands—it seems that in the Melanau culture the wives do not stray. I have not used the latter prayers as my guides feel that they are used against the will or knowledge of the person to whom they are given and therefore not ethical.

The methods for using the written prayers vary. Some, such as the sleep remedy and the addiction remedy, are placed directly on the skin. The sleep remedy is placed on the forehead held on by a scarf and helps one to sleep at night. With the help of a colleague who does homeopathy, I have turned some of the prayers into homeopathic remedies. The vast majority of the prayers are traditionally placed in a bucket of water. The Bomoh blows his guides into the water and then throws a bucket of water over the person. This method works well if you live in the tropics and bathe out of doors. However, I did not think I would get many volunteers to receive the prayers on a chilly New England day, so I adapted this method. I bless the prayer in water as the Bomoh had done and then put part of the prayer in a bowl for the client to drink and the other part I put into a plant spritzer and spray the client as if I were misting a plant. Somehow it seems to work.

The prayers seem to defy all rational logic. How is it that a written prayer, whose contents I do not understand, has the power to alter the vibrational and psychic structure of a person? I have been told that the Tibetans have oral prayers that when chanted have the same impact. Are there sacred words that have the power to break down existing defenses and call forth a person's true essence? It is my belief that there is a combination of factors involved in the power of these prayers. The words are sacred, the intent as to the use of the prayers is sacred, and spirit guides are utilized and intermingle with the power of the written words magnifying the potency of the prayers.

When I go to study with the Bomoh, I often take pictures of people who have requested healing from him. Judy sent a picture along with a pack of American cigarettes. The Bomoh spent a great deal of time studying Judy's picture, as American cigarettes are valued commodities. At one point he asked me, "Is this person man or woman?" I replied, "She is mostly woman, but somewhat man." As you may recall, Judy has thirteen different personalities, some of whom are male. I did not know how to explain the concept of multiple personalities with the limited common language between us so I left my response ambiguous. He went back to studying her picture and then wrote out a prayer just for her. I asked, "What condition is it for?" The Bomoh replied, "It is for Judy." So I brought the prayer back to her with a detailed set of instructions as to the type of ceremony, but without a clue as to what problem or condition it addressed. Judy said that she was willing to try it and to trust in what would happen.

Moments before the ceremony was complete, Judy cried out, "make it stop, make it stop" and began to tremble. Until this moment Judy did not have co-consciousness with her thirteen personalities. This means that she neither had been aware of what any of the personalities were thinking or feeling, nor did she have access to any of the memories of the other personalities. All communication between the personalities was either through writings, drawings, or direct communication with me, which I shared with Judy. All of a sudden she had thirteen different voices of a variety of ages talking in her head at once. Those familiar with the integration of personalities into the core ego structure know that it is done very slowly and carefully, one personality at a time, so that the client is not flooded with too many memories at once. It took three months of intense work to help Judy find a sense of equilibrium and relative quiet within her mind. In retrospect, Judy is relieved to have co-consciousness and not to worry if a personality was "out" at the wrong place and time, saying or doing something inappropriate. Judy claims that she would do it again. I'm not so sure I would.

From this experience I learned some important things. The prayers do have the power to work on a very deep level and that the success I had seen when I had used other prayers with clients, was not the result of a placebo effect. This particular prayer has the power to break down the defensive barriers and structure in the psyche in a rather immediate and profound way. I have used this prayer gingerly with clients with whom I have a long-standing relationship and who want to break through a barrier that is holding them back. For the most part, it has helped clients to remove blocks and defenses that heretofore had kept them from making important changes in their lives. Yet for a few people it had little or no impact.

I pondered why it is that one would have such a powerful experience, others very positive experiences, and still a few little impact at all. It is well known that the same medication affects people differently. I have had clients who have done beautifully on Prosac, while others have had negative side effects with little positive gain. The philosophy underlying plant, spirit, medicine and homeopathy is that each remedy or herb is selected for a particular person rather than a remedy or herb be selected for a symptom. The Bomoh had selected a prayer specifically for Judy, which had a powerful effect on her. But this analysis did not fully satisfy me. Why is it that some people did quite well with the prayer while a few received no benefit? I journeyed to learn what my guides had to say.

Teachings from My Guides

I traveled with several of my guides to the upper world. I was in an open space with many different people, floating as if inside a giant embryo that contained everyone and everything. I first noticed the energy field of each person. The field moved in and out of the physical body and was holographic in nature. For some the physical layer or the layer closest to the body predominated. For others it was the emotional body or the mental body. There were a few whose energy radiated to the outer edges of their field with a brilliant warm light. Then as I looked at each person, I could see cords coming out of each person's body and field. There were faint threads that connected each person to her various past lives. Some had relatively few connections, others a moderate amount, while there were those whose fields were laden with hundreds of threads that connected them to many lifetimes.

I noticed cords streaming out to other people and things—such as televisions and cars. I watched as all of the cords, one by one, connected each person to someone else until I was struck with the realization that on some level we are all interconnected—that we are all part of the same energy inside this giant embryo. As I observed the multitude of ways that we are part of each other's fields, the scene before me became quite chaotic and the thought passed through my mind that those who came up with chaos theory must have had a similar journey to the one that I am having.

Then I began to focus my mind on the question at hand and asked my guides, "How do we each become who we are?" Shenla Odkar, a wise and all-knowing divine being from the Tibetan Bon tradition, appeared and said, "Let's go back to the beginning." He took me to a still place where a soul essence was readying to become incarnate. The soul essence's guides and teachers surrounded the light being. First there was a discussion regarding the path of the soul in the up-coming lifetime and what was to be healed from other lifetimes in this incarnation. The soul had been a warrior in many of the previous lifetimes. "Did the soul essence want to continue the warrior path or try something different?" As the question was asked various scenes of past lifetimes flashed before us as did scenes of possible future lifetimes. As the weight of the horror of battle fell over the soul essence, the decision was made to commit to a life of service to atone for some of the suffering caused that comes from being a warrior. Then there was a scan of the universe for the soul essence's clan. Was there anyone that the soul essence had known in other lifetimes that was ready to receive a child? The largest grouping of familiar souls was in India. There was a family waiting to receive the soul essence. So the soul essence went off to India to live a life of service, to heal, and to learn.

Then Shenla Odkar showed me another soul essence that was ready to become incarnate. This essence had lived several lifetimes of impoverishment, hunger, and early death. It was time to experience and learn the lessons that come from being materially comfortable. The soul essence went to a family in Switzerland that was relatively well to do and who was known to this essence and had also experienced lifetimes of hardship.

Then Shenla Odkar said, "It does not matter so much what lifetime one chooses in the beginning of one's evolution on earth as there are so many important lessons to learn. But as one nears the end of one's stay on the planet, it is important to have experienced everything, to have made amends for all one has done, and to give back some of what has been learned throughout the various incarnations. This is why older souls may experience a more difficult time than those just beginning."

With that teaching, Shenla Odkar left. I called after him, "but I still do not know how to help all who come to see me." My three healing guides, Fish, Hekate, and Shin Shu, materialized as rapidly as Shenla Odkar had vanished and asked me to come with them.

They showed me an embryo inside of her mother's womb. I could see the energy of the tiny embryo reach out to connect to the soul essence that was about to inhabit its body. Overlaying the embryo was the mother's energy field. I was reminded that on many soul retrievals I am brought first to the womb to heal and retrieve part of the soul essence that left before birth given that the environment within the mother's womb was too toxic for the essence to stay. Then I witnessed the birth and the gradual process of the soul coming fully into the body and into the energy field of her new family. The energy field is an amalgam of the mother's energy and all of her ancestors that came before her as well as that of her father's and his ancestors before. Cultural and societal expectations are part of the formation of the field. In some societies the birth of a girl is a cause for celebration, in others it is greeted with disappointment and feelings of inadequacy for not having brought forth a son. Children carry through life a sense of whether or not they were wanted and cherished from the environment in the womb and the conditions in the first few months of life.

As I observed the various milestones that impacted this little girl on her way to adulthood, the complicated and intricate matrix that formed around and within her field and dreambody fascinated me. I saw both thought forms arise from within to process and make sense of what was transpiring and from without as she was inculcated to her family and society. I witnessed vibrational threads to past lifetimes activated as situations in her life triggered memory of the far off past. I watched as the soul essence struggled to hold her own in the midst of all the forces brought to bear on her developing soul.

Then Hekate spoke, "You cannot help everyone. There are many factors at play. There are those who have been so deeply wounded in this and past lifetimes that their soul essences are not strong enough to overcome the imprinting of this incarnation. They need love and care before they find the will to heal and to show up for their lives. There are others who are so stuck in their woundedness that even with love and care, they still do not find the will to change. There are some who are comfortable and do not feel the need or the push from within to change. They come to see you because others want them to change, but it does not come from deep within them. There are those with whom there is not a strong, trusting energetic connection—the ground is not fertile for the two of you to work together. Remember that you can only work as deeply with another as you are willing to work with yourself; there are those who carry the same shadow energy as you whom you cannot help until you are fully healed. You carry a belief or thought form that you should be able to help everyone—it is part of your imprinting. You must give this up as it exhausts you. You work too hard with some who do not have the will to change when there are others who need your help and are open to grow." With that Hekate dematerialized. Fish and Shin Shu gave me a hug and the Garuda appeared to escort me back to ordinary reality. As I returned to consciousness, I noticed that my legs were asleep as I had been sitting in a meditation pose for over an hour.

There are many teachings in this journey. There are two that stand out the strongest. We are all interconnected and will, at one time, be the starving child in Ethiopia or the smiling boatman in Tahiti. The soldier we kill in Iraq was or will be our son, lover, mother, or friend in another lifetime. And at the same time that we are intricately connected, we are uniquely and quite complicatedly who we are. Each of us is in our own energetic cocoon. This accounts for the sense of separateness that we each feel, even though we are quite connected to others. Siblings that are raised in the same family and town, and attend the same schools and share many of the same thought forms and imprinting, are often distinctly different.

There is a hunger that we all have to be seen and understood, to have people agree with us and think that what we are doing is good and noble— to be like us so that we do not have to feel alone. We form groups and teams, join political parties and churches so we can have a sense of belonging. Yet each of us views life from a unique prism. We need to respect both our individual specialness and honor the fact that we are all one. If we can comprehend this teaching, then the need to make our children and our allies just like us will cease as will much of our suffering.

From the journey I was re-reminded of what so many of us already know—the importance of a healthy and loving prenatal environment and the proper care and nurturance of our young. There is an old wives tale that says, "Do not upset a pregnant woman." This adage is, in fact, quite true as the baby does absorb the emotional state of the mother through the walls of the placenta. Our earliest imprinting begins in the womb and is carried over in how we are treated as infants and small children. The first seven years of life are the most crucial in the development of psychic structures and in shaping the energy field of the child.

Child-rearing theories and techniques can shape a generation and bring a layer of collective imprinting. Enormous fortitude was needed to survive the Great Depression and World War II. Dr Spock became the child-rearing expert for this generation. He advocated that babies be kept on strict feeding schedules to prevent spoiling. Some have wondered if the rebellious "flower children" that came of age in the sixties and seventies, was, in part, due to a regimented beginning. Others have wondered if the rigidity of these childrearing practices has negatively impacted the ability to securely attach and might be at the root of half of all marriages ending in divorce. New parents of this period, known as baby boomers, countered with a more relaxed and permissive, and perhaps more competitive, childrearing style, which has brought us generation X and Y. Today the pressure to be successful at work and to raise a near perfect child brings undue stress to the parent-child bond, which often results in anxiety being part of the early imprinting.

In Matu, infants and small children are always held and fussed over. The child's attachment to her parents and culture is much more secure than most children's attachments in the West. Malaysian children grow up to be calm, considerate, and well behaved, and in turn raise their children in the same manner. The energetic imprinting of calmness is both from the family and also the culture.

From immersing myself in the energetics of life I have come to understand that babies and young children may also attach to energetic states. This is particularly true when there is the absence of a loving attachment figure. I was about to do a depossession for Violet, a woman who was born and raised in a cult in South America. Violet had done an enormous amount of healing work and was beginning to own her own power as a healer. Yet there was a dark energy that dodged her and, at times, rendered her incapable of carrying out the simplest of tasks.

I asked Violet, "Is there any reason that you might want to keep this dark energy?" Her mouth fell open as she gasped, "I will disintegrate if it is gone. It is what holds me together."

With this pronouncement I understood that there had been no one or thing for Violet to securely attach to. In view of this lack, Violet attached to the dark energy that enveloped her and her family. This was her container, her energetic imprint. Before we could do a depossession, it was necessary to build an attachment to a more nurturing energy source. Power animals and spirit guides are invaluable in providing a secure source of nurturing.

The Matrix of Thought Forms and Energetic Imprinting

The interplay between our thought forms and our energetic imprint form a web that encases us and provides us with a lens through which we view the world. As I began to explore the concept of energetic imprinting and it's interplay with thought forms, I had to confront the ways in which much of the subtle aspects of my behavior and personality—which I had always taken for granted as just being me—were in fact imprinting. My dad had a shoe business and was quite generous in giving people discounts or even shoes at cost. When I first went to work for him at the age of 14, I did some of the bookkeeping. I was both aware of the extent of his generosity and the complications that it presented in keeping the records straight. Unwittingly I followed in his footsteps. I had a wide sliding scale and frequently waived part or all of insurance co-pays. Each person had his or her own payment plan. Finally my bookkeeper threatened to quit, as it was just too difficult to keep track of the complicated system that I had devised. I checked with my colleagues and none of them ran their practices as I did. Finally it hit me what I was doing and where it had come from. Because I admired my father's generosity, I had taken on or energetically absorbed his way of doing business.

Often the imprinting and thought forms pull us to re-enact behaviors that can be destructive and pull people to us who energetically feel comfortable but keep us from awaking to whom we really are. Before I do healing work for a person, it is important that she is cognizant of the beliefs and patterns that keep her stuck and that she has a willingness to let them go. When I do the healing work, I first remove and heal the energy of all those who have cast an energetic web over my client as well as pluck out those thought forms or beliefs that hold the imprinting in place and impede the return of the soul to wholeness. Sometimes there are layers and layers of dark heavy energy that need to be removed. At times I must struggle to disconnect this energy as it is so strongly held in place with the mind. After I am finished, the client invariably tells me that they feel light—as if I have removed pounds from their being. The challenge then is to help the client work with these energetic shifts so as not to bring the old energy and beliefs back in and to bring the person to a place where she can remember who she truly is before she was hurt in this lifetime and why she came to be on the planet at this time.

When a child is raised with love, acceptance, and the opportunity to explore and make mistakes without judgment, the child's energetic imprint has a relaxed and open feel to it. If a child is raised in a critical, judgmental environment and is left to feel that her parent's suffering is her fault, the child's energetic imprint has a burdened and depressed feel to it. The former child expects acceptance and draws this to her; people want to be around her and do things with her. The child raised with judgment expects criticism and blame and draws that type of energy as well. Just as the child who feels invisible in her family frequently feels and is perceived as being invisible in the world at large.

Within the American culture there is a tendency to blame the parents for the child's problems. Often we do not understand the pain that the parents felt to exude so much negativity and blame as well as the choice, on some level, that the soul made in choosing these parents—the lessons that the soul took on in order to advance the soul's path. Anger towards those who have harmed us is a necessary first step in the healing process. It is one of the easiest ways to break out of the victim role. Staying stuck in the anger, however, keeps one encased in the imprinting. Thoughts of anger and blame become spikes that hold the imprinting in place and keep one energetically connected to the one with whom they feel anger.

The planet earth also has an energetic imprint. There are those[29] who believe that we are in the midst of an energetic global shift as the earth moves out of a cycle that it has been in for the last four thousand years. Some are predicting the end of civilization, as we know it, through great wars, natural disasters, and plagues. Others forecast a significant shift on the planet in which we rise to a more compassionate way of being and treating one another. Some feel that the outcome is still in doubt. In the summer of 1987, many celebrated the onset of the Harmonic Conversion. It is believed that this conversion is a 26-year cycle, beginning 13 years before the millennium and extending until 2013. From journeys I have taken, people I have spoken with, and things that I have read, it seems we are trying to shift to a consciousness that is more open and inclusive—a consciousness that is less focused on the self and more on cooperative action. The dualistic thinking that produces division and conflict will be replaced by a more expansive and compassionate mind. There are forces in the world that steadfastly cling to the old hierarchical models and, it appears, will go down fighting to protect this way of being. There are also hundreds of thousands of people who are using all of their psychic energy and prayer to engender a shift to a different vibrational frequency for the planet—a shift where consideration and cooperation replace greed and judgment and where love replaces hate and where we honor and respect all of the natural resources, animal, and plant life on the planet.

As the energetic imprint of the planet shifts, it pulls on each of us individually to alter our vibrational frequency to accommodate this shift. Those who resist this pull fall deeper into the despair of their wounds, while those who are able to open to the shifting energy find a new peace and freedom heretofore unknown. I have never experienced such a dichotomous time in my psychotherapy and healing practice. There are some who consistently feel good, empowered, and at peace and are ready for termination. There are others who have never felt so depressed and hopeless.

On New Year's Eve that heralded in 2003, a group of close friends climbed a hill that overlooks the Atlantic Ocean. Each year we drum to bring in the New Year. While drumming, a guide came to me and said, "This is the year of the spiritual warrior.[30] All that you have been studying and preparing for is to come to fruition. The time to dwell on your own life issues is gone; the time to act collectively is here."

Later I did a journey in which I saw that hundreds of light beings have come from all over the universe to support the earth in its healing and transformation. I was shown that there is much negative energy that is stored in the earth from eons of acts of violence and destruction and that this energy is up for clearing. The light beings are here to help in this clearing and to help to ground and support all that inhabit the planet as the earth goes through this transmutation. In January of 2003 there were unusually deadly fires. As I journeyed to the nightclub fire in Warwick, Rhode Island, I saw and experienced much darkness—a vortex of very negative energy that had snared the lives of a hundred innocent people. As I looked more closely, I realized that there had been a horrible massacre on this very site in the 16th century. The fire, in part, occurred on this spot so that the energy from the previous disaster could be cleared through the many prayers and healing energy sent to help all that died and were injured.

The light beings showed me how to use their healing energy to shift the vibrational energy of those with whom I work. When I do energy work on a client, I am to envision them floating in space. The light beings send energy from above through all of the major chakra centers through the body to ground this energy in the core of the earth. As I do the healing work, I call upon the higher self or true essence of the client to come forward and then bring this energy in through the top of the spine at the base of the neck and through the heart chakra. The energy from the core of the earth then flows up through the chakra system and connects with the light beings. Through this exercise, we ground our energy in the new vibrational shift while also serving as a channel to bring healing energy into the earth. A few months after I began to bring this practice to the clients that I felt could benefit from it, I was aware that all of the clients who were doing quite well had received this particular healing. Yet a few who received it and reported feeling good at the time did not seem to benefit from the work in the long term.

Challenges in Altering Imprints

For a number of years I have taught an on-going seminar to a group of psychotherapists who want to learn how to integrate shamanic work into their psychotherapy practices. It is an extremely talented and gifted group of healers. All of us have had the same experience of observing that some of our clients we see for healing work undergo quite profound transformations only to have the same debilitating patterns slip back a few weeks later. While for others, the power of the work results in changes that are lasting. We journeyed on the following two questions: What conditions are needed to enable the work to be effective? What advice do our guides have to help us and our clients enable the work to stick? The following are the messages we received from our guides.

When we journeyed on what conditions are needed to enable the work to be effective there was much commonality in response from our collective guides and teachers. A central theme was the importance of a loving and compassionate healing alliance between therapist and client, coupled with a desire on the part of both the higher self of the client and the personality for change to occur. It was also important for both the clients and therapist's guides to be in agreement about the work to be done. Respect for the forces of change and the arduous task ahead needs to be acknowledged. The guides reported that fear is the major block for change to occur as it creates its own vibrational frequency and holds the old patterns in place. The belief that the work can make a difference is essential as the doubt blocks the change from happening. An absence of guilt or shame regarding past behavior and the energy being changed is also essential for the negative patterns not to be pulled back. The energy of fear, guilt, and shame is often on a similar frequency to the energy to be changed and thus keep the negative patterns in place. A willingness to let go of the storylines that perpetuate stuck thought forms is also key for healing and transformation to occur. If I continue to believe that I am stupid because I was the first child to sit down in a fourth grade spelling bee and repeat this story in my head and to others, this story will become my reality. Healers can try to remove the belief and energy that I am stupid, but it is not going to shift until I am willing to disidentify with this storyline.

The guides recommended that there be an initial journey in which threads that connect old negative patterns to the field are identified. Then it is important to grieve these past connections and to honor the role that the patterns played in protecting the psyche. Time and care must be given to envision the future and to develop a sense of the future self. There were strong rooting images that emerged from the journeys. The guides said that it is important to fertilize and root the energy of change in love before the work begins—the metaphor of good seeds and good earth came forth. While doing the work it is important for the healer to merge completely with spirit and to shape-shift[31] into nature to develop a strong root system and then envision the root system holding the transformation. It is important to look lovingly and compassionately at that which is being held and transformed so as not to encourage resistance. Our guides also reminded us that it is essential for the client to do rituals after the work is done to protect and seal the new energy.

We then journeyed to ask our guides what advice they have for us and for our clients to enable the work to stick. There were several similar themes to the previous journey, underlying their importance. The theme of proper preparation emerged especially in regards to building a bridge to the future. The bridge building is to occur in both the cognitive and energetic realm through asking the client to envision herself after the healing and the ways in which her life will be different. It is important to concretely spell out the vision as a map of what life can be. The bridge also needs to be built energetically by sending energy into the future to ground the new cognitive structures that have emerged. If the change will be experienced most at home, send the energy there; if the impact is greatest at work, ground the energy at work; or, if appropriate, the energy can be sent to both places. The idea is that the new energy is there waiting for them when they get home.

The therapist is to be the midwife to the birth of the client's new self. When doing the healing work it is important to ground the client in energy from above and below and then bring the client to the place of the original blockage or trauma to see what life was like before the blockage—to remember whom she was before she was harmed. Then we are to work with both sets of guides to ground the client in this early energy and sense of self while also connecting the energy to the greater whole.

The guides reminded us that all paths lead to the heart and if there are blockages to be flexible in moving in and out, above, and below them—to keep the resistance guessing. They stressed that we are in a global shift and that it is good to remember that the healing is occurring for the higher good as well as for the individual—as each one of us heals, we all heal; as each one of us suffers, we all suffer.

The guides reiterated the importance of ritual to seal off the old energetic threads and to cement the new ones. Before the client leaves the office, it is important to devise a ritual for the client to do. The rituals are to be individually designed for each client. It was advised that the therapist might want to give a post-hypnotic suggestion regarding the integration of the work and the changes that will take place.

Our guides taught us that the ability to believe in one's future, to trust in one's guides, to love and be compassionate to oneself, and to let go of one's fear of change are some of the essential ingredients necessary to shift the deep imprinting and thought forms that hold each of us back from knowing our hearts and living our paths. There is no one magic cure to enact change and to remove the energy and beliefs that perpetuate suffering. But if one is willing to open the heart and mind to change and growth and to listen within, magic can happen.

Later I had a discussion with members of my peer support group, some of whom are in the shamanic study group. We pondered if a significant element in shamanic work being more effective in Matu than it is in Massachusetts is because of attachment issues. People in Matu are so securely attached that they readily open to the spirit world and its teachings. In the West the need for a secure, concrete attachment is so great that many clients attach to the therapist/healer rather than to the work being done for them. In doing so the energy from spirit does not have clear opening in which to enter.

We, in the West, are complicated beings as we tend to honor the mind over the heart and our separateness over our connectedness. Yet, each culture has its myths and beliefs that shape the psyche and the energy of its people. The last few times I have visited Matu, I have been asked by the Bomoh's wife, Hwa Jung, to do healing work for her and for others in the village. It seems that because I am a white woman from America and use a "magic crystal" that I must carry strong medicine. Of course, the medicine that I carry comes from there, but their own internalized racism imbues me with something special that they do not have.

During my last visit, I arrived to find Hwa Jung pale and weak with little or no appetite. Her eyes hurt; she had little feeling in her limbs, which she reported as being quite cold. Immediately my guides told me that she has diabetes. The energy work that I did for her alleviated her symptoms, but I believed that she needed medicine from a doctor trained in western medicine. I took her to visit her daughter who lives in a nearby town where there is western medical care. Normah was very concerned about her mother and had been trying to get her to take medication for the diabetes, but Hwa Jung had steadfastly refused. Hwa Jung had been diagnosed with diabetes earlier that year, but that diagnosis carried little meaning for her. Hwa Jung did not want to take a "pill." She always made a horrible face as if the pill was poison whenever either of us suggested it. After much work and cajoling, she agreed to take the medication, still believing that the only reason that she felt better was because of my healing work.

Others in the village came to see me for all sorts of physical ailments. I am not a medical doctor and have had no training in western medicine beyond what I have learned from work I have done with clients with serious physical ailments. Yet, I believe strongly in the mindbodyspirit connection and trust in my guides to tell me what to do. I rarely had any sense of what was wrong with them as my language skills were so poor after years of nonuse. To my surprise and amazement, each person who came to see me felt better afterward. I think that, in large part, they got better because they believed that spirit and I could help them and because I trusted my guides to tell me what to do.

These two incidences carry interesting teachings in how beliefs and imprinting work. Hwa Jung believed that I could heal her, but I did not. The influence of western medicine is still strong within me, and I believed that she had a condition that needed western medicine. This belief was strengthened by the fact that the Bomoh had been unable to heal her. I do not see myself as capable of doing things that he cannot—even though that could be an erroneous belief in some incidences.

Then I asked myself, "Why then did I trust myself to help the others who came to see me?" I was aware that I had a more neutral stance regarding my ability to help them. When I checked in with my guides, they told me that my healing work is stronger in Matu because many of the spirits with whom I work come from Matu and are part of the energetic fabric of the culture. That, coupled with their trust and belief in me and the spirit world that comes, and my need to surrender to my guides and not use my mind, are major factors in why the work was successful.

When I work in the United States, I strive to find a balance between my western academic training and the intuitive wisdom that comes from my guides. I feel a need for balance as the grounding in the intellectual and academic is part of the belief system and imprinting of my culture and is part of my personal imprinting. I love to work in Matu where I work totally through the directions of my guides. The work feels organic, clear, and sacred and strengthens my trust in the shamanic. But my work is here in the West as I strive to forge a bridge between the sacred and profound of the old ways and the intellectual foundation of 21st century theory and practice.

When I first began to open to the shamanic path more than a decade ago, I was naïve in my expectation of what shamanic work could do. The potential for transformation and change is much greater than I dreamed possible. The extent to which the complicated western mind creates its own suffering is more profound than what I previously understood. The degree to which I must trust and believe in the spirit realm, let go of the chatter in my mind, and surrender to forces unseen is much greater than I imagined. And the forces of darkness, in both ordinary and non-ordinary reality, are much more deeply embedded and powerful than I ever conceived possible.

Each day I am reminded of what I do not know, and each day I am taught what I need to know—if I am only willing to listen. As I have deepened my connection to the work, I have had to let go of many of my most deeply held beliefs and thought forms. I have struggled mightily to shed the energy and expectations of others as I have been propelled by a power greater than I, to understand that which seems incomprehensible. It has been scary and lonely at times, but I would not have missed a minute of it. I am filled with immense gratitude for the Bomoh and all of my guides awakening me to my path and urge all of you to look for opportunities to awake to all that you know and carry deep within your being.

Epilogue
THE ALTERING OF OLD MODELS, THE CREATION OF NEW ONES

In the new millennium, the world is shrinking via telecommunication networks and easy travel. By pooling information from many cultures, we can find new ways to deal with the host of problems confronting us. The integration of shamanism and psychotherapy is but one model to consider as we expand our perspectives and find new ways to bring about transformation. There are many rich traditions and practices throughout the world that are capable of healing in ways viewed as incomprehensible to many in the West. As we bring these practices into mainstream consciousness, there is a tendency to try to find the one method or practice that is the true teaching or the most powerful. I urge us not to compare or judge these methods, but attempt to find the practice and teaching that most resonates with our core being and style of learning and healing.

The health care system in the United States is struggling under a mounting bureaucracy in which 40% of health care costs are for administrative expenses and doctors are often forced to consult with insurance companies before making medical decisions. There has never been a better time for the development of new models of health care to counter the frustration that many feel with the current system.

In the small coastal community of Cape Ann, comprised of three small towns an hour north of Boston, there are three or four different groups who strive to create a healing center. Although the groups have different visions and goals, there is a collaborative spirit as we try to bring to reality a new model of healing. I can only imagine how many other groups there are around the country, which strive to fulfill a similar dream.

I am part of one of these groups. We are a group of alternative health care practitioners who have come together with the intention to imbue our work with the spirits of nature and an appreciation of our interconnection with all. We work from a mindbodyspirit perspective with the goal of bringing each person to a higher level of balance and wellness. We bring together a mixture of different health care professionals, such as psychotherapists, acupuncturists, chiropractors, body workers, energy workers, shamanic practitioners, past life therapists, and yoga and meditation teachers. We hope to bring forth a new model of healing in which two or three practitioners may simultaneously work on the same person in order to maximize the greatest benefit. We want the center to be a place where important life events such as birth, coming of age, and death can be honored in ritual and community. We envision the center to be a training and educational center. If you would like more information about the center, please go to my website at www.anndrakesoulwork.com or to fullcirclecenter.org.

NOTES

[1] Mircea Eliade, *Shamanism: Archaic Techniques of Ecstasy* (New York, NY: Pantheon, 1964); Michael Harner, *The Way of the Shaman* (New York, NY: Harper, 1980).

[2] Eliade, *Shamanism.*

[3] Sandra Ingerman, *Soul Retrieval: Mending the Fragmented Self* (New York, NY: Harper Collins Harper San Francisco, 1990).

[4] Barbara Brennan, *Hands of Light* (New York, NY: Battan Book, 1987).

[5] Karl Pribram, "The Neurophysiology of Remembering," *Scientific American* 220 (January 1969).

Karl Pribram, *Languages of the Brain* (Monterey, CA: Wadsworth Publishing, 1977).

[6] Pribram, *Languages*; see also David Bohm, *Wholeness and the Implicate Order* (London: Routledge & Kegan Paul, 1980).

[7] Brennan, *Hands.*

[8] D. W. Winnicott, *The Maturational Process and the Facilitating Environment* (New York, NY: International Press, Inc., 1965), p. 99.

[9] Winnicott, p. 99.

[10] Brennan, *Hands.*

[11] Shalila Sharamom & Bodo J. Baginshi, *The Chakra-Handbook* (Wilmot, WI: Lotus Light Publications—Shangri-La, 1988).

[12] Brennan, *Hands*, Sharamon and Baginski, *Chakra*, and Anodea Judith & Selene Vega, *The Sevenfold Journey: Reclaiming Mind, Body & Spirit Through the Chakras* (Freedom, CA: The Crossing Press, 1993) have written wonderful books explaining the chakra system, suggesting exercises for opening and cleansing the chakras. I recommend reading these books for an in-depth analysis of the chakra system.

[13] Erik Erikson, *Childhood and Society* (New York, NY: W. W. Norton & Company, 1963).

[14] Carol Gilligan, In a Different Voice (Cambridge, MA: Harvard University Press, 1982).

[15] Judith Jordon, "Empathy and Self Boundaries" *Work in Progress* 84-05 (Wellesley, MA: Stone Center Working Papers Series, 1984); see also Judith Jordon, Janet Surrey & Alexandra Kaplan, "Women and Empathy: Implications for Psychological Development and Psychotherapy" *Work in Progress* 82-02 (Wellesley, MA: Stone Center Working Papers Series, 1983); Jean Baker Miller, *Toward a New Psychology of Women* (Boston, MA: Beacon Press, 1976); and Janet Surrey, "The Self-in-Relation: A Theory of Women's Development" *Work in Progress* 84-02 (Wellesley, MA: Stone Center Working Papers Series, 1984).

[16] Arnold Mindell, Dreambody, the Body's Role in Revealing the Self (Boston, MA: Sigo Press, 1982), p. 32.

[17]Tim Weiner, "Senate unit calls US 'most violent' country on earth" The Boston Globe (3, 13, 1991), p. A3.

[18] Patrick Healy, "Speechmaker, aspiring peacemaker" The Boston Globe (6 6, 2002), pp. B1 &B10.

[19] Patricia Wen, "Household wastes" The Boston Globe, (1/13/2003), pp. A1&A6.

[20] Amy Miller, " 'Good Will' moms play protective roles" Cambridge Chronicle (2, 19/98), p.1.

[21]Steve Newman, "Earthweek: A diary of the planet" The Boston Globe (4,6,1998), p. A3.

[22] Anorexia Nervosa is a disorder that occurs when one's body weight is 85% or less of what it should be for the age and height of the person, accompanied by a fear and obsession with being fat even though one is significantly underweight. Bulimia involves eating excessive amounts of food and then vomiting. Men and boys suffer from these disorders as well as girls and women.

[23]Alice Miller, Prisoners of Childhood (Translated by Ruth Ward, New York, NY: Meridian, 1981).

[24] Bessel van der Kolf, Alexander McFarlane, & Lars Weisaeth,Eds. Traumatic Stress: The Effects of Overwhelming Experience on Mind, Body and Society (New York, NY: Guilford Press, 1996).

[25] Miriam Greenspan, Healing Through the Dark Emotions: The Wisdom of Grief, Fear, and Despair (Boston, MA: Shambala, 2003).

[26] For Buddhist, the mind is centered in the heart.

[27] Jon Kabat-Zinn, Full Catastrophe Living (New York, New York: Harcourt, 1990).

[28] Shirley Andrews, Atlantis: Insight from a Lost Civilization (St Paul, MN: Lewllyn Publications, 1997).

[29] Demetra George, Mysteries of the Dark Moon (San Francisco, CA: Harper Collins, 1992).

[30] The term spiritual warrior purports that one is to stand strong and fierce in one's spiritual beliefs—to be unwavering. It in no way implies that one is to go to battle or to fight.

[31] Shape-shifting is the process in which the shaman energetically moves out of her own form and into that of a particular energy that is helpful to promote healing. In this case the shaman merges with the root structure of a tree so as to ground the energy of change.

Glossary of Terms

The following terms are quite complex and are open to a myriad of interpretation. Thus they are not to be taken as the precise definition of these terms but rather as a roadmap to understanding what I am trying to convey in the book.

Alters is the term given to distinct personalities that reside within the ego structure of one who has Multiple Personalities or who has been diagnosed with Dissociative Identity Disorder.

Buddhist Mind. In Tibetan Buddhism the mind resides in the heart and one thinks with the heart. Westerners tend to think of mind residing in the head near the brain.

The Chakra System is an ancient metaphysical system originating in India, which ties the complexities of the universe to the intricacies of the human existence. There are seven major chakras, 40 secondary ones, and, according to traditional writings, 88,000 in all which leaves scarcely a point on the body that is not open for the reception, transformation, or transferal of energy. Please see Chapter 7 for a deeper explanation.

The Dreambody operates on various frequency bands. Within the dreambody are housed the physical body, the psyche, energy body and the soul. The dreambody is holographic in nature, moving in and out of the physical body, capable of functions beyond those we in the West believe possible. Please see Chapter 8 for a deeper explanation.

Extraction is the removal of energy that does not belong in the body or the energy field. This unwanted energy enters when there is soul loss and causes physical or emotional illness. It needs to be removed before lost parts of the soul can be returned. Spirit guides or power animals remove the unwanted energy by working through a healer who is physically doing the extraction.

Holographic refers to the ability of energy to materialize and de-materialize, to move in and out of matter and to travel on its own and then re-materialize and reconnect with matter as needed. Scientist now believe that phenomenon such as *Star War's* Princess Leia's ghostly image emerging through a light beam from Artoo Detoo is more fact than fiction.

Introjects are aspect of psychic energy from one person being taken into the psychic structure of another. A parent's fear and anxiety may be absorbed and taken into the psychic structure of the child along with the belief that a certain activity or person is dangerous. See Chapter 6 for a deeper explanation.

Multiple Personality refers to a condition when there are two or more distinct personalities residing within the same body and psychic structure and are usually discernable as being uniquely different. Often these personalities do not have awareness that the other exists and each may have activities and friends that only they know and visit. This condition arises from extreme and often repeated trauma at an early age and is considered to be an adaptive way for the psyche to endure such trauma and continue to function. Currently it is believed that there is a Dissociative continuum with distinct personalities being at one end and brief periods of disruption in normal functions of memory, consciousness, and identity at the other end. For instance, if a woman witnesses a horrible car crash, she may not be able to remember that she was even there let alone what transpired. Each time that she sees a car accident, she may go into a Dissociative state and not be present, but the rest of the time she functions normally.

Non-ordinary reality is considered to be a realm that we cannot concretely see but in which we can learn to travel and know through going into a trance state. Traditional cultures refer to this reality as dreamtime or the other time. Power animals live in the lower realms of non-ordinary reality whereas spirit guides inhabit the upper realms. Intuitive wisdom originates in non-ordinary reality.

Ordinary reality is the concrete reality in which we can see, smell, and touch things. In some traditions it is referred to as the middle realm. When one becomes proficient in shamanic journeying, it is possible to travel forward and backward in ordinary reality. Most of us spend the majority of our time in ordinary reality.

Power Animals are guides and teachers that inhabit the lower realms of non-ordinary reality. These animals exist on a vibrational frequency and bring us the teachings or medicine that we need. Some are with us our entire life while others come to us for a specific teaching or task. Most of us have an intuitive sense of which animals we are most connected and who our power animals might be.

Programming is a process in which the beliefs and words of one person or group are placed within the psychic structure of another through torture and/or hypnosis.

Projections are unintegrated aspects of the psyche that are energetically sent to another. If a woman unconsciously feels that she is not bright and capable of being successful, she may project onto others that they feel that she is stupid even if they do not or conversely she may believe that they are stupid or inadequate and send this energetic belief to them. If one of the people to whom this projection was made feels inadequate, then she will take in the projection as truth. This is called projective identification and is when one person feels the energy of the projection, takes in this energy, and believes it to be true. See Chapter 6 for a deeper explanation.

Psychopomp is a shamanic practice in which the shaman, through shamanic journeying, accompanies the soul of the recently deceased to the other side and does healing work on the other side for the dead.

Ritual abuse is when a person is harmed, tortured or abused repeatedly and the abuse has the same pattern or ritual accompanying it each time the torture occurs.

Sado-masochism is a practice or tendency in which one person plays the role of perpetrator and the other of the victim.

A shaman is a healer who has the ability to travel to other realms of reality, communicate and work with spirit guides and power animals to bring about healing for individuals, the community at large and the earth and all that inhabit the earth.

Shamanism is an ancient healing method dating back at least 60,000 that has been practiced in almost every culture throughout the world. It involves working with guides and teachers from non-ordinary reality to bring about healing and to gather information and wisdom from other realms of knowledge.

A shamanic journey is the process of going into a trance state via percussion sound, hallucinogenic plants, or a meditative state to communicate with guides and teachers in non-ordinary reality. A skilled shaman can walk in both ordinary and non-ordinary reality simultaneously.

Shape-shifting is when a person or animal merges with another form of energy and shifts into that being.

The Soul carries an awareness of our purpose and place in the universe. Within the soul are the psyche, energy, and physical bodies that are vibrationally housed in the dreambody.

Soul loss is when part of the soul or essence splits away from the core and is vibrationally disconnected from the core aspect of the person. Soul loss occurs through traumatic occurrences or through the disconnection of the soul to the spiritual realm and to the presence of spirit in everything.

Soul retrieval is when a shaman travels into the dreambody of a person with soul loss and finds the split off part of the soul, does a healing for the soul part, and returns it to the core vibrational frequency of the person.

Spirit Guides are our teachers that live in the upper realm of non-ordinary reality and provide guidance and teaching. Some of these guides are dear friends who have crossed over and who have come to help us on the physical plane. Others may be teachers or loved ones from other lifetimes, while others may be mythic beings who embody the divine energy and wisdom of the universe.

A Spiritual Warrior is a person who is comfortable traveling in non-ordinary reality and in working with negative as well as positive energies in both ordinary and non-ordinary reality.

Tonglen is a Tibetan Buddhist practice in which one breathes in the suffering of another on the in breath and sends out love and compassion to the other on the out breath thereby transforming the suffering through taking it into oneself.

Trance is an altered state of consciousness when one can see beyond the veils of ordinary reality into other realms of existence and communicate with guides and teachers in these realms.

Vibrational Frequency is our energetic mode of operation. Our bodies are slowed down energetic frequencies that have become matter. When we travel to other realms of reality through entering a trance state, we increase or raise our vibrational frequency. The more we journey or enter trance, the further we can travel, bringing us access to greater information and wisdom.

BIBLIOGRAPHY

Andrews, Shirley. *Atlantis: Insight from a Lost Civilization.* St Paul, MN: Lewllyn Publications, 1997.

Brennan, Barbara. *Hands of Light.* New York: Battan Book, 1987.

Bohm, David. *Wholeness and the Implicate Order.* London: Routledge & Kegan Paul, 1980.

Dickson, M.G. *A Sarawak Anthology.* London: University of London Press Ltd, 1965.

Eliade, Mircea. *Shamanism: Archaic Techniques of Ecstasy.* New York: Pantheon, 1964.

Erikson, Erik. *Childhood and Society.* New York: W. W. Norton & Company, 1963.

George, Demetra. *Mysteries of the Dark Moon.* San Francisco: Harper Collins, 1992.

Gilligan, Carol. *In a Different Voice.* Cambridge, Mass: Harvard University Press, 1982.

Greenspan, Miriam. *Healing Through the Dark Emotions: The Wisdom of Grief, Fear, and Despair.* Boston: Shambala Publication, 2003.

Harner, Michael. *The Way of the Shaman.* New York: Harper, 1980.

Healy, Patrick. "Speechmaker, aspiring peacemaker" *The Boston Globe*: June 6, 2002.

Ingerman, Sandra. *Soul retrieval: Mending the Fragmented Self.* New York: Harper Collins Harper San Francisco, 1990.

Jordon, Judith. "Empathy and Self Boundaries" *Work in Progress* 84-05. Wellesley, Mass: Stone Center Working Papers Series, 1984.

Jordon, Judith, and Janet Surrey and Alexandra Kaplan. "Women and Empathy: Implications for Psychological Development and Psychotherapy" *Work in Progress* 82-02. Wellesley, MA: Stone Center Working Papers Series, 1983.

Judith, Anodea, and SeleneVega. *The Sevenfold Journey: Reclaiming Mind, Body & Spirit Through the Chakras.* Freedom, Calif: The Crossing Press, 1993.

Kabat-Zinn, Jon. *Full Catastrophe Living.* New York: Harcourt, 1990.

Miller, Alice. *Prisoners of Childhood.* Translated by Ruth Ward, New York: Meridian, 1981.

Miller, Amy. " 'Good Will' moms play protective roles" *Cambridge Chronicle,* February, 19,1998.

Miller, Jean Baker. *Toward a New Psychology of Women.* Boston: Beacon Press, 1976.

Mindell, Arnold. Dreambody, the Body's Role in Revealing the Self. Boston: Sigo Press, 1982.

Mullen, Vernon. *The Story of Sarawak.* Kuala Lumpar: Oxford University Press, 1967.

Newman, Steve. "Earthweek: A diary of the planet" *The Boston Globe.* April ,6,1998.

Pribram, Karl. "The Neurophysiology of Remembering," *Scientific American* 220. January 1969.

Pribram, Karl. *Languages of the Brain.* Monterey, Calif: Wadsworth Publishing, 1977.

Sharamom, Shalila, and Bodo J. Baginshi. *The Chakra-Handbook.* Wilmot, Wisc: Lotus Light Publications—Shangri-La, 1988.

Stevens, Jose, and Lena. *Secrets of Shamanism: Tapping the Spirit Power within You.* New York: Avon, 1988.

Surrey, Janet. "The Self-in-Relation: A Theory of Women's Development" *Work in Progress* 84-02. Wellesley, MA: Stone Center Working Papers Series, 1984.

Talbot, Michael. *The Holographic Universe.* New York: Harper Collins Publishers, 1991.

van der Kolf , Bessel, and Alexander McFarlane, and Lars Weisaeth ,Eds. *Traumatic Stress: The Effects of Overwhelming Experience on Mind, Body and Society.* New York: Guilford Press, 1996.

Weiner, Tim. "Senate unit calls US 'most violent' country on earth" *The Boston Globe.* March, 13, 1991.

Wen, Patricia. "Household wastes" *The Boston Globe.* January 13, 2003.

Winnicott, D. W. *The Maturational Process and the Facilitating Environment.* New York: International Press, Inc., 1965.

Wolf, Fred Alan. *The Dreaming Universe.* New York: Touchstone, 1995.

"Ann Drake has given us one of the most detailed descriptions of shamanic healing in the literature. The text begins with her shamanic initiations in the jungles of Borneo and takes us through her journey as a clinical psychologist dedicated to he healing of her clients. In so doing, she extends the territory of shamanism into clinical psychology by demonstrating, through clinical case histories, how shamanic techniques such as 'soul retrieval' and 'extraction' enhance the healing of numerous types of traumatic and dissociative disorders. [*Healing of the Soul*] is a must-read for all mental health professionals wanting to integrate shamanism into psychotherapeutic practice."

—Larry Peters, Ph.D.
Teacher
The Foundation for Shamanic Studies